Originally published in 1936
Ordeal By Hunger was praised as

"The tale of wise, prosperous, enthusiastic, and hopeful people ending in a nightmare of cannibalism is a terrifying one that is told calmly, but with deadly interest. The temptation to editorialize must have been tremendous. Mr. Stewart has resisted that temptation and has produced a superb historical narrative that is well worth your reading—if you have a reasonably strong stomach." —*Best Sellers*

"A terrible story, its blackest moments lit up with white fires of high heroism. It is a tale of men in the wilderness, stripped of moral scruples; and some of them came through the ordeal nobly. George Stewart has told their story simply and superbly." —*New York Herald Tribune*

In this new edition of his famous book, the author has added the text of several poignant diaries and letters of people in the Donner Party and an analysis of the new material which has come to light since 1936. The main body of the book stands as it was when first written—an American classic.

ORDEAL BY HUNGER
was originally published by
Houghton Mifflin Company.

Ordeal
by Hunger

The Story of the Donner Party

by
George R. Stewart

New Edition

With a Supplement
and Three Accounts
by Survivors

PUBLISHED BY **POCKET** BOOKS NEW YORK

ORDEAL BY HUNGER

Houghton Mifflin edition published 1960

POCKET BOOK edition published February, 1971

4th printing........May, 1973

This POCKET BOOK edition includes every word
contained in the original, higher-priced edition. It is printed
from brand-new plates made from completely reset, clear, easy-to-read
type. POCKET BOOK editions are published by POCKET BOOKS, a division
of Simon & Schuster, Inc., 630 Fifth Avenue, New York, N.Y. 10020.
Trademarks registered in the United States and other countries.

L

Standard Book Number: 671-77262-6.
Library of Congress Catalog Card Number: 60-9361.
This POCKET BOOK edition is published by arrangement with
Houghton Mifflin Company.

Printed in the U.S.A.

TO HARVEY FERGUSSON

PREFACE TO THE 1960 EDITION

IN THIS new edition the text of the original work is reproduced without change. I augment it with a Supplement—as I hope, thus increasing its interest and usefulness. In this new section I review recent scholarship, reconsider some controversial matters, and consider the impact upon the original work of two collections of Donnerana which have become available since 1936. Also added are three important original accounts which have not been previously published in a book designed for general circulation.

I am content thus to republish the 1936 text. In the first place, I believe that it still holds up, since the possible errors (in the light of the more recently available materials) are neither numerous nor vital, being concerned almost entirely with details of chronology during the early part of the journey. (See p. 239.) In the second place, I may say, paradoxically, that I did not wish to tamper with another man's work; for I am not that man of a quarter-century ago, and to attempt to revise what he wrote would lead to unevenness and patchwork. Finally, I am perhaps deluded enough to think that a text which has existed for such a period of time and has been read by thousands of people has already begun to achieve a kind of classic quality.

With this 1960 edition I hope to put the book into final form—at least for as long as I shall be concerned about it. One may wonder as to whether still more new materials on the story will come to light. Certain papers of Woodworth's, for instance, are believed to be extant, and they will doubtless become available at some time. These papers, however, will probably not change the story significantly, and I know of nothing else, unless some miracle of excavation at Alder Creek should bring to light the diary which Tamsen Donner is said to have kept.

I wish to express my indebtedness to the late Dr. Douglas M. Kelley for having made available to me the Donner materials collected by his grandfather, C. F. McGlashan. Mrs. Kelley has since, in accordance with her husband's expressed intention, generously presented the collection to the Bancroft Library.

The Southwest Museum, through its Librarian, Mrs. Ella Robinson, kindly sent me a photostat of the Virginia Reed letter of May 16, 1847, and permitted the printing of the text.

The Sutter's Fort State Historical Monument, through its Supervisor, Mr. Carroll D. Hall, has generously allowed me to use the Reed diary.

As for the Bancroft Library, I have been under such heavy debt to it throughout so many years that I cannot fully express myself on the subject, and can do little more than refer to the original Preface. In particular, for this new edition, the Breen diary is reproduced from that library's collection. Among present staff-members I am under especial debt to Mrs. Julia Macleod, Dr. George P. Hammond, and Mr. Dale L. Morgan.

On the original title-page my name appeared with a Jr. Shortly afterward, however, I dropped that distinction, and in this new edition my name appears as it does in my later books.

G. R. S.

Berkeley, California
January 28, 1960

PREFACE TO THE FIRST EDITION

THE misadventure of the Donner Party constitutes one of the most amazing stories of that land of amazing stories, the American West. It is worthy of record as a historical document upon what human beings may achieve, endure, and perpetrate, in the final press of circumstance.

This account is intended for a full and critical history of that ill-fated band of pioneers, and has been made possible by the remarkable preservation of detailed records. It is strictly factual, based upon the evidence of the sources and upon reasonable deduction from that evidence; it is not fiction.

More than a hundred characters are involved. I have given most of these some kind of introduction at the time of their appearance, but I found this impossible with the children, and have accordingly appended for reference a roster of the Donner Party.

If in the story I have told much which is unpleasant and much which the actors themselves would have been glad to let be forgotten, I may at least plead that I have told all in charity. I blame none of the emigrants for their acts during that winter, any more than I should blame a man for his acts during a delirium. Upon controversial points I have honestly considered both sides, and have given each a chance to speak, in the notes if not always in the text.

The Bancroft Library of the University of California has made available from its excellent collections the greater part of the materials, both printed and manuscript, upon which this study is based. For the unfailing courtesy and the ready coöperation there afforded me I wish to thank Professor Herbert I. Priestley, Miss Edna Martin, and Mrs. Eleanor Ashby Bancroft. I have also used material from the collections of the University of California Library, California State Library, Huntington Library and Art Museum, and Illinois Historical Society. Mrs. Estelle Doheny permitted me to use from her private collection the important Jefferson map. The volume of Virginia Reed's letters was made available through the courtesy of Mrs. W. W. Gilmore, and Dr. George Henry Hinkle. To these individuals and to the officers of the various libraries and societies I offer my sincere thanks.

Mrs. Theodosia Burton Stewart has, as always, been a helpful advisor. Mr. Harvey Fergusson has been generous of his time, and has given much valuable criticism. Professor George R. Potter has helped me explore the mountains upon several expeditions during which our sufferings were (I have sometimes thought) second only to those of the Donner Party. I wish also to acknowledge advice, information, and aid in the interpretation of data furnished in correspondence or conversation by: The California Fish and Game Commission, the Rev. James Culliton, Professors Herbert E. Bolton, Frederick L. Paxson, Charles L. Camp, and Erwin G. Gudde, Dr. Eric Ogden, Dr. C. W. Chapman, and Messrs. Charles Kelly, P. M. Weddell, and Grant Smith.

For permission to reproduce the Breen diary I am indebted to the Bancroft Library.

G. R. S.

Berkeley, California
December 9, 1935.

CONTENTS

MAPS

ON THE MAPS

The maps, being of such small scale, are merely for the general guidance of the reader, and offer little information not supplied by the text. Je is the chief source. The maps do not attempt to show minor deviations. The crossings of the Humboldt are from Je, and are presumably correct. On the Truckee and elsewhere the recording of individual stream-crossings would require a much larger map.

The precise route of the emigrant road in 1846 has not yet been established foot by foot. The only controversial point of importance, however, is the question of whether the road ran (1) north of Donner Lake and through the pass now used by the railroad, or (2) *via* Cold Creek and through a gap about a mile south of the other. Both routes were certainly used in early times, but I have no hesitation in stating that the former was the earlier, and was used in 1846. Use of the other may possibly have begun as early as 1846, but I think more likely later. In 1849 the route north of the Lake had been abandoned, for on September 15, 1849, E. Douglas Perkins wrote in his diary (MS., Huntington Library): "The road from the Donner huts has been changed—instead of going round Truckie's Lake as formerly it begins to ascend the mountains immediately."

Hastings's detour around the Ruby Mountains stands out even on a small map. He had never explored this route, and why he took it rather than a more direct one can be explained only upon the grounds of his sheer ignorance.

PART I

THE MARCH

"Bear thee grimly, demigod!"
Moby Dick

FOREWORD

To OBSERVE the scene of this story the reader must for a moment imagine himself taken backward many years in time and raised in space some hundreds of miles above a spot near the center of the state of Nevada. Poised there at an aëry point of vantage, facing toward the north and blessed with more than human eyesight, he sees laid out beneath him the far west of the United States of America. Only it is not yet part of the United States. Over it Mexico still claims a nominal sovereignty, soon to be ended by process of the war already begun; actually it is the land of Indian tribes and the haunt of a few white trappers. The year is 1846; the month, July.

Far to his left, westward, the onlooker from the sky just catches the glint of the Pacific Ocean; far to his right, on the eastern horizon, high peaks of the Rockies forming the Continental Divide cut off his view. Between horizons lie thirteen degrees of longitude, a thousand miles from east to west. A sweeping glance reveals a region of high plateau, mountain, and desert, brilliantly alight with a seldom-clouded sun. The far-reaching scene is somewhat lacking in the brighter colors, and in general dull green, drab, and gray possess the land. But, here and there, spots of bright blue reveal lakes and a shining dazzle of white shows the location of alkali plains. Little snow appears in the scene, but it is, we remember, midsummer. The land knows snow in its season.

Having satisfied his curiosity with an impressionistic glance, the observer must now view the country more systematically from east to west along a line following roughly the center of the landscape. From the peaks of the Continental Divide upon the eastern horizon, high plateau country scattered with mountains extends westward a hundred miles to the few log huts which form the trading-post of Fort Bridger. In the next hundred miles, west of the Fort in the present state of Utah, lie the Wahsatch Mountains, lofty, rugged, and forbidding. They are in most places bare of trees except along streams, for they are mountains which face a desert.

Just westward of their base lies the Great Salt Lake itself, a sizeable and very brilliant spot of blue with a wide alkali desert running off from it southwestward in a white shimmer. For five hundred miles westward from that salt inland sea stretches, dun and heat-stricken under the summer sun, the arid country of the Great Basin, which forms now the state of Nevada. A monotonous succession of mountain ranges is this land's most noticeable feature. Treeless, of dark volcanic rock sometimes sinister in reds or tawny yellows, as yet nameless, these ranges run north and south at almost regular intervals. As the sun moves, their shadows swing from west to east across the great empty sagebrush valleys between them. Afternoon looks only morning reversed. It is a thirsting land. Small meadows with springs fringe the bases of the mountains, but dust storms blow over the plains, and rivers are few. The Humboldt, dreariest of streams, threads from east to west between the desert ranges, stretching out toward the Truckee descending from the Sierra Nevada. But Humboldt and Truckee alike disappear in sinks and salt lakes, and forty miles of desert lie between them.

At the western edge of this arid country rises suddenly the sheer wall of the Sierra Nevada. At its foot the drab color ends, and the mountains stand forth notable by the rich green of forests, the blue of lakes, the white of snow, and the clear shimmer of high wind-swept granite. The Sierra and its foothills form a belt a hundred miles wide, and westward of them is the Sacramento Valley of California, now in mid-summer stretching away mellow and golden with its ripe grasses. And in the valley the watcher from the sky may see also the adobe walls of Sutter's Fort.

Between Bridger's and Sutter's the only mark of civilization is a tenuous trace winding from east to west and for a portion of the way swinging off to the north into another region. It is a faint pair of parallel lines—the track of wagon wheels on the California trail.

Even now, far upon his right, the watcher may mark the emigrant trains. Most of them have just come into view, their white wagon-tops agleam as they debouch from South Pass at the Continental Divide. Some are for Oregon, some for California, and even all bound for one destination will not follow exactly the same route, but all who are for California must at last descend the winding way to where the Humboldt dies in the sand. Then they must reach the Truckee, go up it, pass the blue glitter of Truckee Lake, and finally by sheer power of oxen lift their wagons over the Sierra.

It is a long road and those who follow it must meet certain risks; exhaustion and disease, alkali water, and Indian arrows will take a toll. But the greatest problem is a simple one, and the chief opponent is Time. If August sees them on the Humboldt and September at the Sierra—good! Even if they are a month delayed, all may yet go well. But let it come late October, or November, and the snow-storms block the heights, when wagons are light of provisions and oxen lean, then will come a story.

I. THE LONGEST WAY ROUND

TAMSEN DONNER was gloomy and dispirited as the wagons pulled aside; Mr. Thornton noted it in his diary. The others were in high spirits at the prospect of the new route ahead, but she felt they were relying only on the statements of a man of whom they knew nothing personally and who was probably some selfish adventurer.

The place of separation was the Little Sandy. Willows lined the creek where the shallow, clear waters ran over yellowish sand. Lupin bloomed on the camping ground. The grass among the willows was trampled by the hoofs of many oxen. Back from the stream the sagebrush country began, and across sandy rolling table-lands the emigrants could look away toward buttes and snow-capped mountains in the distance.

To the right the wheel tracks, scarcely to be called a road, bore away for Oregon and California over Greenwood's route. To the left was the way to Fort Bridger, leading to the new cut-off south of the Great Salt Lake. With last farewells said, Governor Boggs, Mr. Thornton, and the greater number of the emigrants turned their wagons off to the right, but Mr. Reed, "Uncle George" Donner and his brother Jake, the "Dutchmen," and a few others kept to the left. The day was July 20, 1846.

In the smaller company were twenty wagons, each lurching ahead as its oxen shouldered their heavy way along. To this point their owners had merely formed part of the great emigration of that year, and as companies with confusing rapidity had formed, and broken, and re-formed under different leaders, the emigrants thus finally grouped together had now traveled in company, now apart. Before the time of the separation at the branching of the roads, the Donner Party cannot be said to have existed.

That it ever existed at all, was the result of one man's scheming. On July 17, while the emigrants had been toiling up to the Continental Divide at South Pass, a horseman had come riding to meet them, and had handed round an open letter. With an almost imperial sweep it was addressed "At the Headwaters of the Sweetwater: To all California Emigrants now on the Road." It told of war between the United States and Mexico (although the emigrants knew of that already), and urged that all those making for California should concentrate into large parties against danger of Mexican attack. It gave information also of a new and better route which the writer had recently explored, and urged the companies to take this road to the south of the Great Salt Lake; he himself would wait at Fort Bridger to guide them through. It was signed Lansford W. Hastings.

The letter brought a new subject for talk around the campfires on the three evenings which followed. The very name of Hastings carried much weight, for every one knew of his book describing Oregon and California and the routes thither. It had done much toward inspiring the heavy emigration of this season. And here was the author himself, whose words must be true because they were in print, come to meet the trains and like another Moses guide them through the wilderness. Some of the emigrants had copies of Hastings's book with them, and from it they could see to their greater assurance that this idea of a new and better route was not a sudden notion with the author. In clear black and white on page one-thirty-seven they could read:

The most direct route, for the California emigrants, would be to leave the Oregon route, about two hundred miles east from Fort Hall; thence bearing west southwest, to the Salt Lake; and thence continuing down to the bay of St. Francisco.

Even before receiving the letter, the emigrants had happened to meet near Fort Laramie a few men just come from California, and from them had learned something of Hastings and his latest doings. To explore the way, it appeared, he had left Sutter's Fort in the Sacramento Valley late in April, and risked his life in crossing the still unmelted snows of the Sierra Nevada. Such energy and devotion for the welfare of others (for was he not bringing them warning of the war?) spoke well for the man. Some of these returning Californians, one old trapper especially, gave warnings against the new route—but was not some one like Hastings, who had written a book, rather to be trusted than these un-educated frontiersmen?

As they learned more of Hastings, the emigrants must have been impressed. He was young for a leader, only in his middle twenties. But there was a certain dash about him, and his self-confidence was infectious. Luck seemed to be with him. In '42 he had taken a train safe to Oregon through hair-breadth adventures with the Sioux. He had returned east by way of California and Mexico, and then in '45, just the last winter, had crossed the Sierra in the middle of December, got through to Sutter's on Christmas Day just ahead of the first big snow-storm which would have frozen him stiff as a poker.

And here he was again, turned up chipper as a jay-bird, after crossing a thousand miles of mountains and deserts full of Injuns. It's a good thing to take your chances along with some one who's lucky. Gamblers know that, and if you weren't something of a gambler, you shouldn't be crossing the plains—not in '46. People who weren't for taking chances shouldn't head their oxen west from Missouri.

Nevertheless, a certain shrewdness kept most of them from following Hastings. Didn't he most likely have an ax of his own somewhere to grind? They had taken enough chances to set out on this danged road at all. The way by Fort Hall might be long, but "the longest way round is the shortest way home," as they said back in the states.

At Fort Bridger, a hundred miles away, Hastings was waiting. Some emigrants from preceding parties had already gone to join him. Their wheel-tracks ran ahead, plain-marked in the granite sand, as the Donners and their friends swung off to the southwest.

Along the trail for Fort Bridger went the twenty wagons, high-wheeled and canvas-covered, their long line bobbing and dipping over the hummocks. For some trapper or wandering Indian looking under his hand from a distant mountainside, it was only another emigrant train going west. Weeks of prairie sun and rain and sun again had bleached the wagon-tops to a dead bone-white that shone out for miles over the dull sagebrush plain. Beside each wagon walked the driver calling his monotonous "Gee!", "Haw!", and "Whoa!", cracking and plying the long-lashed ox-whip over his two or three yoke. Driving oxen was man's work. The women sat

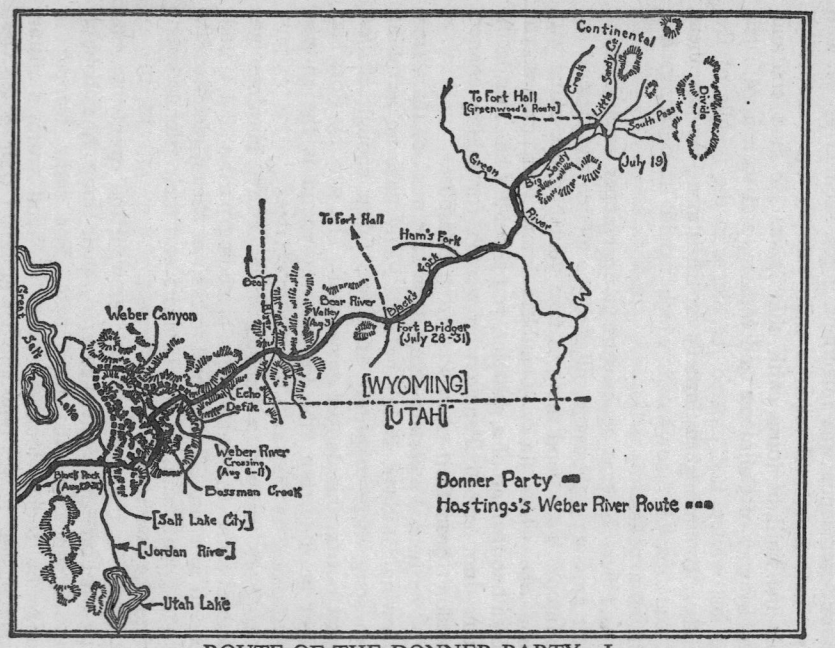

ROUTE OF THE DONNER PARTY—I

in the front seats of the wagons knitting. Children peeped out from front and rear, their heads often bleached almost as white as the wagon-canvases. The family dogs trotted along-side. The few men like Reed and Stanton who were lucky enough not to be ox-drivers explored ahead on horseback, or cantered across the plain with Virginia Reed on Billy, her pony, galloping beside. At the tail of the wagons dust rose from the herd of loose cattle-milch cows, spare oxen, and saddle horses, urged along by some of the boys and an extra man or two.

The only mark to distinguish this train from twenty others was one great wagon looming out over all the rest, rolling along behind four yoke of oxen. Faithful Milt Elliott, Reed's most trusted driver, guided them. The wagon itself was gigantic. Reed had had it built for the special comfort of his family, particularly for his ailing wife and her mother, Mrs. Keyes. The old lady, however, yielding apparently to age rather than to the exhaustions of the journey, had died before they were well out on the plains. The wagon seemed almost a memorial to her. Instead of the usual entrances at front and rear it had easy steps at the side, which led into a veritable little room amidships. Here were comfortable spring seats such as the best stage-coaches used, upon which the women from other wagons liked to sit cozily chatting as the wagon moved along. For warming the compartment on cold mornings an actual sheet-iron stove had been set up, its pipe carefully conveyed through the canvas top. The wagon might almost be called two-storied, for a second floor had been laid across it. On this level were the beds, while beneath, high enough for a child to crawl about in, were compart-ments for storing the food and the canvas bags full of clothing. This was the Reeds' home on wheels, and here Eliza Williams, the hired girl, cooked, washed, and even churned butter as the wheels rolled westward.

Like humanity which is borne always one way in time, so the wagons moved on unreversing into the west, and like humanity which lives unescapably in the vivid present be-tween the half-remembered past and the unknown future, so the emigrants moved overland between the horizon which shut down behind and the horizon which lifted up ahead, half forgetting the traveled road and ignorant of what landscape lay ahead beyond the next rise. As in the greater world, too, noble men and women housed there along with petty, the courteous with the boorish, and the courageous with the cowardly. Yet for the moment in a time of little stress those differences could pass unnoticed. Perhaps no one considered, any more than a man thinks of such matters in any gathering, that in that company were those who might sacrifice themselves along with those who might sacrifice others; those whose love would make of death a little thing, along with those whose hate would be as the venom of snakes. In that voluntarily joined company walked in all ignorance one who was to share the last ounces of food with another, and a third who was to refuse water to the babies of the first. There the slayer walked beside him who was to be the slain, and neither thought of blood. Beneath those wagon-tops lived unrealized the potentiality of heroism to the point of the quixotic, and the potentiality of depravities and degradations of which the emigrants at that moment could not have guessed or have given the name. A microcosm of humanity, to be tested with a severity to which few groups of human beings in recorded history have been subjected, destined to reveal the extremes of which the human body and mind are capable —and yet to the eye of the trapper or wandering Indian merely one more emigrant train going west.

2. MUSTER-ROLL

On the day after leaving the Little Sandy the company met to elect its captain. The task was most likely an easy one, for few of the party could meet the qualifications which the emigrants expected of a leader. The western American in spite of his intense democracy had a profound respect for property, so that the captain of a wagon-train was generally a man of substance. He was also expected to have reached an age which commanded respect, to be an American, and to be able-bodied. Of the emigrants in this particular party, two could meet these requirements.

One of them was George Donner, an elderly, prosperous farmer from the vicinity of Springfield, Illinois. He was of a gentle, charitable spirit; neighbors back home said that it appeared to be a positive pleasure for him to do a kind act. Born of German parentage in North Carolina, he had like so many of his generation come westward by stages—Kentucky, Indiana, and Illinois. He had even spent a year in Texas. Migration by ox-team was nothing new to him, but always he had been behind the first advance of frontiersmen. In spite of his disposition toward wandering, he had attained much property so that he left the children of his first marriage, now grown to maturity, safely in possession of good farms in Illinois. In his sixty-second year and so known in familiar rural fashion as "Uncle George," he was now traveling west in ample manner. Three wagons rolled behind their oxen carrying his goods and the five children of his second and third marriages, all daughters, and the youngest only three years old.

Shepherding this brood was his third wife, Tamsen. Massachusetts-born, forty-five years old, she had gone west and had been a schoolmistress and already once a wife before marrying George Donner. In size she was a mere whiffet: barely five feet she stood, and her weight was less than a hundred pounds. Nevertheless she had sinewy physical stamina. As became her New England birth, she cherished a high sense of duty, but she had also, like her husband, a kind heart. Her book-learning and keen mind gained her the respect of the less tutored emigrants. She it was who had shown her misgivings over leaving the established road and following the promises of Hastings.

George Donner with his wife and his children, his hired servants and his cattle—there is about him something of the gray-bearded Biblical patriarch. Like Job in his prosperity God had blessed him. He did not, to be sure, count his wealth in camels and she-asses, but he had taken the road with twelve yoke of oxen and five saddle horses, along with milch cows and beef cattle and a watchdog. His three wagons overflowed like horns of plenty. They carried food, enough and much more than enough to take his household to California, and besides that, they were crammed with all sorts of gew-gaws to be given as presents to the Indians, and with laces, silks, and rich stuffs to be traded with the Mexicans for California lands. Tamsen had laid in books, school supplies, even water-colors and oils, everything necessary for

the founding of a young-ladies' seminary for her daughters
on the shores of the Pacific. And somewhere stowed carefully away in one of those wagons was an innocent-looking
quilt into which had been neatly sewed bills to the amount,
it has been reported, of ten thousand dollars.

But why, one may well ask, why with old age at hand,
father of fifteen children, with grandchildren springing up
around him, with wealth and position established—why did
George Donner suddenly strike out upon a toilsome removal
of himself and his family to California? He had, it seems,
been reading some of the recently published accounts of the
Pacific Coast, such as Senator Benton's speeches, Frémont's
reports, and Hastings's guide. And what man, shivering in
the November winds of Illinois, could resist those roseate
descriptions of a happier land far away?—"Even in the
months of December and January, vegetation is in full bloom,
and all nature wears a most cheering, and enlivening aspect.
It may be truly said that 'December is as pleasant as May.'"
The road to this paradise, moreover, was represented as beset
with few difficulties and only a spice of danger. It would be,
they thought, "a pleasure trip." So we may consider George
Donner merely one of the first of those many thousands of
middle-western farmers who have felt the lure of balmy
Pacific breezes and set out to "move" to California.

Against the patriarchal and gentle Donner, the only natural
rival for the captaincy was his friend and associate, but a
very different man, James Frazier Reed. Any contest between
them must have been of a friendly nature, for the two had
undertaken the trip in common and had traveled together all
the way from Springfield. Reed was a younger man, only
forty-six, and more practical reasons had swayed him in the
decision to emigrate. For by his move to California he might
well hope to escape the hard times afflicting the Mississippi
Valley in the forties and to prosper even more than he had
in Illinois. He hoped also that the already famous climate
might benefit his invalid wife.

There was a touch of the aristocrat about Reed—and properly, for he was sprung from the line of an exiled Polish
noble. Reedowsky the name is said to have been originally. The fierce and haughty Polish nature had not been greatly
subdued by having its blood mingled with that of the stiff-
necked and restless Scotch-Irish. By virtue of both lines

of descent Reed was a man for quick decisions and decisive action. At Fort Laramie when the old trapper had talked about the Fort Hall road, Reed had spoken up: "There is a nearer way!" It was like him—to choose the nearer way. It was like him also to own the best and fastest horse in all the company, to carry with him the full regalia of a Master Mason, and to hold in reserve for its impression upon Mexican officials a certificate of his character signed by the governor and duly stamped with the eagle, shield, and sun of the Great Seal of Illinois.

Reed had been born in the north of Ireland, but had been in the United States since boyhood, and had spent most of his active life in Illinois. He had served in the Black Hawk campaign in the same company with lanky Abe Lincoln, also from Sangamon County. In Illinois Reed had prospered as a merchant, railroad contractor, and manufacturer of furniture, but lately had suffered some reverses in business.

Nevertheless he was even more wealthy than Donner, or at least made more display of wealth. On the Fourth of July, celebrated in the midst of the Rocky Mountains, he and his friends had toasted the occasion with wine and fine old brandy carried in his stores for a thousand miles. A hired man helped with the rough work of his camp, and hired drivers cracked their whips over the oxen of his three wagons. His wife had Eliza Williams to cook and aid with the three smaller children. His thirteen-year-old stepdaughter Virginia had her own pony for gallops across the prairie. He himself dashed back and forth upon his prized gray racing mare, called in fine defiance of Latin gender, Glaucus.

Maturity, wealth, and long residence in the country made Reed a natural candidate for leadership. In fact his physical vigor, his more active mind, and great experience in handling men gave him preference over Donner. But he had a fatal flaw—he was an aristocrat. For though the westerner always bowed to wealth and position, he insisted that their possessor should act as if he were one of the crowd. Moreover Reed's decisive and somewhat imperious nature had already made at least one man of the party his enemy. But if he had held himself a trifle less stiffly, if Virginia had ridden in a wagon as the other children did, if the mare Glaucus had been a little less clean-cut in the legs, then we might have had the Reed Party, and the story might well have been different.

As it was, on this day after leaving the Little Sandy, the election fell to George Donner. Nevertheless Reed's prestige still remained great enough for Edwin Bryant to write, even after this time, that the party was "known as Messrs. Reed and Donner's company."

Reed was probably well enough satisfied, or indeed may even have preferred this arrangement. As close friend of the rather easy-going Donner he must have known that his influence would scarcely be the less for his lack of the rather empty title.

And in fact the captain of a train of this sort had little real power. He gave his name to the company, but his duties concerned only the smaller matters. He could select the camp-site, give the word for starting in the morning, settle minor disputes between emigrants; but any more important problem, such as a change of route, was decided by the company as a whole. The captain, moreover, was often deposed by mere vote. In practice his powers were likely to vary with the company. If most of its members had come from the same community or were otherwise held by a common bond, they might submit to some discipline. But if they had joined on the plains merely for convenience, they were likely to go their own ways again as convenience changed.

In this respect the Donner Party was perhaps average: many of its members were held together only by immediate self-interest, but it had an unusually well consolidated nucleus in the group which had originally set out together from Springfield. Of its original members one had died and some others had left, but thirty still remained, counting children, teamsters, and the hired girl. They had brought with them from Springfield nine wagons in all: three of George Donner's, three of Reed's, and three of Jacob Donner's.

This last, "Uncle Jake" as they called him, was George Donner's elder brother, also a patriarch. With him were his wife, his two stepsons of fourteen and twelve, and his five children, the last ranging from nine years down. Since George Donner's second wife had been a sister of Mrs. Jacob Donner, the relationships between the children of the two families displayed a complexity pleasing to a genealogist, ranging all the way from double cousins to no blood-relationship at all. Like his brother, Jacob Donner was industrious and kindly, but age was telling on him. Already in his middle sixties, he had passed his best days, and was in frail health.

With the wagons from Springfield had come also several young men. By "bull-whacking" they could earn their way to California, and there the more ambitious ones hoped to attain farms of their own. Although they figure little in the story they should be recorded, if for nothing else, merely for their fine old English names. With Reed were Milt Elliott, Walter Herron, James Smith, and Baylis Williams, the last a sort of utility man and a brother to Eliza the hired girl. With the Donners were Noah James, Samuel Shoemaker, and the English-born John Denton.

After the Springfield contingent the most numerous clan in the Donner Party was that which centered about old Mrs. Murphy, a widow traveling with her five half-grown unmarried children and her two married daughters with their husbands and children. Altogether they numbered thirteen, all of American stock, from Tennessee and Missouri. Unlike the Springfield people, they were not well-to-do, but the two sons-in-law, Pike and Foster, were young and abundantly energetic.

Another young man named William Eddy was the head of the fifth and last American family in the party. In his one wagon rode his wife and two small children. He was from Illinois, a carriage-maker by trade, rough-and-ready, no man to be trifled with in a quarrel and for the same reason a man to be counted on in a pinch. He was enterprising, straightforward, and much liked in the company. Among them all he seems to have been the best hunter and the most skilled in the arts of the frontiersman.

The Donners, Reeds, Murphys, and Eddys must to some extent have looked upon the other families as foreigners. Patrick Breen, indeed, had been an American citizen for two years, but the brogue was still on his lips. He and his wife Peggy were in the full vigor of life, and their family, consisting with true Irish prodigality of seven children, ranged downward from John, a big boy of fourteen, who looked older. Nevertheless Patrick Breen was no mere bog-trotting Paddy of the type which was flooding America in the forties. He could read and write (no common accomplishments for an Irishman of the day), and his diary remains as a unique historical record. He had owned a farm in Iowa, and was by no means poor. Like the Donners and the Reeds he traveled with three wagons, two for food and the third a light one in which the beds and smaller children might be carried. His livestock comprised seven yoke of oxen, together with some cows and riding horses and a dog, Towser, whose tragic end has been recorded for history. With the Breens, but having his own wagon, traveled the unmarried Patrick Dolan, a merry and light-hearted Irishman given to being a comedian for the company.

Another foreigner was a "Spaniard" from New Mexico, known as Antonio or Antoine. He had been picked up somewhere around Independence where the mule-teams of the Santa Fe traders were mingled with the ox-teams of the emigrants for California and Oregon. His special office seems to have been to herd the loose cattle. But as to who hired him, to what family he was attached, and why he had set out for California, the record is silent.

Most of the foreigners, however, were classed by general western usage as "Dutch," although actually with the exception of one Fleming they were all Germans.

Most prominent among them, and owner of two wagons, was Lewis Keseberg. With him were his wife and their two small children. He had come from Westphalia only two years previous. In his early thirties, tall, blond, and handsome, overflowing with the full vigor of manhood, Keseberg made a fine appearance. He spoke four languages, and was probably by far the most highly educated person in the company.

Why did such a man as this come to wander across the barren plains of the west, the comrade of uneducated farmers and boorish ox-drivers? It was not apparently from poverty. But somewhere in his background one suspects a tragedy. His actions sometimes seemed those of a man who is paying off a grudge against the world. Many of the emigrants did not like him, and they had reasons. From what they saw and heard they believed that he beat his wife. Moreover, while still on the Platte, he had been caught in an even greater impropriety. There in company with another German he had robbed an Indian burial-place, actually taking the buffalo robes from the body. At once scandalized, and terrified by the insult to the powerful Sioux, the emigrants had forced him to return the robes and to leave the dead warrior again wrapped in dignified repose upon his scaffold. Moreover, largely through the urging of Reed, Keseberg had been for a while banished from the company with which he had then been traveling. Naturally he bore Reed no good will in return.

The Wolfingers, husband and wife, made up the other German family. They also were reputed wealthy, and the farmers' wives looked with envious eyes at Mrs. Wolfinger's rich clothes and jewelry. Two German men, Spitzer and Reinhardt, are reported to have been partners, and so probably had their own wagon. "Dutch Charley" Burger was, presumably, Keseberg's teamster.

The owners of wagons with families and teamsters and a household servant or two constituted the bulk of the Donner Party, but there were also, as with most wagon-trains, a few unattached men making the journey, perhaps with intentions of emigrating or perhaps merely for love of adventure. They usually rode horseback, and paid some owner of a wagon to transport their food and baggage.

One of these was "old man" Hardkoop. He counted as a Dutchman, although he had originally come from Antwerp. He was a cutler by trade, had lived in Cincinnati for some time, and had prospered there. Some strange prompting had led him when past sixty to set out for California, apparently expecting after the journey to return to his children in Belgium.

Another stray was Luke Halloran. As the company had been breaking camp at the Little Sandy he had approached George Donner with his story—he was attempting to reach California but had fallen sick; he could no longer ride horseback and the family with whom he had traveled could not accommodate him further. The mark of consumption indeed was already upon him, and George Donner was no man to refuse the stranger in distress. From then on, young Halloran, daily growing more gaunt, rode in the Donner wagons.

Those same ample wagons seem also to have carried the goods of another bachelor, Charles T. Stanton. He had been born in New York state, but for eleven years had been in the swiftly developing village called Chicago. For a while he had made money rapidly as a merchant, but hard times had been too much for him and about 1844 he had failed. For two or three years he had been unable to make a fresh start, but in the spring of '46 he had eagerly taken up the idea of going to California. He was about thirty-five, diminutive in stature, but hardy. In spite of his lack of inches most of the emigrants looked on him with some awe, for he had trained himself in geology and botany, and enjoyed practicing his accomplishments along the trail. His training and natural capacities threw him into association with the Reeds and Donners rather than with the ruder emigrants.

Upon the whole, the members of the Donner Party were substantial people, farmers and business-men seeking a new field of endeavor. Many of them were surprisingly well-to-do. Even young Francis Parkman, who in his journey to the plains this same year had carried with him all his Bostonian snobbery, was forced to note: "Many of the emigrants, especially of those bound for California, were persons of wealth and standing." Certain moderns love to dwell upon the poor qualities of the western emigrant, to picture him as a ne'er-do-well, a rolling stone, a fugitive from justice, or a "poor white." His type has become the Pike, trained to knock the eye out of a squirrel with a rifle bullet, but shiftless, lazy, boorish, moronic, and lacking equally in morals and table manners. These ideas cannot be made to fit to the Donner Party. Among the teamsters may have been some Pikes; among the Germans possibly a criminal or two; but by and large they were the strong timber of which commonwealths are built.

But, curiously enough, their good qualities were not the best for the immediate problem. From the very journey which they made they must indeed be called pioneers, but they cannot be called frontiersmen. They were merely country-folk and townspeople of the middle-west, not mountain-men. Far back on the prairies Edwin Bryant, then in company with the Donners, had commented in his journal upon the great amount of sickness prevalent, and noted that few of the emigrants were accustomed to camping. By now they had adapted themselves to the routine. To the mere hardships of the life they were inured, used as they were at best to but few of the comforts of civilization. But this was not the life to which they were accustomed.

They had, moreover, left behind even their familiar natural environment. Many of them had never seen a mountain.

As inhabitants of a low-lying, well-watered country of forest and prairie, they saw the land through which they now moved as a continual prodigy presenting almost daily some new and often dangerous situation for which they had no precedent. Matters which to mountain-men were mere commonplaces of existence were to them portents to be noted in their journals. A hot spring! Frost in July! A salt lake! To them a dry river-bed was almost a crime against nature, and a stream which grew smaller as it flowed from its headwaters was evidence of a world gone topsy-turvy. Even their vocabulary lacked the far-western smack. They talked of "farms," not "ranches"; they would not have known what was meant by an "arroyo" or a "cavvyard."

Moreover, they were lacking in all sorts of skills needful to one who would cope successfully with the strange new environment. Even Eddy was only an amateur at the wiles of the real frontiersman. To read trail signs, to find water where no water met the eye, to talk sign-language, to know when to smoke with an Indian and when to shoot him, to hole up in a canyon in a snow-storm—the whole lore of the farther west, of desert and plain and mountain—all this was a closed book to these solid farming people plodding along by their oxen through the scattered sagebrush on the trail to Fort Bridger.

3. THE TRAP CLICKS BEHIND

IN the barren upland country through which they now were passing, stream crossings marked the progress. Leaving the Little Sandy, they crossed the Big Sandy and followed its course down. Green River, shrunken in late summer, was low; as they forded, the water scarcely splashed the wagon-beds. They passed Ham's Fork and Black's Fork. The going was good.

Days were hard and monotonous enough with the pulling sometimes heavy over boulders and coarse granite sand. But supper, as the campfires began to glow in the dusk, was a pleasure to be anticipated. The buffalo country was left behind now, but meat of antelope or mountain sheep was likely to be sizzling over the fires. The poorer families might depend upon their staples of salt pork, beans, and hominy, along with bread baked freshly in a Dutch oven. But people like the Reeds had plenty of delicacies—fresh butter, cold ham and pickles, cheese, and dried fruit, with tea, coffee, or milk to wash down the broiled antelope steak.

Then in the cool evenings of the high country the young people had abundance of life left for skylarking. They chattered gaily around the fires. For their songs they could draw upon all the rich balladry of their race from *Springfield Mountain* to *Lord Lovell and Lady Nancy*. Often they laid down the hind-gate of a wagon so that some one like jolly Patrick Dolan, who had already that day walked a dozen miles beside his oxen, could do a break-down or an Irish jig. For to the westerner of that day the overland journey was nothing appalling. The wagon pointed west was part of his life. He remembered other journeys—from Kentucky to Illinois, from Indiana to Iowa. The present one was a matter of months rather than of weeks; the trails were rougher, and the country strange, but the march was in no way a cataclysm, and was sometimes very like a picnic. Not a few that summer were undertaking it for mere love of change and adventure. Granted health and average luck, you enjoyed life as you journeyed, at least during the first part of the trip. Of this time Virginia Reed declared years later: "I know I was perfectly happy." The writers who were to transform the ordinary overland wagon journey into a combination of constant superhuman labor and desperate Indian fighting were not yet born.

They passed more crossings of Black's Fork, and on the twenty-eighth came to Fort Bridger. There, in spite of the military name, they saw nothing more than a pair of double log cabins joined by two lines of palisades forming a horse-corral. Jim Bridger, the famous trapper, had built it three years before as a place where emigrants to Oregon might halt and refit, and where he might pick up some Indian trade. He maintained a blacksmith shop, and sold bad whiskey and other supplies at high prices, occupying the post with his partner Vasquez during the summer and in the winter letting it shift for itself. The spot was a pleasant one on the bottom where Black's Fork parted into several channels and supplied water for much fine pasturage. As a business venture the Fort was not so well located, for just when it was well established, the trains had started using Greenwood's cut-off, which missed Fort Bridger entirely. On the other hand, it lay right in the course of wagons using Hastings's route. Not unnaturally, therefore, the Donner Party heard good things from Bridger and Vasquez of what they might expect ahead on the new trail.

Yes, it was shorter, saved three hundred and fifty miles, maybe four hundred. No bad canyons to cross, and the trail mostly smooth and hard and level. What about Indians? No danger, nothing but low-down Piutes and Diggers. Grass and wood in plenty. Water? Well, there was one dry drive, thirty miles, or say forty miles, at most. But you could cut grass at the springs and carry it in the wagons for the oxen. Maybe the party ahead could even explore a way to avoid the dry stretch. Anyway, it couldn't be so bad; forty miles—that was the same as the one from Big Sandy to Green River on Greenwood's cut-off, and wagons took that rather than come a few miles round by the old road.

This was what the emigrants learned from Bridger and Vasquez, and Reed wrote a letter home to Springfield praising the honesty and fair dealing of the partners—"two very excellent and accommodating gentlemen." What Reed did not know was that somewhere around the Fort was a letter written to him by his friend, Edwin Bryant, who on the twentieth had gone on by pack-train. This letter, which Bryant had entrusted to Vasquez, urged Reed by all means to avoid Hastings's route, but it was never delivered!

Hastings himself was not at the Fort as they had expected. He had waited there, as the Open Letter had indicated, talking with the emigrants as they arrived, and he had even held a meeting to urge the advantages of their accepting him as guide. Some had gone on by the old road, but he had collected a party of sixty-six wagons. Then since the season was getting late and most of the emigrants had already arrived, he had set out, leaving directions for any who wished to follow him.

So they halted for four days. It was a pleasant place, good feed for the cattle, and much of interest about the Fort. Probably, for instance, they saw Old Bill Williams, the mountain-man, still limping about rather the worse for an accident. A few days previous, he had come into the Fort, and bought from an emigrant for $20 what seemed to be an excellent rifle. He loaded it, drew his bead on a mark, and pulled the trigger. The rifle exploded with a roar knocking Old Bill end over middle and filling him with splinters. They picked him up for dead, but Jim Bridger brought him to with whiskey. Whereupon he stood up and proclaimed aloud to the world: "Since I come to these here mountains I've been wounded a hundred times, and struck by lightnin' twice, and no god-damn mean rifle can kill me!" "Old Bill" probably seemed to the emigrants a rough character, no good influence for their children, but a few of his kind in the company would have helped.

Needful repairs were the real reason for a halt at the fort. Wagon tires must be reset, and a dozen minor matters adjusted, for this was the final jumping-off place, nothing between here and the Sacramento Valley. Reed bought some oxen to replace two yoke lost by having drunk bad water. George Donner hired a driver to take the place of Hiram Miller who had left him. The new one was a youngster known as Jean Baptiste, a little frontier mongrel from New Mexico who claimed a French trapper for a father and a Mexican for a mother and probably had a strain of Indian from both. He boasted of knowing much about the Indians and the country on the way to California.

Also they picked up another American family, the McCutchens, husband, wife, and baby, from Missouri. These had probably been left behind by a preceding party, forced to halt on account of sickness, loss of oxen, or the breaking of a wagon. There is no evidence that they now had a wagon, and they most likely made arrangements to take passage with one of the other families. McCutchen himself was a promising recruit. He stood six feet six and was powerful in proportion; his vocabulary was counted picturesque even in the West.

On the last day of July the Donner Party got away from Fort Bridger. A short distance out they came to the fork. To the right the old road led off; to the left were the wheel marks where Hastings's party had turned aside on the new route. It was the last chance. But they had apparently abandoned all thought of Fort Hall, and no Mr. Thornton was present to record whether even Tamsen Donner was downcast as they made the fated turn.

Soon they entered difficult country, rough and mountainous, much worse even than the crossing of the Continental Divide. The road, too, was rougher, for they had left the Oregon trail, beaten down by four years of travel, and were following merely where Hastings had broken the way through. In fact it was often just barely passable, and that was all. In some places the track ran down narrow ravines and along dangerous side-hills; at some places the wheels had to be locked at the top of the descent; the wagons slithered precariously down. Still they got along, making ten or twelve miles a day. They found much to wonder at—soda-springs with queer-tasting water, and a little streamlet so rich in some reddish mineral that it looked bloody. They crossed a high ridge and on the fourth day were in the valley of Bear River; they forded the Bear, went over another ridge, and came to the headwaters of a westward-flowing creek which led them down into an awesome canyon. Here the trail wound close beneath towering red cliffs from which the rattling of the wagons over the stones reëchoed back like the sound of carpenters' hammers tat-tatting far back in the ravines, and a rifle shot magnified itself and went rolling off like grumbling thunder. They came out of this canyon to a stream flowing northwest. This they knew to be the Red Fork of Weber River, which ran into the Great Salt Lake. They followed Hastings's wheel-tracks down the stream for four miles, and then as the trail came to the crossing, they stopped.

Stuck in the top of a bush beside the road was a letter. It was from Hastings. Briefly it informed any who might be following him that the route below, in Weber canyon, was very bad; he feared that his own party could not get through; he advised them to go into camp and send a messenger forward to overtake him; he would then return and guide them across the mountains by a better and shorter route than that down the canyon.

This was disconcerting news, to say the least, but no time was to be lost. The company held a meeting. Three men agreed and were appointed to go forward—Reed, little Stanton, and the gigantic new recruit McCutchen. They clattered away on horseback down the canyon.

The others settled down in camp. They probably expected

the three others to be back in a day, but several days passed. Idling was a pleasant change but the older heads must have worried. Had the three riders been cut off by some war-party of Snakes or Utes? Besides, time was passing. Even before leaving Bridger they had been almost the last party on the trail; it had been the sixth of August when they found the letter. Already provisions in some of the wagons were getting a little low; and the snow on the distant peaks had an ominous look. Besides, what kind of man was this Hastings, anyhow? Hadn't he said he explored this way? How was it he'd blundered right into that hell of a canyon with all sixty-six wagons, women and children and Sunday clothes and everything? It didn't look like a man they'd ought to be following. But what could they do now? They couldn't go all the way back to Bridger and then by Fort Hall. That way they'd never get to the mountains before the snow came. And people said the snow in those Sierras was bad, worse maybe than the big snow in Illinois when it snowed three feet on the level and there was sledding for nine weeks. No, there wasn't any going back. If this was a trap, it had clicked—behind at least. The only thing to do was to go ahead and see if they could come out the other end.

4. THE WAHSATCH

THEN at last on the evening of the fifth day a horseman came riding back up the canyon. He was alone. It was Reed! The camp swarmed into excitement. He looked as if he'd had a hard time, and he was riding a different horse from the one he'd gone away on! What about the others? What had happened? Oh, they were all right. Their horses gave out. So had his own. He had got this one at Hastings's camp.

But again no time was to be lost in mere excitement. That very evening the men met to decide their course of action. Reed's report was clear. He and the others had set off down the Weber, and had soon come to the bad place. Following Hastings's trail they had no trouble in seeing what the difficulty was. The canyon was so narrow that the wheel tracks scarcely had room beside the river. Boulders blocked the way, and the emigrants had been forced either to get these to one side somehow, or to pile up rocks and brush for a road over them. For a week the train had not made over a mile and a half a day. In places the canyon was wholly impassable, and the wagons had been taken right over the spurs of the mountains. Here the way was cleared through thick brush. Then some one had rigged up a windlass at the top of the ridge, and the wagons had been lifted up with ropes almost bodily. These places were so steep that an ox could not keep his feet. In one spot a wagon with its team had slipped right over the precipice, had fallen seventy-five feet, and now lay a tangled mass of ruin.

After getting through the canyon Reed and the two others had come out on the plain of the Great Salt Lake and had finally overtaken Hastings camped on the south shore of the lake at a place where a big black rock was a landmark. Here McCutchen and Stanton had stayed with their jaded horses, and Reed had started back with Hastings. But in spite of the promise contained in the letter, he had been unable to make Hastings return the whole way. They had camped one night at the edge of the mountains, and in the morning Hastings had taken him to the top of a peak and pointed out the general course which he should follow in returning to the Weber. There they had parted, and he himself had ridden on all day, following an Indian trail part of the time, and making blazes on trees so as to find the way back. This route across the mountains was the one which Hastings had taken in coming east; on the word of one of his men who had been ahead exploring, he had tried the canyon route with the wagons, although he had never actually seen it.

As the assembled emigrants listened to Reed's report, a choice of desperate measures faced them. Reed gave as his opinion, supported by those of Stanton and McCutchen, that in spite of the work done by the preceding company, the wagons could not be got through the canyon without the greatest difficulty and most likely the loss or breaking of some of them. The other company was large, and strong in men. They themselves were comparatively weak. On the other hand, the way across the mountains was difficult also, and would take much labor with both shovels and axes.

Finally the company voted unanimously to take the route which Reed had explored. For the last night the fires burned themselves low in the camp on Weber River.

The next morning they set out. A half mile down the river they turned off sharply to the left, following up a creek and leaving Hastings's wheel-tracks, the last trace of civilized man except as they came upon Reed's blazes. Breaking road as they went, they moved ahead only a short distance, and camped that night on the creek. The next day they did not move at all, but had to spend the whole time cutting a way through the thick underbrush along the creek and making a road across the rocky higher ridges. It was tiring work. Up to the top of the first divide they scratched out a winding road, "exceedingly rough and crooked and very dangerous on wagons." The down-grade was even worse, for the only way was to make the road skirt around the open hillside, and with their high-wheeled and top-heavy wagons the emigrants hated side-hill slopes like poison. On the third day they took the wagons without accident across the eight or nine miles of the divide.

Here they came down to what they knew as Bossman Creek. Its real name was Beauchemin, called probably after a French trapper; but if it had been named as being a "fine road," that was a mistake so far as the Donner Party was concerned. Reed's blazes led up its course toward the south, but the road-making, as they soon discovered, was a matter of hewing out the way yard by yard. In the narrow bottom of the canyon willow, alder, and aspen twenty feet tall, intertwined with service-berries and wild rose, made a tangled mass. The emigrants camped, and the next morning the men went forward with axes, picks, and shovels. It was exhausting labor, and not to be finished in a single day. Night after night they came back to the same camp, and every night they were more wearied and disgruntled.

For the unceasing labor rapidly wore them down both in body and in temper. They were for the most part hardy outdoor men, but even so they were not used to this sort of work. After a few days there must have been sore backs and blistered hands. Many of the men had reason to grumble and could justify themselves at shirking, for they had hired out for ox-drivers, not for pick-and-shovel men. Often it was ax-work, too, in the thickets, and the Germans probably had no skill at such labor. It was easier to grumble at Reed who had mapped the route than to cut through the interlocked alders. As dissension grew, work fell off. Besides, they were really too weak in man-power for the task which they were attempting. To clear a road for twenty wagons was as much labor as to clear a road for a hundred, and not so many hands were available for the work. At most, counting even seventeen-year-old Bill Murphy, they numbered only twenty-seven men, and of these Luke Halloran was sick, and the two Donners and Hardkoop too old for the hardest work. Moreover, Stanton and McCutchen were still away, and a searching party had been sent after them. Fewer than twenty axes could be kept working. No wonder that progress was snail-like. Even the oxen were suffering from lack of good pasturage. Service-berries were in season, but the company could have done without the luscious fruit to be rid of the bushes.

On the third day of this struggle they were surprised to be overtaken by three wagons, hauled by the usual ox-teams, with drivers, women in the wagons, and the rag-tag of children, loose cattle, and barking dogs. It turned out to be the caravan of Franklin Ward Graves, called "Uncle Billy," an elderly farmer from Illinois. With him were his wife Elizabeth, his married daughter with her husband Jay Fosdick, his daughter Mary of twenty, his son Billy of eighteen, six smaller children ranging down to a nursing infant a few months old, and finally a young man named John Snyder who was driving a team. They had come on with a party across the plains, but after reaching Fort Laramie had paid little attention to whether they had company or not, and had finally gone ahead to Fort Bridger by themselves. There they had heard of the Donners, and had decided to push on and overtake them.

Altogether the newcomers numbered thirteen, and on being accepted into the company they swelled its enrollment to the final total of eighty-seven. Best of all they furnished four fresh men, as yet unwearied by the labor of road-making.

Thus aided, the discouraged emigrants pushed the road on. After eight miles they left the main creek bottom and began working up a side-canyon westwards. Here the ground rose steadily; the timber was larger; ahead was a discouragingly big mountain, a higher ridge than anything they had had to cross before. Putting through the road, such as it was, eight miles up the Bossman and four or five over the big mountain —even with the aid of the newcomers it took six days! And what a road it was that they hacked out! Along the creek-bottom it twisted and ducked and writhed; it was full of hairpin turns and crossed the creek almost twice to the mile. Two bad swamps gave variety. In the branch canyon the creek must be crossed several times more; the wagons had to be taken around side-hills and jolted over boulders and big stumps. It was horribly rough country. Then toward the top of the big mountain the ascent was steep, and the descent was bad enough to call for the locking of wagon-wheels. Part way down they had to bridge a steep little ravine by cutting small trees and laying the trunks to form a fill.

Even bringing the wagons through after the road was made was a big job. One of Reed's tipped over, but was righted again without much damage done. They had not had time to clear out the overhanging branches, so that at times the canvases were almost torn from the wagons. How Reed's great van got through at all was a wonder. It was August 20 when they finally took the wagons over the big mountain— hard work and dangerous almost all the way.

But from the summit a man could see far off over lower mountains to the wide valley of the Great Salt Lake, and it seemed no great distance off. Heartened, they pushed ahead down the steep western slope. Here the tired men had cleared out only the roughest kind of road. Big stumps stood up jaggedly. The wagons plunged down; it was only luck that wheel or bolster didn't break. They got across the ravine on the fill of tree-trunks. Then the slope eased off, and full of the hope of soon reaching the plain the tired emigrants brought the wagons into a little opening in the mountains.

And here at last they had another cause for rejoicing, for they found the searching party with Stanton and McCutchen. The last two had been really lost in the trackless mountains and when found were in a starving condition, ready to eat their horses.

But rejoicing turned into consternation when these two scouts reported that to reach the valley the train must still go a long way around. The big mountain across which they had just come was not the main ridge, but only a divide between two branches of the Bossman. They must therefore turn off upstream to their left again, and cross another watershed.

At this news the company almost went into a panic. It was too much! Had Reed lost the way? Were they doomed to wander as in a nightmare cutting their way blindly through canyons and over divides? They were plains-people of Illinois and Iowa used to half a universe of sky, but down among these mountains the sky narrowed to a mere slit above, and a person couldn't get a good look around him. To go back was unthinkable, and the idea of carving their way ahead was more than they could face.

They steadied themselves, however, and led by Stanton and McCutchen planned the route ahead. Again there was nothing for the overworked men but to go ahead with axes. The creek-bed was thick-grown, and the ridge higher up was a jungle of service-berries. With the addition of the Graves contingent and the rejoining of the scattered parties, they had now about thirty men available, but fatigue and dissension had grown, too. Slowly, with some fagged and some shirking, they cut the way forwards. For five days they struggled as if still in the nightmare, to open about six miles of road, cutting timber and hacking through brush, digging down side-hills, rolling out boulders, and leveling for creek-crossings. It was as bad country as along the Bossman, and now they were worn out and lacking confidence. The way which they cleared was merely a passage strewn with boulders and ugly with stumps; the wagons took the chance in coming through. By a crooked and steep road they got to the top of the divide, and thence cut an even steeper road down the other side. Then on the sixth day they took the wagons over and descended into a meadow which led on down to a canyon opening into the plain.

They camped for the night, and in the morning made a desperate decision. The canyon farther down seemed narrow and blocked with more thickets, and although they were almost through, the emigrants were completely wearied and simply could not face more labor. So they crossed to the north side of the creek. Then they double-teamed the wagons, and took them sheer up the steep north wall of the canyon.

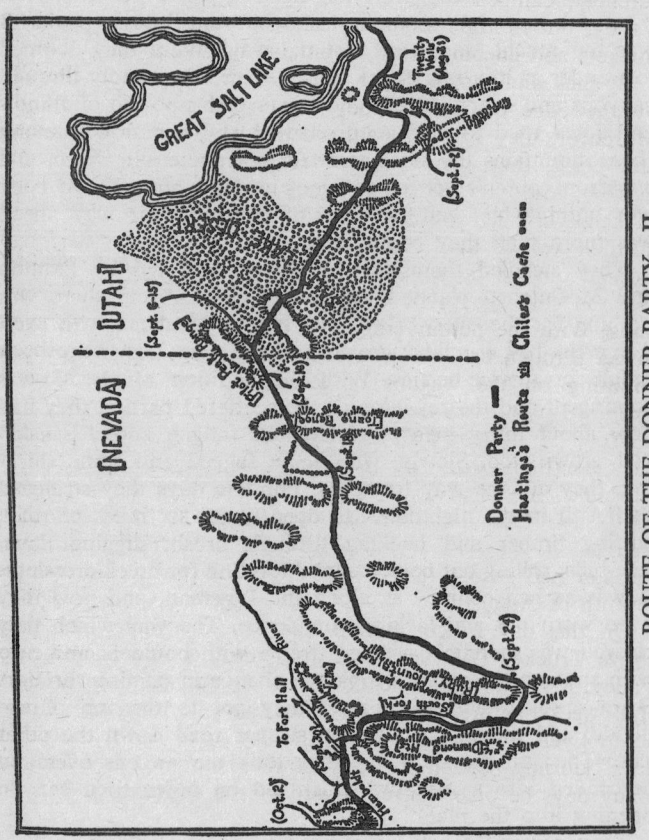

ROUTE OF THE DONNER PARTY—II

It was a gambler's chance, for a slipping ox might have rolled wagon and teams together for three hundred feet down the slope. But they all got over safely, and the canyon on the other side was open and easy. That night they rested serenely, camped there on the open expanse of Salt Lake Valley, out of the woods at last, with the hideous bristling thickets and encompassing mountains behind them.

By pick and shovel they had beaten the Wahsatch; literally by the edge of the ax they had cut their way through. Moreover, they had met with no serious accident. But, man and beast, they were tired. Oxen were lean, and wagons racked. And for the men, even worse, their morale was shaken. They had lost confidence in Hastings their guide, and in their own leaders, and in one another. Too many had shirked on the labor. Fear, too, was coming among them, like the cold breath of wind from the snow-capped mountains. With the poorer emigrants, provisions were low; even to get through to California at all they must now have been counting on the wagons of Reed and the Donners, well crammed with extra supplies.

Worst of all, they were playing—and they knew it—against Time, and they had lost the first game. Twenty-one days it was since they had first camped by the Weber. Twenty-one days—and they had moved thirty-six miles! Daily, as they watched it with the practiced eyes of men living outdoors, the sun had swung farther to the south. It was the twenty-seventh of August.

On this day Edwin Bryant had already topped the pass above Truckee Lake and was descending to the Sacramento Valley. Mr. Thornton and Governor Boggs had been at Fort Hall weeks before, and were already well down the Humboldt. Even Hastings had made the dry drive and was several days' journey beyond it. They of the Donner Party had by many days become the rear guard of the emigration.

5. THE DRY DRIVE

NEXT morning they pushed on again, not even taking a day to recover after the struggle in the mountains. The open plain seemed a paradise, and with the eyes of farmers they noted it as a good place for settlement. It offered easy going for the wagons, too. They forded the river flowing northward to the lake, and then at last came upon the trail of Hastings's wagons. It ran straight across the open country. They followed it till evening, covering more distance in this one day than they had in the ten preceding, and when they camped by a spring only a mile or so from the shore of the lake, they must have felt that at last their luck was on the rise. The next problem would be the dry drive, but they did not know just where that started; and at Fort Bridger they had been told that Hastings might avoid it entirely.

The following day was more difficult, with rough going as they rounded the point of a mountain close to the lake. Here one of Reed's wagons suffered a broken axle, and his men had to go fifteen miles to find timber for a new one.

But much though the wagons jolted over the rocks that day, one member of the party was past caring. During the passage of the mountains the poor consumptive, Luke Halloran, had grown worse. Tamsen Donner had nursed him as she might one of her own children, but in spite of every care he had coughed steadily and grown thinner. Now the paroxysm was upon him. In the afternoon the emigrants saw the wagon halt and fall behind. Inquiries brought only the reply that he was not much worse. But that evening at eight the wagon came into camp bearing a dead man.

Their camping place that night of August 29 was at the black rock by the shore of the lake where Reed had found Hastings, three weeks before.

Next day they merely moved camp to a better location, and out of deference to the presence of death did not attempt to travel. For coffin some one gave boards from a wagon. They buried him with a Masonic service close beside John

Hargrave, a member of Hastings's company who had died at the same place.

Halloran had been a waif, traveling without family or comrades. His possessions—a horse, bridle and saddle, an old trunk and its contents—he left to the George Donners who had befriended him in his necessity. On opening the trunk they found to their surprise, besides clothing and keepsakes, the emblems of a Master Mason and $1,500 in coin. On the plains in '46 even the waifs seem to have been people of substance.

On the next day they followed the trail again; it swept westward in a great curve along what was obviously one more wonder of this strange country, the beach of some long-vanished lake high above the present. Occasionally the trail cut across spurs of the hills to avoid the marshes lower down. At evening they came to another marvel. "Twenty Wells" they called the place, for they counted that number of curious holes seeming more like dug wells than natural springs. These varied from six inches to nine feet across; each was full of pure cold water clear to the brim, but not one overflowed. If water was taken out, the well immediately filled up to the former level. The ground, moreover, was hard and dry right up to the edge of the water. Truly, no one could tell what to expect in a country like this where even a friendly thing like water did not behave after its kind. They curiously cast a sounding-line, and in some of the wells saw a seventy-foot rope disappear without getting bottom.

Next day the trail took them around the point of a range of hills and then almost due south away from the lake. On their right, isolated in the plain, stood up a strange mass of rocks resembling a castle or redoubt. They passed a spring flowing a good stream of water, but so salty that no one could drink it. After a long, hard drive with barren hills close on the left and an arid plain of sagebrush stretching off to the right, they came at last to a fine meadow and springs like those of the previous night—and then suddenly dismay came upon them.

Lying there was a board. Any kind of a board was strange enough in that wild country, but this one had obviously been intended for a sign-post. Scraps of paper still clung to its surface, and others lay about on the ground. Marks of writing showed on them. Had birds pecked them off to eat the paste, or had Indians wantonly destroyed the marker? The simpler emigrants, to whom reading and writing was at best a somewhat marvelous matter, stood frustrated and gaping. What message, what warning, had thus been destroyed for them?

But to the former schoolma'am writing offered nothing mysterious. Kneeling before the board Tamsen Donner began to pick up the scattered tatters and piece them together. Seeing what she was about, the others searched here and there and brought her what they found. She laid the board across her lap and, making use of the shape of the scraps and the marks of writing, pieced out the puzzle. The script was that of Hastings. The others gazed on, as she worked. The message began to take shape as the bare notice—two days and two nights of hard driving to reach the next grass and water.

That was all. The meaning was clear enough, as far as it went. But why could he not have told them more? Something ominous lurked behind such brevity. This, then, was the dry drive. Thirty-five miles, or forty at most, they had been told; but even forty miles was only a forced march of two days broken by a halt for rest during the darkest time of night. Two days and two nights had stretched the dry drive out to fifty miles or more; that is, unless Hastings was just unduly careful and was giving this warning to be sure they looked well to everything before starting.

They spent the next day in preparation. Thirty-six hours of rest would put the cattle on their feet, and although oxen are not camels, still with some grass and little or no water they could go the two days and two nights well enough. The men filled all receptacles for water, and cut grass in the meadow. The women cooked food to last the passage; there would be no chance of fuel later on.

At daybreak of the third they were under way. It was a Thursday; they could not hope to get across the dry stretch before Saturday morning. Hastings's trail, merely the line of wheel-tracks marked by the broken sagebrush, led out almost due west across a great open valley ten miles broad, pointing straight at a range of rough hills high enough to be called mountains. These must be either skirted or crossed before the dry drive was ended—crossed probably, from the way the trail headed. Farther out in the valley the sagebrush was more scanty; the country was getting drier.

It was well on in the day when beneath the desert sun they got close to the foot of the hills and saw the trail rising to the north toward a pass. It was a stiff climb—up and up. No one had told them that a mountain lay in the middle of the dry drive. They toiled up more than a thousand feet above the valley before finally they topped the pass. It must have been late afternoon. The sight that unrolled before them as they looked into the sun might have shaken the boldest.

Below the steep descent ahead lay another plain even more thinly scattered with sage than the one they had just left. After a few miles it ended against a ridge of volcanic hills, rocky and completely barren, offering no chance for water. Over the top of this ridge stretching off for miles they saw a perfectly flat plain unbroken even by sage, and dazzling white, like frost, with the glitter of salt. Beyond this plain, so far in fact that unless the day had been clear they could not even have seen them, rose mountains, the first hope for water. A more sickening sight has seldom faced men tired from a hard day's march, with water-buckets no longer full, and oxen already suffering. Any one could see that even from where they stood much more than forty miles of desert lay ahead.

Most likely they got down from the mountain before night, and made some sort of camp in the valley. The oxen must be rested even if they could not be watered, and probably each animal was doled out a quart from the scanty supply. Men and women shivered in the piercing chill of the desert night, and overhead a great white moon swung through the desert sky.

Whether they waited for daybreak or slogged on desperately in the hours of awesome moonlight, no one has ever told. The way up the next ridge was an agony of steepness, and coming down, the wagons plunged and threatened to break themselves among great volcanic rocks, in spite of the road-making done by Hastings's men. Hours were passing, and the cattle suffered more and more.

At the bottom of the ridge, well on in the second day now, they came into the heaviest going yet. Dunes alternated with level spaces, and the wagons lurched heavily over the dunes only to sink inches deep in the light, ash-like sand of the levels. It was terrible until they had accomplished the descent from the ridge; in such a place need might arise for many hands and extra oxen. But now no more ridges could be seen ahead, and by this second day differences in teams and in temperaments would begin to show up. As the sand began to put a premium on light loads, men with less-burdened wagons or stronger oxen pushed ahead; men less favorably equipped and those who husbanded their teams for the long pull brought up the rear. The march became a go-as-you-can, each family or group for itself. The line began to stretch out over a mile or two, Eddy and Graves ahead, the heavily-laden Donners and Reed's great wagon at the tail.

All day on Friday they struggled on, scarcely seeming to get any closer to the mountains in front. The oxen stumbled beneath their yokes. The first wagons had got through the dunes, and found easier going on a hard surface of salt; the line stretched out further and further as the leaders gained ground.

But if some made faster progress, all suffered equally. The desert sun of September beat down from above, and struck back blindingly from the white surface below. As Eddy plodded by his wagon, he suddenly saw twenty men in single file marching at a distance from him. He stopped astounded; the men stopped with him. He moved; they moved. He realized that a mirage was tricking him; the men were a multiplied image of himself. The others also had visions. Their minds, distorted by thirst, saw lakes in the desert distance. Once the image of the train appeared to them, even with the dogs trotting beside, for a moment so vivid that some of them cried out, thinking that they had actually overtaken the wagons of Hastings.

But if the second day saw suffering, what of the third? Already they had ended the two days and two nights of hard travel for which the message had prepared them. The good going across the hard salt flats had not lasted for long. Next came the sink marking only the middle of the desert crossing; here the wagons broke through the thin crust and sank several inches into sandy slush oozing with salt water. In such a place the wagons could not follow one behind the other, but they fanned out, each driver getting what benefit he could by crossing an unbroken surface. Every one was thirsty now; even the children had to suffer. Tamsen Donner gave hers small lumps of sugar moistened with peppermint. Later on each had a flattened bullet to chew on; it was supposed to keep the mouth from feeling so dry. The hardest pushed teams, now miles ahead, probably got through the sink by Friday morning, but the Reeds and Donners, their heavier wagons losing steadily, were struggling through the slush all that day.

Thursday, Friday, Saturday—and at last dawn broke on Sunday, and found the last wagons still miles out on the salt plain. They had been three days and three nights in the desert, and still no sure end in sight. Water was getting so low that every one faced actual danger of dying of thirst. It came noon. The oxen were about done up; they could never pull the wagons much further under the sun, with no water. In this extremity Reed volunteered to go ahead, reach water, and return. With definite information they could decide whether to abandon the wagons, and push ahead for their lives.

Mounted probably on his racing mare Glaucus, reserved for such an emergency, he prepared to set out. He instructed his teamsters to take the last ounce of pull from the oxen and finally when they could no longer advance to unyoke them and drive them on to water. A little ahead now the trail swung to the left, a good sign. For why should it bend, if not for water? It passed an isolated volcanic crag thrust up through the salt crust, and then not so far beyond reached a mountainous ridge showing a grass-like green; there one might hope for a spring.

Even on his jaded horse Reed soon left the wagons far behind, but the further he went the worse the situation appeared. The emigrants were in all stages of disaster. Some still pushed ahead with their wagons; some had taken their oxen out, and were driving them on for water. The deserted wagons loomed up like tombs; here and there lay exhausted cattle. He reached the mountain, but no water appeared. The green was merely greasewood, treacherously alluring. The trail, mounting, swung around the point of high land, a mountainous promontory thrusting out into the salt desert. It was no great climb, fortunately, but still the sun must have been well in his eyes before Reed topped the rise, and looking westward beheld another disheartening sight. Still the salt plain stretched out ahead, a dozen miles to the foot of the mountains on the other side! Nothing for it now, but to push ahead for water; the horse could not take him back without it. As well as he could on the stumbling horse, he went on. He passed Eddy's wagon, standing deserted, the oxen driven on for water. Finally it was evening when he came to the willow thickets around the spring at the foot of the mountain, just a few rods beyond the edge of the sand. From noon until evening he had ridden; the place where he had left the wagons must be almost thirty miles from the spring.

A few emigrants were already there with their cattle. Eddy was among them; he had got to water at ten that morning, and had been recruiting himself and his oxen through the day. Reed gave himself only an hour. Then in the early dark, probably on a borrowed horse, he started back with Eddy. The latter carried a bucket of water, hoping to find and revive one of his oxen which had lain down. A full moon was rising.

On the return the misfortune of the train unrolled in the opposite direction. Women and children plodding along forlornly or huddling frightened in the standing wagons; cattle frenzied and half-blind with thirst; men driving cattle, carrying water-pails over their arms, and cursing Hastings who had enticed them into this disaster. About eleven o'clock Reed met Milt Elliott and another teamster driving his own cattle and horses. The moon neared the zenith. He began to meet the emigrants who had been with him in the rearguard, the Donners among them, driving in cattle. Finally he passed Jacob Donner's wagon; only his own remained beyond. He struck out into the great salt plain again and at last, only a few miles from where he had left them, he came upon the three wagons looming out gigantically on the plain. The five family dogs greeted him. It was almost daylight. Mrs. Reed, Virginia, and the three little ones were still safe, but they were a perilously long way in the desert. With them were two of the men, and probably Eliza the cook, but Walter Herron, one of the men, immediately took the horse and set out again for water—no need to let the poor beast perish.

All day long under the merciless sun Reed watched the westward trail for his teamsters returning with the oxen. Water was nearly exhausted. Finally at evening they were forced to the last desperate step, and set out on foot. They took what water was left, and a little bread. Mrs. Reed was in weak health and not strong at best. Virginia of thirteen and Patty of eight could shift for themselves after a fashion, and even little Jim who was only five walked manfully, but Tommy a mere baby of three had to be carried in his father's arms. The five dogs followed along—Tyler, Barney, Trailer, Tracker, and little Cash, the children's pet.

In the course of the night the cold of the desert settled down on them; the children became exhausted. Their father laid down a blanket, huddled them upon it, and covered them with shawls. Soon a cold wind was blowing fiercely, and even under the coverings the children whimpered with the cold. The father, his ingenuity fertile with the necessity, ordered the five dogs to lie down on the blanket close to the children and outside the shawls; he and Mrs. Reed sat with their backs to the wind sheltering the children from its worst attack. The whimpering ceased. But it was only a short respite. Suddenly one of the dogs leaped up, barking; the others followed, and all dashed into the night, giving warning and making an attack upon some approaching danger. Reed seized his pistol. In a moment a large animal loomed through the darkness, charging directly upon the family; but the dogs dashed in valiantly and swerved it; as it passed by, Reed recognized one of his steers. Unguardedly he called out that the animal had gone mad. Wife and children sprang to their feet at the words, the children starting to scatter like quail into the night. They could scarcely be calmed.

But the incident had one good result, for fear of worse things now kept the children moving in spite of weariness. They labored on for the rest of the night, and at last, about daylight, they came up to the wagons of Jacob Donner, where they found his family sleeping.

Here Reed learned more of what had happened in his absence. His drivers, it seemed, had not obeyed orders to put the oxen to the limit, but as soon as the animals began to show considerable weariness had taken them from the yokes and driven them ahead. The other emigrants had whipped their oxen on, and even Jacob Donner had taken his wagon some miles beyond where Reed's had been left. But there was worse news; Reed's men had been out searching cattle; nine yoke were missing! Shortly after they had passed Reed, the story ran, a horse had lain down, and while the teamsters were engaged in getting him up, the cattle had disappeared into the darkness, stampeding for some vague scent of water. Unless they could be found, this amounted to a disaster.

Leaving his family with Jacob Donner's, Reed set out again for the spring to spur his teamsters in the search for the cattle. Again he crossed the last stretch of salt plain. Many people were abroad in it now. Some were after cattle which, like Reed's, had been lost. Some had assembled their teams, and were driving them back to bring in wagons. Among them was Jacob Donner, who after meeting Reed on Saturday night had got his cattle to water early on Sunday morning; he would bring Reed's family in with his own.

For by now the passage of the desert had been accomplished. It had been a catastrophe, measured in terms of dead, lost, and worn-out cattle, of equipment jettisoned to lighten wagons, of wagons themselves ruined by the dryness of the desert air. But it had not been a complete disaster. No lives had been lost. A few had at last managed to get through without deserting their wagons. Other wagons had already been retrieved, and the rest could probably be brought in. On Thursday at dawn they had left the springs; now it was Tuesday.

Yes, they had got across, although the price had been heavy. For none had it been heavier than for Reed, who on this morning for the second time got to the spring among the willows, full of the daunting realization that, unless his men found the cattle before the Indians did, he himself was left with one ox and one cow to retrieve three large wagons from the desert and transport them, no one knew just how many hundreds of miles, to California.

6. THE LONG PULL

THE Jacob Donners, bringing the Reed family, came in during this same day of the eighth, so that after six days of continuous struggle everybody had finally got across the desert safely.

Nevertheless, the camp at the spring was a far from cheerful place. Tired men and boys, on jaded horses, were out scouring the country for cattle. Thirty-six head of working oxen were missing, and if they could not be found, it was serious. A few had died in the desert, but most of them following scent had probably got to water somewhere and remained hidden in a canyon, unless (worse luck) the miserable Indians of the country had already found and killed them. Two Indians came into camp once, and made signs which the emigrants took to indicate the missing cattle. But with many of the men away, the women were nervous at having Indians around and were glad when the visitors left, even though they took away with them a clue to the lost oxen.

As they gathered at the camp, the emigrants were in confusion, almost in despair. They openly cursed Hastings for betraying them by concealing the true distance across the desert. Thirty-five or forty miles! By God, it was eighty! Here they were, next thing to stranded, with nearly a quarter of their oxen lost, in a country of Indians. They would have to leave some of the wagons, that was certain. Well, it was nearly an even match between oxen and wagons, for some of the wagons had dried out so with the desert air that they were falling to pieces. But they couldn't go back, that was sure. And as for going ahead following that man Hastings, that seemed almost as bad. But then they couldn't stay where they were, either!

One thing they must do, and that was to bring out the wagons which had been left in the desert, for these wagons held much of the food still available. So some of the men went back into the sink with horses and mules. With these, they could make the journey faster than with oxen, and did not run the same risk from thirst. But since Reed had lost his teams, there was no use of bringing in all of his wagons, and so the men merely transferred the food and other necessities to the big family wagon; then they made an attempt at caching the rest of the property. But there in the sink, as soon as you dug a few inches, the hole filled with salt water. So they laid a wagon-bed on the sand, put the goods into it, and heaped sand over them. It was a conspicuous mound, not likely to escape the Indians, but nothing better could be done. Besides, what real chance was there of his ever coming back to get the stuff, anyway? They left Reed's two wagons there in the desert, and got back to camp with the others the next evening.

By this time the cattle which remained had had about a

week of complete rest and had recovered a little. Young Billy Graves and Milt Elliott, whose unlucky mistake had caused the loss of his master's oxen, were still out somewhere ahead on the lookout for missing cattle, but most of the men were ready for pushing on. Adjustments had to be made before they could start. Reed managed to arrange for the loan of one ox from Graves and another from Breen. These, together with his own remaining ox and cow, made a weak team at best, unable to pull the great wagon so heavily loaded with supplies taken from the two others. The other emigrants would not carry his food in their wagons without being allowed to use it, and so Reed was forced to distribute most of his supply. And some of the others were by this time in distinct need of it.

In the morning only nineteen wagons were ready to start, for besides the two which Reed had had to leave, George Donner and Keseberg had each abandoned one. It was on the whole a sorry-looking caravan that took the road. The wagons showed the wear of the desert-crossing; the oxen were gaunt. Here and there a cow was under yoke. The horses were jaded, and the herd of loose cattle was shrunken in numbers. The men and women, too, were dispirited. Weary and shaken, they went ahead with their only guide the wheel-tracks of that Hastings whom they no longer believed.

They moved out along the base of the mountain range which rose out of the desert. This day the weather changed, and instead of the desert heat a sudden snow-storm burst upon them. It was as chilling to the spirit as it was to the body. Snow in this strange country by the middle of September! And at home the corn would be heavy on the stalk and the nights thick with heat. If it was snowing already here, what would it be in the mountains? They plugged along soddenly, and at three in the afternoon met Milt Elliott and Billy Graves. These two reported that a camp-ground with a spring was near, but added the discouraging news that beyond that point was another waterless stretch of forty miles!

Since the two in hunting cattle would not have been likely to ride so far afield, one assumes that they had found another note from Hastings. And the finding of such a note would make clear the next stage of the journey, for Hastings at a certain point had gone off north of west for close to a day's journey, and then on the following morning had turned back sharply almost upon his own tracks, directly south for a full day's journey, to reach the next springs. The route for the Donner Party struck out directly across the dry plain toward these springs, and so merely crossed the base of the triangle which Hastings had followed around two sides. But in compensation their one day's drive without water was to be longer than either of Hastings's two.

To rest and prepare for this, they halted at the camping-ground, having made, what with the snow-storm and the early stop, only about five miles for the day. At dawn they yoked up for the dry drive. They followed Hastings's wheel tracks for ten miles across an open plain toward a gap in the next mountain range; then after crossing through an easy pass they turned aside to the left and struck out, straightaway, southwestwards. Night fell and it was the dark of the moon. As was the custom on dry drives, they probably halted somewhere to bait the oxen, to throw them out a little dried grass cut at the last pasture, and to let the weaker ones have a quart or two from the water casks. Some of the cattle were in a bad way. Then yokes had to be put on again, and relentlessly the march was pushed on through the dark. Straight they went into the southwest, as straight almost as if they steered a compass course. The cattle became mere stumbling skeletons. Some of the weaker ones dropped, and had to be taken out of the teams and left behind. If Hastings had told any more lies about the distance, this would be the end of everything! But at last, just at dawn, they sighted the green of grass ahead, and came to a fine meadow with many springs, some cool, some lukewarm. They slipped the yokes from the drooping oxen, and rested for twenty-four hours.

They couldn't go on this way. Something had to be done. The cattle were done up, and twenty-four hours wouldn't put them on their feet, either. Twenty-four days, maybe. If the country didn't get better soon . . . ! No use sending back to Bridger's, but they couldn't be so far from Californy now, and people said that Cap'n Sutter always tried to help emigrants in a pinch. If they stopped to rest the critters, they'd be too late to get over the pass, account of the snow. Anyway, they'd just as likely starve before they got there. Hell!— if you pushed the teams too hard, they died on you; and if you didn't push them hard you took too long and got caught in the snow or starved before you got that far—hell! And there were Injuns, too. Wouldn't a fellow like a chance to boot that man Hastings! But, anyway, they could send some one ahead, and maybe he could persuade Cap'n Sutter to send back some food. But what man would you send? A married man wouldn't leave his family and wagons out here in the desert, and if you sent a man who wasn't married, maybe he'd just skip out on you and sit tight once he got to Sutter's. He'd be a fool at that to come back, once he'd got over the mountains. You couldn't blame him a lot. Anyway, two men would have to go, account of Injuns. Even a trapper didn't cross alone, if he could help it.

At last they compromised by choosing Stanton and McCutchen, who had previously made the journey through the Wahsatch in company. Stanton had no family, but he was a gentleman and the kind that could be trusted. And big McCutchen left behind him his wife and baby. A queer-looking pair they must have been as they set off, the gigantic McCutchen and little Stanton a good foot shorter, the big man on a horse, the little one on a mule. They disappeared ahead over the first rise, upon a journey full of dangers, pledged once they had escaped those dangers to return into worse ones.

At the springs the rest of the company prepared to set forward. It was plain that more sacrifices must be made, or the cattle would never get through. So Reed buried most of the little property that he had remaining. Eddy put his team to Reed's wagon; Pike took Eddy's wagon and abandoned his own. The line was still shortening; only eighteen canvas-tops took the trail next morning.

Steady toiling for another day took them across still another easy pass with a fine valley beyond. The country was really improving, and they were getting the hang of it, too. You left a spring, crossed some hills by a gap, went across the plain beyond, and came to another spring under the hills at the far side. The water seemed to be always at the western edge of the valleys. But the country was getting better; there was no doubt of that; maybe they were closer to California than they thought. Many Indians were about, but they seemed friendly and acted as if they had never seen a white man. The broad, treeless valleys were dotted with antelope herds, and mountain sheep browsed on the rocky hills. Fresh steak was a welcome relief to beans, bread, and salt pork—and not so much of those, either.

For two more days they kept on generally westwards through fine country. Of course it was dry compared with Illinois, but there were always well-watered meadows under the eastern slopes. Then one night they camped not far from a range of mountains higher than any they had seen for a long time. It ran across their path, north and south, as most of these desert hills ran, but it did not seem to have any gap in it as the other ranges had. Perhaps Hastings had found a pass somewhere, for the emigrants wanted to go west and not to spend their time playing hide-and-seek with mountains. But next day the trail went off south, paralleling the range; and taking them in the direction they did not care to be going. The country was finer than ever, but even that was not much comfort as the trail ran for a second day southwards. Even when the third morning broke, no gap showed in the hills.

Hastings's trail led off across the plain, still southward. It must be several weeks old. Broken sagebrush, ground scarred by wagon-wheels, the droppings of animals, marked it. On the right the mountains were still close at hand; on the left a broad valley stretched away. The sun rose flaming over far-off desert ridges, and in the evenings, when still high in its course, was cut off by the mountains. Nothing happened to distinguish one day from another. Every night they camped where Hastings had camped. It was past the equinox now, and the moon was waxing. But even so, at some point they actually lost track of time, and got a day off in their reckonings.

There must have been something dreamlike in thus following a trail with no map or guide, or any known landmark, a trail which existed merely between the last rise behind and the next in front, a trail, too, which defied geographical necessity and ran south when every one knew that California was to the west. That was a point! Was Hastings crazy? Was he taking them to Mexico? Did he know *where* he was going? They breathed more easily when after three full days of southing, the trail one morning bore off to the right, and found at last a gap in the mountains. They crossed, came into the valley beyond, reached the springs under the eastern slope of the mountains, and camped there.

Next day, as if out of sheer perversity, the trail led out due north, and for three days they merely reversed what they had done. Again the sun rose behind the distant mountains and sank behind those close at hand, only now for a mocking variety it beat upon their backs, not in their faces. It was a discomfort to realize that each day's journey actually brought them nearer to the place where they had camped several days before.

"Nothing transpired for some days of any note"—these are the words which one emigrant used to describe this part of the journey. Only one variation marked one day from the next, and that was that each man took his turn at leading the train and taking upon his oxen the hard work of breaking trail. So if Foster led on Monday, he fell to the rear on Tuesday, and let another team take the lead. But if monotony ruled, still every day came the steady, tiring pull of fifteen miles or more through the heat and dust, days without even the savor of danger or great endeavor. The story of such days is to be told only in the petty details which no one ever records—little irritations of weariness, and indigestion, and lips splitting with the dryness, of crying babies and women's gossip, such irritations as show themselves only in the tragedies of a larruped boy, a dog kicked and yelping, or oxen too heavily lashed. Yet such irritations could grow and fester in the inescapably close contact of life in the same wagon train. There might come a time when tempers would snap.

No one could have felt the strain more than Reed, naturally a proud and high-strung man. He had been the wealthiest of all—three wagons, five hired servants, oxen and horses of the best. Now oxen and wagons were gone. His family shared with the Eddys. He still had the hired hands, but now they were useless and merely ate up the supplies. He had also, to be sure, enough money about himself to buy up most of the emigrants, but money meant little on the desert and was not a thing to be advertised. Moreover, he knew himself to be unpopular. Even at the Little Sandy they had disliked him for being an aristocrat; now many held him responsible for the delay in the Wahsatch. Probably he suspected that many of the poorer emigrants viewed his present downfall with not a little complacency.

At last on the evening of September 28, after three days of going due north, they camped at the entrance to a canyon.

Stark-naked Indians hovered shyly about the camp, but did not approach. Ten miles to the east, the emigrants could still see mountains, and it was no pleasure to realize that about a week before they had camped just at the other side of those mountains at no greater distance than a man might walk between dawn and evening.

In the next two days they went down the canyon making small distance on account of the roughness of the way. Finally at the end of the last day of September they came to a westward-flowing river which they knew must be the long-sought Humboldt. They forded it, and after dark came to the well-beaten road, following down the north bank. They had rejoined the main California trail.

7. KNIFE-PLAY BY THE RIVER

CUSTOM had not yet settled the river's name, so that the emigrants often called it Ogden's or Mary's River rather than the Humboldt. By any name it was, as by the next morning's light they got some acquaintance with it, an un-prepossessing stream, scarcely more than a series of half-stagnant pools of water, warmish and unpleasant to the taste. Bushes and scrubby willows lined its margin, and grass grew in the meadows. Back from the water sagebrush and grease-wood spotted the benches and hills. It was not such attractive country as that through which they had passed during their long wandering toward the south. Nevertheless, there was rejoicing among the emigrants that they had now done with wandering uncertainly through nameless valleys; henceforth for many miles the river would be a guide and a sure guarantee against the extremes of thirst.

Just how far they were from California, none of them knew. They hoped that Hastings's trail had joined the river far down its course, and that any day now they might meet Stanton and McCutchen returning with supplies. This hope was destroyed, however, by some friendly Indians who wandered into camp and through the uncertain medium of signs gave the emigrants to understand that they were yet two hun-

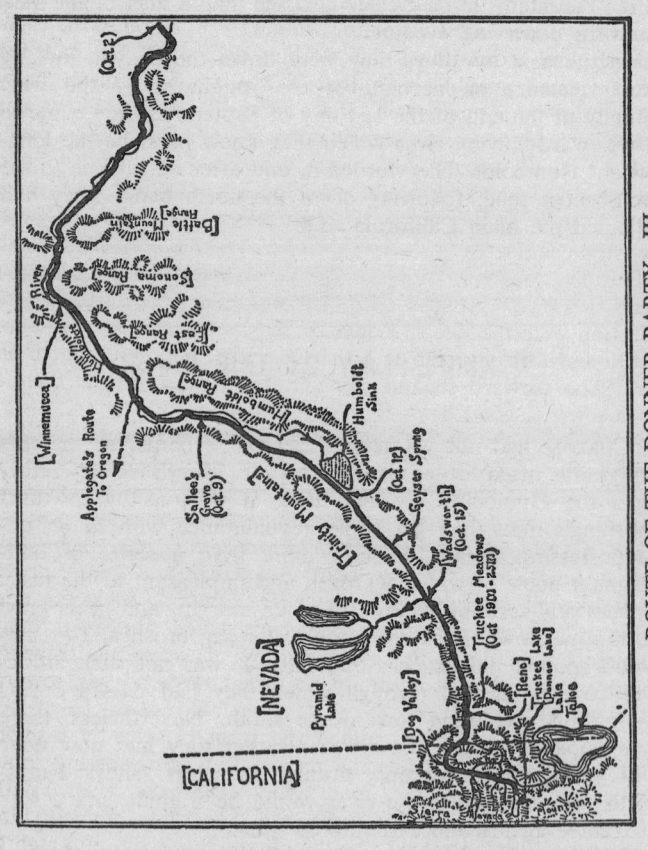

ROUTE OF THE DONNER PARTY—III

dred miles from the place where the river flowed into its sink. In any case there was nothing for it but to go on. The other emigrant trains must be a long way ahead.

By this time the cattle had failed badly. The struggles in the Wahsatch, the thirst and hunger of the desert crossing, and the unceasing wear of the winding trail through the sagebrush had worn down the working-oxen. But no halt for rest seemed possible, now that it was come October; every day must be a steady pull, and a long one. Moreover, at this time of year grass was scanty along the Humboldt, and probably for this reason the company decided to split into two sections so that by camping at different spots they could give the herd a better chance to graze. So the Donner brothers, whose oxen were in better condition, pushed on ahead with their five wagons; with them went Reed's teamsters, except for the faithful family retainer Milt Elliott. In the second section were the Reeds, Eddys, Breens, and Graveses, together with the Murphy clan and the Germans, a dozen wagons in all. The forward section gained rapidly, and in less than a week was a good day's journey in advance.

The new arrangement had the one disadvantage of offering twice as much chance to the Indians. This was the country of squalid desert tribes, known derogatorily by the general name of Diggers, degraded creatures living in filth, poverty and nakedness, not possessing horses and armed only with weak bows. In a stand-up fight they might well be despised, but like all weak peoples they were cunning tricksters and thieves. Having sometimes been mistreated and seen their kinsfolk shot down in cold blood by unscrupulous trappers and emigrants, they naturally cherished no good will toward the whites.

One of these Indians joined the train in friendly fashion on the second day, while the rear section was crossing some hills which forced the road away from the river. With thoughts of Robinson Crusoe the emigrants named him Thursday, thinking this to be the day of the week, although it was really Friday. Thursday spoke a few words of English, picked up from emigrants. Later in the day another Indian came in; this one could call out "Gee!" "Whoa!" and "Huoy!" in imitation of a driver yelling at his oxen. The two went along, made camp with the emigrants, and did good service in helping put out an accidental grass fire which threatened to consume three of the wagons. They were gratefully given food, and then lay down to sleep on the best of terms with every one. Next morning they were gone, and with them a shirt and two oxen belonging to "Uncle Billy" Graves. Two nights later a horse was missing, again part of the Graveses' property. The first section suffered also, for one night the Indians crept up through the darkness and shot arrows into several oxen.

A mountain-man, if there had been one in the company, could probably have put a stop to such troubles. He could have out-wiled the skulkers, shot and scalped one or two, and left the bodies as an ugly but plain warning for all the Digger nation not to fool around with white men's property. But these were farmers, not mountain-men. They might remember their Bibles—about the arrow that flieth by day and how the Lord would guard them from it. But here the arrows flew by night, and the Lord seemed grown careless; perhaps like the law even He did not care what happened west of the Missouri. The best they could do was to set a closer watch at night, a watch which was often ineffectual and which robbed the men of sleep and still further wore down their tempers.

All the while they were pushing hard, and averaging twenty miles a day. They were actually gaining on Hastings, but they could see by the camps that he was still a long way ahead. Every one able was walking in order to lighten the loads. The women and children toiled on beside the wagons, which were still heavy with household goods, but woefully light of provisions. Every one now was on short rations, for game was not plentiful as it had been for a while. Eddy ranged the country for antelope, now and then in his own turn being stalked and shot at by Indians. It had come autumn now. Nights were colder and days shorter. Even the desert sun struck down less viciously. The wild geese were going south, honking through the night.

Petty disagreements grew more irking. The company had been together for too long. By this time they should have been in California, ready each to go his own way, to see new faces and forget the irritations of companionship too long enforced. As it was, they plodded daily along the scrawny stream. South of west they followed it first, and then north of west; and then about noon on October fifth, the second section reached an unusually high and long sand-hill, covered with rocks at the top. It was no worse probably than twenty others they had passed, but it was the final point of strain.

The hill was difficult enough to call for doubling teams. Two of the Graveses' wagons were got over in this way, but John Snyder, who drove the third, thought that his team could make it without assistance. Next in line, driving the wagon shared by the Reeds and Eddys, was Milt Elliott. He had joined Pike's oxen to his own team, and had grown tired of waiting. Probably thinking that Snyder would not move until Graves's oxen returned, Milt swung his wagon aside and tried to pass. The way was narrow; the lead-yoke became unruly, and tangled with Snyder's team. Sharp words passed between the drivers, and Snyder, enraged, fell to beating the oxen violently over the head. Reed rushed forward protesting, and Snyder's rage shifted. Cursing furiously and whip in hand, he threatened the owner of the oxen with a cowhiding, too. Soft words did not put him off, but instead he became so menacing that the fiery Reed, who was not a man to take a beating from any one, drew his hunting-knife. Alarmed in his turn, Snyder suddenly reversed his whip and struck out viciously with the butt. The blow caught Reed across the head, laying open a long gash, but as he tried to dodge he struck back with his knife, driving it home just below the collar-bone. Mrs. Reed rushed between them, and Snyder, still fighting, struck her once and Reed twice more. The last blow felled Reed to his knees.

The encounter must have been only a matter of seconds, too sudden and brief for any of the men to interfere. Snyder turned, and went a few steps up the hill, then staggered. Young Billy Graves caught him, and eased him to the ground.

"Uncle Patrick, I am dead," he spoke out as Breen came hurrying up.

Reed, the blood running down over his own face and shoulders, was in an anguish of remorse. He tore himself away from his wife and daughters as they strove to staunch his wounds; he threw the knife into the river, and pressed in to the dying man. Some said that Snyder spoke once again, saying to Reed, "I am to blame." Certain it is that he was dead in a few minutes.

The train encamped at once with the Reed family a little apart. All was confusion, and the resentment engendered by minor irritations and hardships and kept smothered down for weeks, suddenly burst out. Some sort of council was held with Reed excluded. Written statements were taken with a view to bringing him to trial when they arrived in California. But Snyder, who had generally been a merry young blade, had been vastly popular, while the haughty Reed was correspondingly disliked. The cry rose for more direct action.

Reed's situation was desperate. The Donners and his own teamsters, who could have been expected to stand by him, were headed with the first section. His offer of boards from his own wagon as a coffin only raised greater indignation. Mrs. Reed, at best little better than an invalid, was prostrated by the misfortune and by the blow which she had received. The small children only added to the terror. Reed himself was badly wounded, with the blood caked about the three cuts in his head. Young Virginia pluckily dressed these, washing off the blood, clipping back the hair from the cuts, and bandaging the head.

At evening the crisis came. Keseberg, cherishing the grudge of his former banishment, propped up his wagon-tongue with an ox-yoke, for the hanging. The Graves clan was crying for vengeance.

Only two men, Eddy and the faithful Milt, stood with Reed, but all three were armed to the teeth, and two of them at least were not men to be trifled with. A conflict would have meant death on both sides and the possible crippling of the caravan as a whole. Eddy finally effected a compromise, that Reed was to be allowed to leave the camp and go on ahead. Reed at first refused to be banished and leave his family deserted, but the others promised that they would care for his wife and children. These latter urged him for his own safety and theirs to depart. His wife would scarcely be safe if he should remain. Besides he could do them all a service by riding ahead and bringing back food in case Stanton and McCutchen failed them.

In the morning Reed sorrowfully assisted at the burial of Snyder. No coffin had been made, and the poor fellow was laid away merely wrapped in a shroud with a board below for decency and a board above to keep off the coyotes. When the grave had been filled in, Reed amid the tears of his wife and children took his leave, mounted upon Glaucus. They were a sorry pair, the man haggard, worn, and swathed in bandages, and the once proudly stepping steed now so gaunt with hard fare that she could scarcely carry a rider.

Although they had commuted the death-sentence, the resentment among the company was still extreme, and the final decree had been that Reed should depart without firearms. Had it not been that the Donners were in advance, this inhuman decision would have been the equivalent of death; even so, it exposed him defenseless to the Indians for a day's journey or more. Reed acquiesced in his hard fate, apparently willing to do anything to insure the safety of his family. After he had left, however, some one (Eddy according to one story, Virginia and Milt according to another) followed after and brought him gun and ammunition.

He disappeared from sight, and the company plodded on behind. Upon this section of the trail, the passing wheels of many wagons had pulverized the light alkali soil; it rose in clouds of dust about them as they walked. It settled upon the men's beards like gray powder; the oxen were chalky specters; the faces of the whole company looked pale. Snyder's corpse had not been whiter.

Moreover, the evil feelings that had been loosed that day by the sand-hill upon the Humboldt were not to be again confined. The emigrants were no longer a "company"; they were only a number of family groups each for itself, some of them ready to coöperate only when manifest good was to be gained for themselves. Hatred and inhumanity walked beside the wagons.

8. THE LAST DESERT

SNYDER had died on October 5, and Reed had departed on the next day. The day after that was a bad one for the second section. They were now rounding the big bend of the Humboldt, shifting their course from northwest to southwest. In the morning Eddy and Pike, out hunting, were shot at several times by Indians, and when after a long hard day the company finally made camp, they found a note from Reed, a disconcerting note warning them that one of the advance companies had had a battle with Indians. Then they looked around the camp; they found that the old Belgian, Hardkoop, was missing. Like all the others he had walked for a while, but being not far from seventy he had given out entirely, and for the last few days had been carried in Keseberg's wagon. Keseberg said that he knew nothing about the old man, but the matter had an ugly look, and a scout sent out on horseback found Hardkoop about five miles back on the trail. He said that Keseberg had put him out of the wagon to walk or die.

Next morning more adjustments had to be made. Eddy's oxen had been hauling Reed's family wagon, but this great lumbering van was too heavy; it was abandoned and a lighter one belonging to Graves was substituted. Mrs. Reed, driven from pillar to post, transferred what few belongings she had left.

Upon this morning of the eighth Eddy, who in the exchange of wagons had had to cache some of his goods, was probably the last to leave camp. When he had been upon the road only half an hour and was working to get his wagon through some heavy sand, old Hardkoop approached him, and saying that Keseberg had again put him out, asked Eddy to take him into the wagon, since he could not possibly keep on afoot. Eddy promised to do what he could for him, if only the oxen could get to the other side of the sandy stretch, and Hardkoop said that he would try to get as far as that by himself. In the toil of the day, hard pressed by his own troubles, Eddy neglected to find out what had become of the old man, probably supposing that some one else had taken him in. But at night he was missing again, and all that could be found out was that some boys driving cattle had seen him sitting along the trail by some sagebrush. He had been wholly played out, and his feet had swollen until the skin had split.

Eddy, conscience-stricken, built a large fire on the side of a hill, and since he had the first watch, kept it burning as a signal, hoping that with the aid of the full moon the old man might find his way in. The night was bitter cold. Milt Elliott, who relieved Eddy, kept the fire up till dawn. In the morning Mrs. Reed, Eddy, and Milt went to Keseberg and urged him to return, but Keseberg in a manner which seemed brutal and inhuman refused flatly. Of the emigrants in the second section, only Breen and Graves still had saddle horses. Both of these refused to lend them, Breen saying that old man would be dead, anyway, by this time, and Graves with a burst of anger declaring that he would not kill his horses to save the life of Hardkoop. Elliott, Pike, and Eddy offered to go back on foot, but the others even refused to wait—the threat of snow in the mountains and of starvation before they got even so far was already hanging upon them like a death-sentence.

They went on, and that day at eleven came to the place where Applegate's cut-off branched off for Oregon. Here at the nooning Breen and Graves were again approached for their horses, and again refused violently. The company took the road again, not liking to think about what might now be lying beneath the sagebrush.

The country was getting worse all the time now, drier and less hospitable. Pasturage was scanty. Almost daily, as they followed it down, the river by strange perversion grew smaller instead of larger as a proper river should. The road that afternoon of the tenth was heavy with sand, and they struggled through it until four in the morning. Then they came to a camping place where they found the Donners. It was an ill-omened spot, for the Donners on arriving had found the bones of one Sallee, a member of Hastings's company, who had died of an arrow wound, been buried, dug up by the Indians, stripped of his clothes, and left to the coyotes. The reunion was almost as ill-omened, for wranglings and accusations were rife about the deaths of Snyder and Hardkoop, and some were almost frenzied by the hardships and emotional strain so recently endured.

Reed, as those of the second section now learned, had overtaken the Donners on the eighth. He had departed after breakfast the next morning, taking with him Walter Herron, one of his teamsters. The two had taken food for only a few days, but had hoped to live off game. Herron was not mounted, but this would probably not hold Reed back, for in the hard desert country a man on foot could get along about as rapidly as a half-starved horse. Two men, moreover, were much safer from Indians.

The bad luck of "Sallee's grave" continued during the stop of a few hours which the recombined train made there. For that morning the Indians managed to run off all of the

Graveses' horses, as if in penalty for their not being sent back after Hardkoop. Also, another wagon had to be abandoned.

The train was now well down on the final reach of the Humboldt to the southwest. The sink was not far ahead, and correspondingly the grass was scanty and the water in the river hardly fit to be drunk. For the people, too, starvation rations were getting to be the rule, unless some one shot a wild goose.

On the first night after their reunion the emigrants camped in a spot with little grass and very poor water. Such conditions made the cattle tend to scatter and be restive, and the Indians, seeing their chance, pounced down and ran off eighteen oxen, and a milch cow to boot. The loss fell mainly on Wolfinger and the Donner brothers; the latter were stripped so clean that they had to yoke up some cows.

The next evening found the train at an equally bad spot. The water was in pools or sloughs, surrounded by mud, hard to get and unwholesome to drink. A mare of Breen's bogged down in a sinkhole. He asked Eddy for aid in getting her out, but Eddy coldly told him to remember Hardkoop, and the poor mare smothered in the mud. During the night there was trouble also. The Indians along this part of the river were enterprising, and besides were emboldened by success and aided by the darker nights which came with the waning of the moon. This night they did not get a chance to stampede any stock, but they crept close through the darkness, and shot arrows at the oxen. Several were wounded, but none killed, for the Diggers' bows were weak.

October 12 was a long, hard drive across a desert plain with mountains close upon their right and the sink of the Humboldt the goal ahead. They reached it at midnight, an ox or two having dropped by the way. For the rest of the night the cattle were kept corralled, but at daybreak were driven out to grass under guard. Everything was quiet, and the guards rode in for breakfast. Whereupon the Indians pounced again, and shot twenty-one head! It was maddening thus to find the poor creatures stuck with arrows, not always dead, but too badly hurt to keep up with the train. There was nothing for it but to slaughter them, cut off a few steaks to be used before they spoiled, and go on, knowing that as soon as the last wagon disappeared, the dark naked savages would steal down from the hills for feasting. The desert and the Indians together had taken a toll of nearly a hundred cattle.

For some of the emigrants this disaster at the sink was the final stroke. Only one ox was left to Eddy, and only one to the German Wolfinger. Thus near the end they must abandon their wagons, that is, all their worldly possessions, and push on afoot. However, as far as food was concerned, the loss of transport mattered little; it was practically exhausted, anyway, except for odds and ends such as tea and sugar, which could easily be put into the remaining wagons.

Of the emigrants caught by this last disaster, Wolfinger was in perhaps a slightly less desperate state than the others; for he had no children. But even so, it seemed harder than could be borne to have to leave all his property so near the goal, and enter the new land as a pauper. The company, now in imminent danger of starvation, refused to delay a moment over a mere question of his chattels. Two other Germans, however, had been traveling with him, and they, Reinhardt and Spitzer, remained with him to make a cache. Mrs. Wolfinger decided to go on ahead, walking with the other women.

By this loss of cattle poor Mrs. Reed and the children were left finally stranded, for during nearly a month they had traveled with the Eddys. All the bad luck of the journey seemed to be piling upon the Reeds. For the last week every day's journey had been filled with haunting dread, as around every bend of the road they feared to find a scalped body. Eagerly they looked about for camping places to see the fresh ashes of his fire, and sometimes they rejoiced to see goose-feathers scattered about, good sign that he was not yet starving. Since rejoining the other section they had a little easier time of it, for now they had the support of their friends the Donners and not merely the dogged loyalty of Milt Elliott. With the forward section, also, the Reeds had two saddle horses which could be used to carry the smaller children on the march. But this more hopeful time had lasted only a few days, and then came the loss of what little comfort Eddy's wagon had been. From the plenty with which they had started, they were now reduced to a change or two of clothing and some robes and blankets. They dumped their little bundles into one of the Breen wagons, and they themselves set out to travel with the Donners. The two horses remained for the littlest ones; the others must walk. Even Billy, Virginia's pony, was gone now; he had failed somewhere along the road, and Virginia, looking back wistfully as the wagons moved along, had seen him grow smaller and smaller in the distance and then disappear.

Eddy's case after the loss of his oxen was the most pitiful of all. He had his wife, a boy of about three, and an infant daughter. Moreover, his gun had been broken some days before, and he had left it behind. His shoes had gone to pieces, and he was reduced to wearing moccasins, a poor protection against the jagged desert rocks. In the depths of despondency he hastily cached the few goods remaining to him; almost nothing now was left to the family except the clothes which they actually were wearing. That morning they ate their last mouthful of food except for three pounds of lump sugar. He could see Indians looking down from the hills, positively laughing at the hapless plight of the white men.

Ahead lay the long desert reach between the Humboldt and the Truckee. Most emigrants counted this stretch as the worst of their experiences, but for the members of the Donner Party who had suffered so much worse things before, and were to suffer still more terrible ones in the future, this was merely an incident.

It was a sorry-looking train which led out from the sink that morning of October 13. Only about fifteen wagons were left, hauled by scrawny teams of mixed oxen and cows, all half starved. The emigrants themselves were tattered and disheveled. To lighten the wagons, they were even carrying odds and ends of household goods, like people escaping from a fire. One of the Murphy boys walked with a copper camp-kettle held upon his head. Each family group was fending for itself as best it could. Daily the journey seemed to become more of a rout.

So great was the need of sparing the oxen that, inhuman as it seems, no one took the Eddy children into a wagon. Sullen but plucky, Eddy took up the three pounds of sugar. Since he might be able to borrow a gun, he put some bullets into his pockets and slung a powder-horn over his shoulder. Then he lifted up the three-year-old Jimmy into his arms. Eleanor took up the baby, and they set out.

That day was sheer horror. Across the heat-stricken sand

of the sink naked mountains of rock, luridly sinister in brown, red, yellow and poisonous green, leered out at the straggling train like devil-haunted hills in a dream. The road was the mere scratching of wheel-tracks. The ash-like surface of the desert showed only the thinnest scattering of sage. The sand and dust were in places so light that horses sank almost to their knees. In other places the trail crossed ridges of jagged volcanic rock, the sharp edges of which cut through moccasins. Hunger and thirst, heat, dust, exhaustion, and fear for the future combined to torture the emigrants.

The Eddys toiled in the rear. Night found them still on the desert. The parents ate nothing; the children had only the sugar to suck at, and grew more and more prostrated. An old moon rose at last, and finally (it was nearly daybreak) they struggled up to a place where the party had made a halt to rest the oxen.

It was a diabolical place, a very outpost of hell. From a hundred or more holes bitter, boiling-hot water oozed out, and from one of them a fountain of steam jetted spasmodically twenty feet into the air. The water was too hot for drinking, but if kept in a bucket until lukewarm, it relieved thirst in spite of its bitterness. Here one of the kindly Donner women gave Eddy a little coffee. This he prepared in a hot spring and gave to Eleanor and the children, stubbornly refusing to keep any of the scanty supply for himself. It was sufficient joy to see the children revive.

But the Geyser Spring, as it was called, was a mere halting place. It offered water of a sort, but no grass. The George Donners lightened their load by taking out some heavy boxes of books and caching them. Then, stringing out along the trail, the company pressed on again toward the Truckee over another twenty miles of desert. On this march Eddy's children suffered so for water that he feared they were actually dying. Breen had a water-cask in his wagon but refused to share his supply, saying that every drop was needed for his own family. The desperate father finally had to take the water, bluntly threatening to kill Breen if he interfered.

At sunset the emigrants came to a wide reach of bare sand stretching itself across their way as a final barrier. They struggled on across it all night. The horses labored painfully as their feet sank into the loose surface. The oxen managed a little better in the sand, but they had to pull forward against the weight of the wagons. Three yoke failed, and lay down to die. The men and women set their faces the firmer, and toiled on.

Then well on toward daybreak they sighted the trees of a river bottom. They dragged their feet along down the final two miles, and came to the Truckee—clear, flowing, pure water. They had passed the last desert, and all the people had got across, that is at least, all except the three Germans who had stayed behind to cache Wolfinger's goods.

9. —AND CLOSES IN FRONT

THE last desert was crossed! Whatever else might still happen, they would never again be beyond reach of water. Here the cool stream from the Sierra rushed past, fifty feet broad, swift-running, sweet water with no taint of alkali. In the bottom-land grass and wild peas gave luxurious pasture, and trees were growing, actual trees, tall cottonwoods in whose shade a man might rest, the first trees which the emigrants had enjoyed in five hundred miles of scrubby sagebrush. Such loveliness following upon such desolation inspired one emigrant-poet, casting about for a metaphor, to hail the Truckee as the River of Heaven itself.

As they rested for a day in the bottom and let the cattle feed up, they were not altogether without reason, hard as their situation was, to think well of themselves. Since they had first struck the Humboldt, they had been no longer forced to camp each night where Hastings had camped, and in full knowledge of the lateness of the season they had begun to stretch out their daily marches. And they had done well in spite of oxen whose hip-bones loomed through the tight-stretched skin, in spite of troubles with the Diggers and of troubles among themselves. Down the Humboldt they had made it to the sink in twelve days, and they could count that an average of twenty miles a day even without allowing for the half-day they had halted on account of Snyder's death. They could tell pretty well from Hastings's camps that he had spent sixteen days in making the same distance. Four days' gain in twelve was good going!

They and the cattle, too, deserved a rest, but they were not going to get it for a while. Lingering in this little paradise by the river was not for them. To cross the desert was only to solve one problem, and two others at once pressed forward —to pass the mountains before the snow flew, and to avoid the present danger of actual starvation. The latter was more imminent. Had Stanton and McCutchen failed—or deserted? The emigrants must have begun to eye Mrs. McCutchen and the baby a little queerly. Wasn't Mac going to come back even for *them?*

Eddy had not eaten for forty-eight hours. Eleanor was almost as badly off, and even the babies had had nothing but the sugar and some coffee since leaving the sink. He applied to Mrs. Graves and Mrs. Breen for a little meat, but they refused him. Hearing some wild geese, he borrowed a gun, and after two hours along the river returned with nine fine birds. This sudden surfeit he shared with the other emigrants. During the day also the Indians again killed some cattle, so that the need of food was supplied at the expense of transport.

After only a day's rest for the oxen, the train pressed on up the Truckee. The bottom land lasted for only two or three miles, and then narrowed into a canyon winding straitly between high rocky mountains, red, brown, and black in color. To follow the plentifully flowing, green-banked river and look up at these parched desert heights was like sitting comfortably in a warm room at home and looking out into a raging snow-storm.

Unfortunately the going was hard, doubly so for the worn-down oxen, many of them suffering with arrow-wounds. The road ducked and dodged almost as badly as the one which they themselves had cut through the Wahsatch. They had to ford the river more than once to the mile.

On this day Reinhardt and Spitzer came up. Wolfinger was not with them, and they told a briefly tragic story. The Indians had come down from the hills; they had killed Wolfinger and driven the others away; then they had rifled and burned the wagons. Mrs. Wolfinger almost collapsed at the news. The story had an ugly look. To return without your companion was a bad business by western standards.

Wolfinger was believed to be rich, and to have much money with him; every one remembered the rich clothes and the jewelry which Mrs. Wolfinger had worn at the beginning of the journey. But it was just as well perhaps for Mrs. Wolfinger to believe the story. The ever-charitable Donners took her in, and the train moved on. They might all be with Wolfinger soon enough.

For three days, scraping at the bottom of the flour-barrels, they labored up the canyon, and then suddenly he came! Three riders and seven pack-mules clumping down the trail. It was little Stanton.

Food in camp again, boys! Flour and jerked beef! And bread baking in the Dutch ovens! You never could tell. Here they had sent out a married man and a single man, and it was the single man who came back. Good little Stanton!

Where was McCutchen? He was taken sick, had to stay at Sutter's. Yes, they had both got through all right; nothing much had happened on the way; they had passed Hastings's company. McCutchen had found friends with Hastings, and they had tried to get him to go back, had even offered him food, to go back and get Amanda and the baby. They thought the Donners were not far enough along, and couldn't ever get across before the snow. But McCutchen had gone on. He decided to stick to his promise to the whole company instead of trying to pull out his own family.

Yes, Sutter had given all the food and the mules, gladly. And these two others—they were Indians, good fellows though. They were two of the ones that Sutter had to herd his cattle, *vaqueros* they called them in Spanish. They could catch steers in the most curious way you ever saw, by throwing a noose. No use trying to talk English to them; Luis understood a few words, that was all. The other one was called Salvador. Spanish was their lingo, and they were Christians, Catholics, that is. You could trust them, even if they were Indians, for they were afraid of Captain Sutter, and he had said he would hang them if they lost his mules.

Yes, he had seen Reed, too; Reed and Herron had just managed to get through. Four days ago as he came into Bear Valley on the way back, he had found part of Hastings's company camped. And that day, down the steep mountainside where the wagons were let down with ropes, two men had come falling rather than walking. A gray mare, tottery and gaunt, too weak even to carry a saddle, came with them. The two were so worn with fatigue and starvation that no one recognized them, but they turned out to be Reed and Herron.

The pair had gone on from the Donners' camp, it seemed, riding turn and turn, until the mare failed. After their few days' rations were ended, they had been able to kill geese by the rivers, and so get along from day to day. But after leaving the Truckee they had had nothing. They decided not to stop and hunt, for fear that they might have no success and would starve by delaying. For several days they pressed ahead, eating nothing but a few wild onions, and at last Herron demanded that they kill the now useless animal. Reed pled for his favorite mare, but promised to sacrifice her if they did not find help soon. They went on. Herron became delirious. That afternoon Reed found in the road a treasure which had spilled from some wagon—*one bean!* He gave it to Herron. After that they walked with their eyes keen for anything more which might have filtered through that wagon-bed, and held themselves well rewarded by finding four more beans. This was their ration for the day, but Herron ate more heavily than Reed, for he had three beans to Reed's two. Next morning they struggled on, and soon came to some abandoned wagons. They searched eagerly for food, but emigrant wagons at the end of the trail were always as bare as Mother Hubbard's cupboard. Reed found the usual tar-bucket beneath one of the axles, but scraping away with the tar-paddle on a despairing hope he discovered that the bucket had previously held tallow and that a little rancid fat still stuck to the bottom! Close by, Herron was sitting on a wagon-rack, but at Reed's words he got up hallooing joyfully. Reed handed him the tar-paddle on which he had scraped together some tallow to the size of a walnut. Herron swallowed it without even a smell. Then Reed ate a little, but even in his starving condition could hardly swallow the ill-smelling filth. The stouter-stomached Herron ate a second helping, and demanded still more. Reed refused, out of fear that to a starving man more of such food might be fatal. Strangely enough, Herron digested the meal, but Reed had scarcely left the wagons before he became so sick that his companion for a few moments thought him dying. When he recovered somewhat, they proceeded. Not far from the scene of the tar-bucket, they came to the steep

descent into Bear Valley, and when part way down caught
sight of more wagons. Stumbling down the mountainside,
shouting weakly, they at last got to the camp and found food.
There, too, they had met Stanton.

That had been four days ago, and since then Stanton had
crossed the pass, finding it still open in spite of some early
snows. He himself now went on with part of the pack-train
to meet and relieve the rear-guard of the train, a day's
journey down the canyon. Afterwards he traveled with the
Reeds, and the Reeds themselves marched on a little more
hopefully for knowing that the family protector did not lie
scalped in some gully. Moreover Stanton took them under
his care, and they no longer had to walk. They had one of
Sutter's mules for their clothing and blankets, and one for
Mrs. Reed and Tommy. Patty and Jim each rode behind an
Indian, and Virginia behind Stanton.

To the plucky little rescuer the condition of the company
which he had come to save must have been a shock. He himself in the noblest spirit of self-sacrifice and social duty had
ridden back across the fateful pass, to save—what? It was
no longer even the fairly unified party which he had left.
Now under the stress of circumstance almost too great to be
borne, the cruel individualism of the westerner had gained the
upper hand, at least with many of the emigrants. These,
more and more, fought wolfishly for their own families alone.
An old man had been allowed to die on the trail; babies with
tongues thick from thirst had been refused water. To rescue
these people Stanton had come riding like a knight upon a
quest. Having once delivered his provisions, he would have
been justified, any one would think, in taking Indians and
mules, and spurring for the pass. Three days would have
taken him to safety in Bear Valley. Instead, he took up
Virginia Reed behind him on the mule, and thus they came
into the broad-stretching Truckee Meadows.

Here the company reassembled, and the emigrants encamped in the fine grassland which reached along the river
for several miles. They were really leaving the arid country
behind now; on the mountains round about the meadows
pine trees were growing. This was the best place to recruit
cattle before attempting the passage of the mountains, and
so the emigrants faced another dilemma. It had come to
October 20. The weather was cloudy and threatening, and

some snow had fallen on the higher mountains around them. Prudence bade them press on with all haste. But prudence also bade them stay, and let the oxen rest and build up their strength. To attempt the passage of the mountains with worn-out teams was only to invite catastrophe. Above Truckee Lake, as Stanton could tell them, the trail went right up over broken domes of granite. It was steep, worse even than the Wahsatch, much worse. Even with the strongest oxen it was a struggle. Every one had to double or triple teams, and many used windlasses and all sorts of devices with ropes.

And more strongly than even the threat of snow, what had happened in the last few days must be considered. On the Humboldt they had gained four days on Hastings, but coming up the canyon of the Truckee he had made it in three days and they had taken four, some of them even five. The teams had been pressed too hard and were at the breaking point. Then, too, Stanton, who of all the company had the best right to make the decision, spoke out for their taking the chance of waiting a few days. At Sutter's the people said that the pass would really not be closed till the middle of November. Hastings, every one knew, had got through on horseback the year before, toward the end of December. This season his company crossing the summit about October 7 had met a heavy snow-storm, but had got through all right. At this time of year the snow would melt between storms. So they took Stanton's advice, although some of them had misgivings, and they let their cattle pasture upon the rich grass of Truckee Meadows.

Then death struck again. The two brothers-in-law, Pike and Foster, sat by their camp-fire as Pike cleaned a pepperbox pistol. Some one called for wood to replenish the fire, and Pike rose to get it. He handed the pistol to Foster, but as he did so, it exploded, and he himself got the bullet in the back. In an hour he was dead.

They buried Pike, and his burial showed the progressing rout of the company. Halloran had been laid to rest in a made coffin; Snyder had been wrapped in a shroud with a board above and a board beneath; but Pike was merely laid into the ground. Sorrow fell on the company with his death. Halloran, Snyder, and Hardkoop had been unmarried; Wolfinger had been childless; but Pike left a widow and two babies. Foster, the accidental slayer, was now the only grown man left among the twelve members of the Murphy family.

Snow fell as they buried Pike. Still they stayed in Truckee Meadows, restless, their eyes shifting from the clouded wintry sky to the gaunt, rib-lined flanks of the oxen. To go or to stay? Stanton's reasoning still held them, but after about five days they began to get under way. They did not leave in a body, but the more nervous and those with the better cattle got off first. No one thought much any more of having the company act as a whole.

First of all went the Breens. The luck of the Irish had been with them; they had lost fewest cattle from the Indians and being in the best condition to move had fretted most at having to halt. With them went their friend Dolan, the Kesebergs, and the wagonless Eddys. Stanton, the Reeds, the Graveses, and the Murphys made a second section. The Donners, solid people and not to be stampeded, took their time, and brought up the rear.

For the first time, from Stanton's story, they had some detail of the road ahead. A day's journey above the meadows it crossed the river for the forty-ninth time in the eighty miles, then swung sharply to the right, left the river to avoid another canyon, and crossed a fairly easy range of mountains. Next it descended into a beautiful little valley, crossed a divide, and went on southwards over rolling, heavily forested country with the main range of the Sierra looming up on the right. Then it came to a cabin built two years before by winter-bound emigrants. A quarter of a mile above the cabin was Truckee Lake, and from the lake you could look up at the great wall of the pass. The whole distance from the meadows to the pass was close to fifty miles.

At the first camp which the leading section made after finally leaving the river, an Indian crept up to the cattle and began shooting arrows. He struck nineteen oxen, but failed to kill any of them. Eddy caught him in the act, and drew a bead. At the crack of the rifle the Indian leaped high into the air and with a horrible shriek fell down a bank into some willows. The score was evened a little for so many cattle.

But in the game which the emigrants were playing against Time, the score could not be evened by a rifle bullet, and it stood heavily against them. During those last days of October snow fell as they moved along. The cattle had to nose through it for grass. On the distant mountains it lay white upon the pine branches. Winter was in the air; it was bitter cold, and the sky was bleak.

On a steep downward pitch a front axle broke on George Donner's family wagon. They hauled little Georgia out through the back of the wagon-sheets, and then dug madly into the heaped-up mass of household goods, calling to baby Eliza, who did not answer. At last they pulled her out, limp, smothered, and unconscious for the moment, but not really hurt.

Abandon the broken wagon! Abandon all the wagons! Let the cattle fend for themselves. Take the children and the horses and push on for life. Get across the pass at any cost —the only chance! Perhaps such thoughts of panic ran through their minds. But the German farmer is not the man lightly to surrender his household goods. Hastily the two brothers cut timber for an axle. Just as they were finishing its shaping a chisel slipped, and the blood spurted from a long gash across the back of George Donner's hand. It was bound up, and he made light of it; there were other things, he said, more to be worried about than a cut hand. There were!

By the time of this accident the Breens far ahead must have been approaching the lake which lay beneath the pass. As they marched, clouds rested upon the high mountains to their right, but occasionally the clouds lifted displaying solid masses of snow. On the night of October 31 they made camp shortly before reaching the cabin. Snow lay on the ground, an inch or more deep. The cattle could not find grass, and made a poor meal of boughs which the men and boys cut for them.

The morning was very cold, and the clouds still hung over the mountains ahead. The Breens and Dolan, the Eddys and the Kesebergs, pushed on. Then the clouds, as if in mockery, rolled away and revealed towering peaks and the pass itself solidly covered with snow. This sight almost sank the emigrants into despair, but still they went on. They passed the deserted cabin, and followed along the north shore of the lake, where the road ran so close that at times the wagons almost seemed to be toppling into the water. They worked on beyond the head of the lake, but the snow was soft and deep, and deepened still as the road rose toward the pass. They reached a point which they thought to be only three miles from the summit, but the snow was five feet deep, and they had no way of telling where the trail was. They could go no further. They turned about and got back to the cabin, which was only a mile in advance of where they had camped the night before. It seemed the end.

The Breens took possession of the cabin. The others camped as best they could. The day had been clear, and in the evening the sky was bright with a nearly full moon. But around it was a ring, and by that sign every one knew that they should expect a storm. Their folklore was right, and the Breens soon found that the cabin roof of pine boughs merely impeded the rain slightly. They took refuge in their wagons. The rain fell in torrents. All the next day they remained in camp, saying hopefully, like the plains-dwellers that they were, that the rain would wash away the snow and melt it down so that they could cross. At dark those of the second section came up, Stanton with them. The Donners did not arrive.

On the next morning the weather was better. Some of the emigrants were in despair and made no further effort, but with Stanton and the Indians as guides those who had previously made the trail and some of the others turned their faces toward the pass. They yoked up the teams, and started with the wagons. But even near the lake the snow was three feet deep by this time, and the oxen after three days of browsing upon branches were weaker than ever. As the men laboriously broke out a way for the wagons, the snow seemed to grow deeper with every yard of advance toward the pass. Soon even the mules were floundering, up to their sides in snow. The emigrants saw now how foolish their hope had been that the rain would beat down the snow, and they realized, what mountaineers would have known before, that at this time of year rain in the valleys meant snow on the heights. As soon as this knowledge had been forced upon them, every one saw that they must abandon the wagons, pack what goods they could upon the oxen, and press on afoot.

Already it was getting late in the day, and indecision over what should be taken along and what left behind caused still further delay. One spoke for a box of tobacco, and another argued for a bale of calico. The packing of the oxen took more time, for the animals were unused to such procedure and objected by bucking off the unskillfully slung packs, or by lying down in the snow and wallowing. Children were so numerous that almost every adult was burdened by carrying one of them. Keseberg had to have a horse, for he had hurt his foot and could not walk. They hoisted him up, and tied his leg up to the saddle in a sort of sling.

At last they got under way again. Clear ahead was the gap at the summit, and it seemed no great distance as one looked at it. Carrying children, driving unruly oxen, and floundering through snow waist-deep, they got ahead but slowly. The road, if here on the pass it could be called a road at all, was buried deep under the snow, so that Stanton and the Indians could follow only its general route. A certain mule proved to be the best trail-breaker; so with little Patty Reed clinging on behind him one of the Indians went ahead, the mule plunging into drifts but making progress. The emigrants advanced on foot for a distance which they thought to be two or three miles; they must by this time have been well beyond and above the lake; the summit as they guessed from looking ahead was anywhere from one to three miles farther. But the labor of the advance was killing, and it came near evening. The leading mule began to plunge headlong into snow-filled gullies, and the Indian could no longer keep to any sort of road. So everyone halted while this Indian and Stanton went ahead to find a route. The two pushed on, located the road, and actually reached the summit. For the second time Stanton came back in the face of death to rescue the company.

In the meantime the halted emigrants had become somewhat demoralized. They were all so worn out with carrying children, that resting seemed best of all. Then some one found a dead pine full of pitch, and set fire to it. The flame leaped up into the higher branches, and the poor, half-frozen women and children gathered about its comfort. The oxen, untended, were rubbing off their packs against the tree-trunks. By the time Stanton returned, the emigrants were half encamped, and only the strongest pressure could make them move. Twilight was already at hand. And Stanton's report was not the most encouraging; they could get through, he thought, if it did not snow any more. Sensing the crisis, some of the emigrants urged a bold push forward, but most of them were too exhausted to make a further effort.

So they prepared to spend the night as best they could upon the snow. They gathered about the fire, and had something to eat. Then they laid blankets and buffalo-robes on the snow, put the children to bed bundled up as well as possible. The men and women huddled about, some making themselves beds, and some sitting crouched by the fire. They were too weary now; they would cross in the morning.

Then it began to snow.

The children slept as the snow covered their blankets warmly. The men and women also slept, or else drew close about the fire. One of the Indians stoically wrapped himself in his blanket, and all night stood leaning against a tree. Now and then a mother shook off the snow from the children's beds as it grew too deep. The night was freezing cold. The wind hissed through the pine trees. The snow fell steadily and fast, mixed with cutting sleet. No one needed to say anything; all knew what had happened. By morning a foot of new snow had fallen. The drifts around them were ten feet deep.

They turned back, and even working down-hill they had consumed the morning and the afternoon until four when they finally reached the cabin. The Donners had not yet come up. Back across the lake, as they looked through the darkening atmosphere of the short winter afternoon, they could see the solid rampart of the pass, a mass of snow unbroken except where bare precipices stood darkly out. It was November 4. The trap which had clicked behind them at Fort Bridger had closed in front.

PART II

THE SNOW

There is no timber that has not strong roots
among the clay and worms.
John M. Synge
Preface to Poems and Translations

___

FOREWORD

ONCE again the reader must imagine himself withdrawn
to a point of vantage in the sky, but this time he need rise
no higher than the flier of the air-mail over this very point
must sometimes attain. He must, however, consider himself
endowed with an even keener sight than that of the most
clear-eyed pilot.

The place in the sky is above a point halfway between
Sutter's Fort in the Sacramento Valley of California and the
mountain-girt body of water known then as Truckee, and
now as Donner, Lake. The narrow strip of country which
is to be observed runs northwest and southwest, and is about
a hundred miles long. The time is early winter, 1846.

The first glance reveals a marked color contrast in the two
halves of the view. The line is not sharp; there are sinuosities
and isolated blotches. But generally speaking, north and east
toward the lake the land is white; south and west toward the
Fort it is green. The white is snow; the green, forests and
grassland. Except for the stretch of featureless plain around
the Fort the view is marked everywhere by the corrugations,
shadow-masses, and gleaming high-lights denoting mountainous country. The whole landscape, moreover, is on a tilt, so
that the plain around the Fort, which is low enough to feel
the ebb and flow of tide, seems farther off than the high
peaks on the northeast, which reach well up toward ten
thousand feet.

These highest points lie along the watershed close above
Truckee Lake on the extreme northeastern edge of the view.

In fact, unless one were at a very unusual height, part of the Lake would remain hidden behind the crest of the pass. The Lake is a little under six thousand feet in altitude; the pass about twelve hundred feet higher; the peaks flanking the pass, a thousand feet higher still. The distance by direct line from the head of the Lake to the pass is only two miles. But this rapidity of rise upon the east is not matched by a comparable fall on the western side, and even if following a straight course, one would have to travel more than ten miles down the gentle western slope before descending to the same level as the Lake.

The most notable feature of the view, its division into white and green, is also the feature most subject to change with the seasons. In some summers the white will disappear completely; in the dead of winter an occasional snow-storm will blot out the green clear down to the walls of Sutter's Fort. But during this winter of 1846 and '47 the irregular boundary line between white and green will usually run somewhere near the middle of the landscape, about the three-thousand-foot level. This will mean for the Sierra Nevada a severe winter.

But the observer in the sky, returning with more careful scrutiny to the mountainous country beneath him, will notice that aside from the superficial division by color it may be separated into three zones. Around the pass lies a region of high peaks, interset with small and very blue mountain lakes; it is so rocky and precipitous as to be largely treeless. At the other end, the plain which surrounds Sutter's Fort yields almost imperceptibly to low foothills, gentle in slope and confused in design, wooded but thinly on account of summer drought. Between these high and low zones extends a broad belt of country magnificently forested with pine, cedar, and fir. It shows a pattern almost regular enough to be the plan of some landscape architect. Great mountain ridges remarkably smooth along the top run almost parallel, each separated from the next by an enormous V-shaped canyon two or three thousand feet deep. At the bottom of each canyon flows a stream, blue and green in the pools, flashing white in the falls and rapids.

These streams are the main branches and the feeders of the three rivers which drain this whole country above Sutter's Fort. To the north is the South Fork of the Yuba, in 1846 known merely as the Yuba and spelled Uber, Yuva, or otherwise. It heads at the pass above Truckee Lake, flows west at first, and then at the upstanding granite dome of Cisco Butte bends northwestward through a narrow canyon and departs from our interest. Along the southern edge of the view the North Fork of the American, fed by many smaller streams, flows out to the west and south through an awesomely deep and precipitous canyon. Beginning not far from the point at which the Yuba swings off to the northwest, the smaller Bear River flows between the two others. Near its source it winds gently through Bear Valley, a fine mountain meadow two miles long by a half mile wide. Below this it runs between the usual ridges, cut through occasionally by tributaries. The chief of these enters from the north, and as if in recognition of the fact that it is a very small stream in a large canyon is called merely by the name of Steep Hollow, in disregard of the stream altogether.

In 1846 almost the only mark of man upon all this country was the emigrant road. Although since late October snow has covered its upper course, we may presume to trace its route. After climbing the rocky wall immediately above the Lake, it traverses for a mile or two a mountain meadow known as Summit Valley. It then leaves the course of the Yuba, keeps to the southern lip of the canyon for several miles, and then descends sharply to some level stretches along the river, called Yuba Bottoms.

There beneath Cisco Butte, where the region of peaks begins to yield to that of canyons, as the Yuba swings off to the northwest, the road leaves the river, climbs a divide, and crosses the heads of several of the little streams which feed the American. It descends a small depression known as Dry Valley until a distinct notch, a hundred feet deep, shows in the low ridge to the north. This is Emigrant Gap, where the trail ceases to be a road, and becomes an incline. To descend the precipitous slope the teamsters must uncouple the oxen and by means of ropes snubbed around trees let the wagons down to pleasant Bear Valley. This is distant from Yuba Bottoms about twelve miles.

Passing on down the stretch of rich meadow-land in the Valley, the road enters the canyon of the Bear, but soon rises again to a ridge, this time the one between the Bear and Steep Hollow. It follows this divide, the twin marks of the wagon-wheels sometimes almost straddling the narrow saddle-backs. Keeping to the top, it goes right over the hummocks rather than skirting the dangerous side-hill slopes. Water is scarce on the ridge, and Mule Springs, ten miles from Bear Valley, is the only good camping-spot. After the distance of another day's travel the ridge comes suddenly to an end when Steep Hollow swings south to enter the Bear. Again the wagons must be let down with ropes. Beyond this point the canyon country yields to the foothills; slopes are more gentle; and after some forty miles the trail debouching finally into the plain arrives at Johnson's ranch, the first settlement. From here it runs, fairly straight and well marked, forty miles more across the plain to Sutter's.

10. IN CALIFORNIA

[Extracts from Edwin Bryant's *What I Saw in California*, based upon his journal of the year 1846]

[October 17, Sonoma] The last two mornings have been cloudy and cool. The rainy season, it is thought by the weather-wise in this climate, will set in earlier this year than usual. The periodical rains ordinarily commence about the middle of November. It is now a month earlier, and the meteorological phenomena portend "falling weather." . . .

[October 28, Sutter's Fort] On the 28th, Mr. Reed, whom I have before mentioned as belonging to the rear emigrating party, arrived here. He left his party on Mary's river, and in company with one man crossed the desert and mountains. . . . His object was to procure provisions immediately, and to transport them with pack-mules over the mountains for the relief of the suffering emigrants behind. He had lost all of his cattle, and had been compelled to cache two of his wagons and most of his property. Captain Sutter generously furnished the requisite quantity of mules and horses, with Indian vaqueros, and jerked meat, and flour. . . . Ex-governor Boggs and family reached Sutter's Fort to-day.

On the evening of the 28th, a courier arrived with letters from Colonel Fremont, now at Monterey. The substance of the intelligence received by the courier was, that a large force of Californians (varying, according to different reports, from five to fifteen hundred strong) had met the marines and sailors, four hundred strong, under the command of Captain Mervine, of the U.S. frigate *Savannah*, who had landed at San Pedro for the purpose of marching to Los Angeles, and had driven Captain Mervine and his force back to the ship, with the loss, in killed, of six men. That the towns of Angeles and Santa Barbara had been taken by the insurgents, and the American garrisons there had either been captured or had made their escape by retreating. What had become of them was unknown. Colonel Fremont, who I before mentioned had sailed with a party of one hundred and eighty volunteers from San Francisco to San Pedro, or San Diego, for the purpose of co-operating with Commodore Stockton, after having been some time at sea, had put into Monterey and landed his men, and his purpose now was to increase his force and mount them, and to proceed by land to Los Angeles.

On the receipt of this intelligence, I immediately drew up a paper which was signed by myself, Messrs. Reed, Jacob, Lippincott, and Grayson, offering our services as volunteers, and our exertions to raise a force of emigrants and Indians which would be a sufficient reinforcement to Colonel Fremont. This paper was addressed to Mr. Kern, the commandant of Fort Sacramento, and required his sanction. The next morning (29th) he accepted of our proposal, and the labor of raising the volunteers and of procuring the necessary clothing and supplies for them and the Indians was apportioned.

It commenced raining on the night of the twenty-eighth, and the rain fell heavily and steadily until twelve o'clock, M., on the twenty-ninth. . . .

II. TWO FATHERS

THE thirtieth was clear with the shimmering clarity of California after the first heavy rain. Sutter's Fort lay steaming in the sun—a rectangle of adobe walls with buildings inside, squat bastions mounting cannon to sweep the approaches, gates south and east with more cannon. It was now officially Fort Sacramento, and was held by an American garrison. For the moment Captain Sutter was not master of his own house.

That morning he and Reed looked out toward the mountains where they could see snow. It was low down and heavy, the Captain said, for the first fall of the season.

Next day the pack-train got away from the Fort, the horses clumping slushily in the adobe mud. Four riders were with it. Two were Indian *vaqueros;* the third was Reed, and the fourth a giant of a man with his feet well down below the horse's belly. Big McCutchen was going back after

Amanda and the baby. Now well of his sickness, he had joined Reed at the Fort. Honor, no less than love, demanded his return, for no man could have held up his head in the West of those days who had left wife and child and was not ready to risk his life to bring them out. There was also his promise to the company.

As for Reed, he owed nothing to the company which had exiled him, but he had even more fear for his own family. Edwin Bryant and the others at the Fort had elected him captain of the company about to be raised, but he had felt justified only in accepting the lieutenancy; for the captain must march with the company, and more pressing duty called him east instead of south. As lieutenant he had promised to be a recruiting officer, and like a Paul Revere to rouse the country as he rode.

The water splashed white as twenty-six horses took the ford of the American, and then the long *caballada* headed off north, on the emigrant road, across the plain.

Three days later with everything ready for the final push they struck out from Johnson's ranch toward the hills, thirty horses and a mule now, with two Indians to help drive and the pack animals laden with jerked beef, beans, and flour. Nothing more had been heard of the Donner Party, but they expected to meet it somewhere this side of the summit, probably near Bear Valley, and in a starving condition, perhaps reduced to eating the draught oxen.

As Reed and McCutchen threaded their way through the foothills, the good weather had yielded to another storm. The streams were not yet high enough to be dangerous, but riding and camping in the steady rain was a dreary enough business to wear down the hardiest man. It was cold, too. As they topped the rises and got views ahead, they could see that the higher mountains were white. On the second day after leaving Johnson's they came to snow, somewhere on the ridge by Mule Springs. Next day they made the lower end of Bear Valley. It lay a white expanse of snow, a foot and a half deep—no sign of wagons! They camped in a storm of rain and sleet so heavy that they could not even get a fire going, and so went supperless. But they kept the provisions and horses safe.

Next morning they plugged ahead slowly. At the head of the valley the snow was two feet deep. Here the two fa-

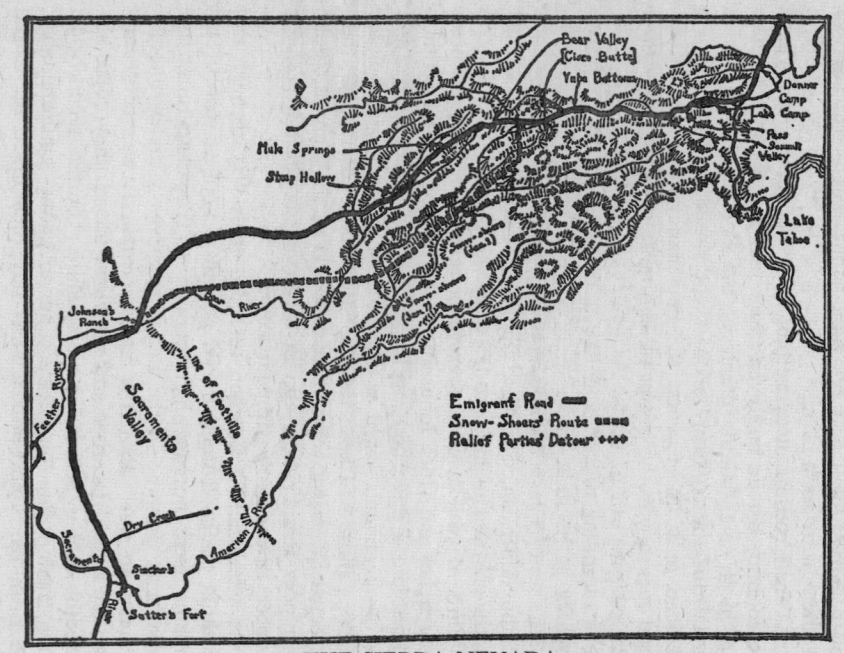

THE SIERRA NEVADA

thers were amazed to be greeted as saviors by a haggard and thoroughly frightened man and woman. A certain emigrant, Jotham Curtis by name, deceived by the pleasant autumn aspect of Bear Valley and having quarreled with his company, had decided to halt with his wife, and winter there. The two of them were now huddled in a sort of pen roofed with a tent. Their cattle had taken the back trail in the storm, and starvation had reduced man and wife to killing their dog. The last piece of this best friend of man was even now baking in a Dutch oven. Reed and McCutchen assured the Curtises of a share of the pack-train's supplies, but they themselves were in a bad state, having been unable to get at the packs or cook anything for more than twenty-four hours on account of the storm. Curtis as a fair exchange of favors offered them some dog, and Reed raising the lid of the oven found the roast done to a turn and emitting a fine, savory smell. He cut out a rib, smelled at it gingerly, at last brought himself to taste it, and to his surprise found it delicious. He handed the rib to McCutchen, who smelled it for some moments before he persuaded himself to the tasting point; he also approved, pronouncing it "very good dog." With the taboos of European civilization thus overcome, they fell to upon the roast. Mrs. Curtis getting some flour from the packs set to work, and in a short time all had supper.

In the morning Reed and McCutchen at Mrs. Curtis's entreaties gave their word to take the two out of the mountains when the pack-train returned with the women and children of the Donner Party, and they also left one of the Indians and nine horses in the camp to be picked up on the way back.

Leaving Bear Valley, the remaining three men and twenty-two horses set out to scramble as best they could up the six-hundred-foot slope where the emigrant wagons had to be let down with ropes. In the deep snow it was a killing labor, even though Curtis's runaway cattle had broken a trail through. On the ridge above, the going was scarcely better. Here the snow was three feet deep, and instead of being somewhat solidified by rain as at the lower levels, it was dry and feathery. With exhausted animals they camped in Dry Valley only three miles from their starting point of the morning, and not far from the wagon in which Reed and Herron had found the tallow bucket three weeks before.

That night Reed and McCutchen heard the sound of horses. Springing up suspiciously they ran to where the Indian had been sleeping and found that he had deserted. McCutchen hastily mounted and set out in pursuit. But the fugitive had the better start, and the pursuer after descending all the way to Curtis's camp found that both Indians had fled down the trail half an hour before, taking with them three horses. Curtis said that he had thought any attempt to stop them would have been useless, but McCutchen, who held no high opinion of his former host, suspected that Curtis might have advised the departure in hope that it would cause the return of the whole pack-train and with that his own escape to the plains. McCutchen gave up pursuit, and with iron-like endurance turned about and got back to the camp in Dry Valley about midnight.

A cold fear that they would be too late for any rescue must have been settling about them, but in the morning they again drove the pack-animals forward. Snow was falling, and with every hour progress grew harder. The trail of Curtis's cattle helped for a while, but then it turned off to the left. The snow got worse steadily. Three miles from camp it was four feet deep, and by the time they had reached the top of the next ridge, it had deepened still more. Here the pack-animals began to give out and lie down with nothing but their noses protruding from the snow. Leaving them, the two men desperately forced their saddle horses on, still hoping that the next turn of the road might bring the sight of wagons or camp-fire smoke. Each yard of advance became a struggle. The horses had to rear high on their hind legs, and breast the snow with a sort of leap; then as their fore feet came down the whole animal would disappear except for the nose and part of the head. This could not keep up for long; a mile beyond the pack-animals, the saddle horses failed, too.

Refusing even yet to admit defeat with all that it implied, the two fathers dismounted and plunged forward on foot through snow almost to their necks. It was light, wintry snow, too, which let a man sink in deep at every step. Nevertheless they made about a mile. Then they came to the point where the road descended to the river, and where they could get some sort of a view ahead. But the snow-surface in Yuba Bottoms was broken only by the silent pine-trees. Not the faintest wisp of smoke curled upwards. Downcast, they paused for a few moments in deliberation.

(At that moment, of the eighty-seven men, women, and children who had crossed the Wahsatch, only one was safe in the promised land of California. That one was Walter Herron, who had just enlisted for the comparatively not very dangerous undertaking of a campaign against the Mexicans. Of the others, five were dead, two sat in the snow upon the ridge above Yuba Bottoms, and seventy-nine were trapped beyond the pass. Among these last was Stanton, who had once been safe through to Sutter's, and the two Indians, whose addition raised the total of those beyond the pass to eighty-one. By coincidence the day on which Reed and McCutchen had entered the mountains bearing relief had been, as closely as can be determined, the very day that the emigrants had entered the mountains from the other direction for their last trial at the pass.)

Reed and McCutchen from the snow-buried ridge looked out toward Yuba Bottoms. They were blocked. They were not more than a dozen miles from the summit, but not even a man with the strength and height of big McCutchen could flounder as far as that through snow which with every hour and every mile grew deeper. But even if they could struggle forward and reach the camp on foot, they would accomplish nothing. What the camp would need was more food, not more men. It was a terrible thought that their wives and children might be beleaguered deep in the snow just around the next spur which cut off the view, but there was nothing more to be done just now. They had achieved all that men could; their honor was white.

They turned back. The horses had to be dug out of the snow. That night they got to Bear Valley again, exhausted in body and equally despondent in mind. Mrs. Curtis was sick, and Curtis was grown so churlish that he could not even keep a civil tongue as McCutchen built up the fire and got supper.

Next morning they found their mule dead from cold and lack of food. They cached the jerked beef in trees and the flour in Curtis's wagon, hoping that it would serve for some later relief expedition or might even succor some of the Donner Party, if any should get as far as Bear Valley. Then they packed a few of Curtis's belongings on a horse, and driving the others light they moved down to the lower end of the valley where bushes stuck out of the snow and offered some poor browsing for the starved horses. Next morning they set out for Johnson's; the bitterness of defeat was upon them.

A few days later, back at the Fort again, Reed told Sutter the story. The Captain was sympathetic and in no way surprised that the crossing had proved impossible. Reed gave him the number of cattle which the train had, and Sutter estimated that, if the emigrants would kill the cattle and preserve the meat in the snow, they would have enough to last them through till spring. As for relief, there was no possibility of that until February when the winter storms were over and the snow a little hardened. Besides, the country was swept clear of men; there were not more than a hundred or two white men in all the Sacramento Valley, and most of these had ridden south to join Frémont. Sutter's only advice was to go to Yerba Buena on San Francisco Bay and there to apply to the naval officer in command. McCutchen at the same time might see what could be accomplished toward raising help around Sonoma and Napa, north of the Bay.

So again Reed rode away from the adobe walls of Sutter's Fort, this time heading south and west and soon leaving out of sight the baffling wall of mountains which might hide behind its imperturbable white expanse he knew not what horrors.

12. BEYOND THE WALL

ACTUALLY that white wall hid as yet no horrors. If Reed instead of riding southward could have lifted himself to overlook the pass above the mountain lake, he would have seen the smokes of three cabins. The snow-trapped emigrants with the adaptability and hardihood of their pioneer blood had already established themselves.

They had built among the pines in the level land below the outlet of the lake. The little creek flowed close by the cabins. North and south, pine-covered mountains hemmed them in close. To the east, if you got clear of the trees, you could see a mile or two down the creek valley. By walking westward a few hundred yards, you could look the length of the blue lake, and up to the high white barrier of the pass beyond, not seeming much lower than the jagged peaks, its bastions. By a direct line the summit of the pass was only five miles distant. The site of the winter camp offered the advantages of easily obtainable water and wood. They had paused here merely because this was the first suitable place which they had found as they back-trailed from their last attempt at crossing. Here, too, the one cabin was already standing.

This one and the two others which had been built all looked much alike. They were squat log-cabins, built more hurriedly and so more primitively than was even the usual frontier custom. Mere openings served as doors, and there were no windows. All the newly built ones had flat roofs, composed of green poles laid across flat from wall to wall and covered with tents, wagon-canvasses, hides, or whatever was available. Two of the cabins were double, thus making use of both sides of one wall. The emigrants had not built close together. The original cabin stood about a quarter of a mile from the outlet of the lake; one of the others was a hundred and fifty yards up the stream and the third stood isolated a good half-mile farther down.

About each cabin was a scene of confusion. Some of the wagons had been left snowed-in beyond the head of the lake, but the few which remained stood about more or less unloaded and dismantled. Here and there on the slushy ground stood a few cattle, mere walking skeletons, together with some horses and the seven mules which Stanton had brought from Sutter's. Many oxen had already been slaughtered and their quarters were stacked up like cord-wood, frozen stiff. Dogs were still about, including little Cash, the Reed children's pet.

In this camp were huddled sixty people—nineteen men counting all of eighteen years and older, twelve women, and twenty-nine children. Of these last, six were mere babies, several still at the breast. Seven family groups were represented, and in general the cabin arrangements preserved, although with no great nicety, the family organization. The Breens, by right of first arrival apparently, had taken posses-

sion of the original cabin and repaired its leaky roof. Along-
side this, Keseberg had built a sort of lean-to for his family.
The up-stream cabin housed the Eddys and the Murphy clan.
The down-stream cabin was double, sheltering in the western
end the Graveses and in the eastern—strange coupling—
the Reeds. With the Reeds lived their servants and teamsters,
and also Stanton and his two Indians. Mrs. McCutchen and
her baby were probably with the Graveses.

The Donners themselves had never got so far as the lake.
Along a small creek about five miles back on the trail, on the
evening probably of November 3, they had been forced to
make camp. With some snow already falling and a storm
threatening, they had that evening cut some logs for cabins.
But in the night a heavy snowfall had covered the ground to
the depth of two or three feet, and lacking the man-power to
build cabins quickly, they had decided to erect some sort of
shelter as soon as possible. The George Donners had cleared
the snow from a space just under a large pine tree, and had
set their tent south of the tree and facing east. In front of the
tent and using the tree for the north wall, they had hastily
built a crude semi-circular lean-to of pine branches. This
they covered with old quilts, rubber coats, buffalo robes, and
odds and ends of cloth. In the ground near the base of the
tree they scooped out a hollow for a fireplace. Inside the
tent and the lean-to they drove stakes into the ground, to
these fastened poles, and on the poles safe from mud and
dampness laid their beds. To strengthen the tent against the
snow they reinforced it with poles and brush. The Jacob
Donners built a similar composite structure, and across the
stream the four young men, teamsters, raised a sort of Indian
wigwam.

Snow had fallen as they worked, but by evening the rude
structures had been made habitable. The families moved in,
Mrs. Wolfinger with the George Donners. The hovels were
cold, muddy and damp, but with the invincible knack of
the westerner to make himself comfortable under any circumstances, they soon had fires going, got supper, and tucked the
children into bed each with a scrap of loaf sugar as a com-
forter.

These three shelters housed twenty-one people—six men,
three women, and twelve children.

The two camps soon established communication, but

neither had much in the way of encouraging news to share. The immediate situation, to be sure, was not critical. Against the cold and the snow they were secure. They had plenty of clothing; firewood was available; and their shelters, poor as some of them were, gave protection from the immediate fury of the storms. But the outlook for the future—that was the terrifying thought. They had now exhausted both their own supplies and what Stanton had brought from Sutter's. Almost nothing remained except a few odds and ends such as coffee, tea, and sugar; even the supply of salt was at the point of being exhausted. The animals were the only hope; first the oxen, then the horses and mules, and when the time came, the dogs. By the middle of November, the cattle had mostly been slaughtered; the poor beasts were dying, anyway, not being able to find grass beneath the snow. The emigrants did not kill them all, however, doubtless fearing that a spell of thawing weather might spoil the meat. Captain Sutter had figured optimistically that if they killed all the cattle they would have plenty of meat to support themselves through till spring. What the Captain did not know was the nightly toll which the Indians had taken along the Humboldt. The emigrants could figure also, and their figures told that starvation would be stalking close before the winter was half over.

Hunting and fishing offered the only possibilities of supplementing the food supply. The lake was as yet not frozen over, and the emigrants following its shores with pole and line frequently saw fish. These refused to bite, however, and the men and boys used to fishing for bullheads and suckers in muddy mid-western streams had neither equipment nor skill for luring mountain trout. Attempts at hunting were scarcely more successful. With a borrowed gun Eddy ranged the woods through snow a foot deep, but he found a land of desolation. By this time the deer had descended to levels below the snow; the bears were beginning to hibernate, and except for a few stragglers the migrating ducks and geese had passed on to the south. On the first day he managed to bring home a coyote, which made a far from palatable supper for the Eddys, Murphys, and Fosters. On the next day he shot an owl. From his third day's hunting he returned despondent and empty-handed. Three days spent in the woods by the most skilled hunter of the company, and the result one coyote and one owl!

Obviously they could not get through the winter by hunting, and so each family hoarded its own supplies the more avariciously. Communal sharing was not part of the westerner's way of looking at things, and besides, too many personal hatreds split this particular group. Of all the families the Breens had lost the fewest cattle, and so were in best condition for the winter; in addition their close friend was Patrick Dolan, who, though a bachelor, had his own cattle and more than enough for himself. The Eddys and the Reeds were the worst off. The former had only one ox. Mrs. Reed was to a greater or less degree responsible for the support of eight people, and for them she had not a single ox remaining of the fine herd with which her husband had started; it is doubtful if even her two horses had got so far as to the lake. The other families varied in their resources, but all were badly enough off.

The result was some very inhumane readjusting in which those having cattle drove hard bargains with those who must buy or starve. Mrs. Reed managed to obtain two oxen from Graves and two from Breen, promising to pay two for one when they got through to California. One of Graves's oxen starved to death, and although refusing to save the meat for his own use, he would not let Eddy have it for less than twenty-five dollars. Some days later Breen sold Foster two beeves, taking a gold watch and other property in security.

The company had finally settled down at the lake on November 4. At that time the ground had been covered with snow, and more snow had fallen with little intermission for the eight days following. It had to some extent melted as it fell, and on the ground about the cabins had never been more than a foot deep. A period of clear weather followed, and under the noonday sun the snow melted from the exposed places until the valley was nearly bare. The cattle and Sutter's mules could manage to pick up a living again.

When food was insufficient and none could be obtained by hunting, sheer necessity demanded that the stronger members of the party attempt an escape. Accordingly thirteen of the hardiest men, and two young women, Mrs. Fosdick and her sister Mary Graves, decided to brave the pass on foot. So urgent was the need of husbanding food that the three fathers, Eddy, Graves, and Foster, decided that they would do better to leave their families than to stay with them. None of the

Breens, who were best supplied with food, joined the adventurers.

On November 12, the very first clear day, the fathers took leave of their families, and the fifteen, each with a small piece of beef for provision, set out. The attempt was a complete failure. Beyond the head of the lake they found the snow soft and still ten feet deep. They were absolutely unable to advance, and had to return to the cabins without having been absent even one night.

Eddy had been with this party, and although he must have been exhausted by the struggle in the snow, he nevertheless set out hunting on the next day, and killed two ducks. One of these he had to give in return for the loan of the gun.

On the following day he went out again, and soon had the very dubious pleasure of seeing the tracks of a large grizzly bear. In those days of muzzle-loaders a single hunter generally left grizzlies alone, and Eddy must have heard many terrifying tales of the ferocious giant of the western mountains. But at this time, although actually faint from lack of food, he followed the trail eagerly. At length at the edge of an opening, ninety yards distant, he sighted the monster, head to the ground, digging roots. Eddy concealed himself behind a large fir-tree, and prudently put his only extra bullet into his mouth to have it ready for quick reloading. He took deliberate aim, and fired. The bear reared up, and then sighting the smoke from the gun, charged furiously. In the few seconds available, Eddy poured his powder and rammed home the bullet. But the beast was upon him. He dodged around the tree. The bear impeded by its wound tried to follow, but could not turn quickly. Eddy leaped around the tree, came upon the bear from behind, and firing into the shoulder at close range inflicted a disabling wound. Having no more bullets, he finished the conflict by cracking the animal over the head with a club.

Eddy and Graves went out after the carcass, probably with some of the latter's remaining oxen. Superstition was beginning to make itself felt among the emigrants, and as the two walked Graves gloomily voiced his fear that he would die in the mountains struck down by the hand of the Lord in judgment for his refusal to go back and rescue Hardkoop.

The bear, they estimated, weighed eight hundred pounds. Foster got half for the loan of his gun. Mrs. Reed and Graves each received a share. Eddy, who had risked his life, had the remainder. This success encouraged the camp for the moment, but spirits sank again when Eddy came back from another day's hunting with only a duck and a gray squirrel. From this time on, no success at hunting was recorded.

The third week of November had come now. Nothing much happened from day to day. Every one was on starvation rations, and all were gradually getting weaker. They had vague hopes. Surely there must come a thaw sometime; even the big snow in Illinois had lasted only nine weeks. If a thaw came, a man could get across the pass. "Uncle Billy" Graves knew about things called snow-shoes; you could walk right on top of snow with them; he knew about things like that because he was born back in the Green Mountains in Vermont. But in Illinoy, and Ioway, and Mizzoury, where they came from, most of them, there wasn't ever snow enough for using things like that. The Dutchmen didn't know about them, either. Maybe Reed, and Herron, and McCutchen would get up a rescue party and come back. Sure, they hadn't treated Reed very well, but still he would want to get the family out; so would Mac. But as they looked westward to the pass, no one ever came across the top and started working down the snowbanks on the steep eastern slope.

Despondency was settling down upon them. Some were half sick from worry and despair as well as from lack of food. Keseberg's foot was still bad. Breen was ailing, too, with what he called "the gravel." Peggy, his wife, had to oversee the slaughtering of the cattle. She was capable of it—a big, raw-boned, masculine-looking Irishwoman; some people said that she was the man of the family, anyway.

At this time Breen apparently sensed that the events through which they were passing might be worthy of record, for the nearness of death often gives men a feeling of importance. He began to keep a diary. The first entry was a recapitulation:

Friday Nov. 20th 1846 Came to this place on the 31st of last month that it snowed we went on to the pass the snow so deep we were unable to find the road, when within 3 miles of the summit then turned back to this shanty on the Lake, Stanton came one day after we arriveed here we again took our teams & waggons & made another unsuccessful attempt to cross in company with Stanton we returned to the shanty it continueing to snow all the time we were here we now have killed most part of our cattle having to stay here untill next spring & live on poor beef without bread or salt it snowed during the space of eight days with little intermission, after our arrival here, the remainder of time up to this day was clear & pleasant frezeing at night the snow nearly gone from the valleys.

Next morning, the twenty-first, another party set out to attempt a crossing. Matters were growing sensibly more pressing, so that sixteen men, three more than before and almost all, in fact, who were at the lake, joined in this trial. The number of women had risen from two to six. Even old Mrs. Murphy and three of her half-grown children were included, and the whole party comprised twenty-two people, more than a third of the entire number encamped at the lake. They took Sutter's seven mules with them.

This time they got along better. Ten days of clear and slightly melting weather had consolidated the snow even at higher levels. The day was fine, and the party making good progress on the snow-crust actually got across the pass. In a little valley on the west side they made a camp in six feet of snow. They were exhausted with the labor of the day and weak from starvation; they knew nothing about camping in deep snow, and had the greatest difficulty in getting a fire started. To add to their troubles a fatal difference of opinion arose. Eddy, always active and now encouraged by momentary success, was for going ahead at all odds. But the mules had had a bad day, breaking through the crust over which the men could slide; Stanton and the Indians refused to go further without the mules. Eddy strove almost to the point of violence, but in vain. He argued that Captain Sutter would never blame any one for abandoning mules in order to save human life; he offered to become personally responsible for the mules; he even threatened the Indians to make them advance against their will. But Luis and Salvador were apparently convinced that Captain Sutter would hang them, if they returned empty-handed. Stanton and Eddy both were in anger. But Stanton held the whip-hand; without him or one of the Indians as a guide no one could go ahead. The others of the party were exhausted, faint, and disheartened in the cold of a November night at seven thousand feet. They could see, as young Billy Graves put it, "nothing but snow and the tops of pine trees sticking out of it." In the morning they stumbled back over the trail, taking the unlucky mules with them. At midnight they got back to the cabins, where only despair and further starvation could be in store for them.

After only two days of rest Eddy and some of the others were again planning to attempt the pass. They intended to start on Thursday the twenty-sixth, but toward evening of Wednesday, it began snowing. At first there was something desultory about the storm. On Thursday—it was Thanksgiving Day—as much rain and sleet as snow came down, so that the ground was deep in mud and slush. On Friday it snowed, but melted mostly as it fell, so that bare ground still showed about the cabins. The mountain-party, baffled, sat about waiting for the bad weather to break. But this somewhat languid storm, the more it continued the more it seemed to settle down to work. By Saturday the snow came down fast; it lay now eight or ten inches deep on the ground, soft and wet. Sunday morning it was still snowing; the wind came steadily from over the pass bringing no rift in the clouds; the snow was about three feet deep. Things had a serious look. In the storm and deep snow the men, weakened by long privation, began to have difficulty in getting wood. During a lull on Sunday Breen slaughtered his last yoke of oxen. It had been snowing for four days now.

It continued. On Monday Breen's diary ran:

Snowing fast wind W about 4 or 5 feet deep, no drifts looks as likely to continue as when it commenced no liveing thing without wings can get about.

And on Tuesday:

Still snowing wind W snow about 5½ feet or 6 deep difficult to get wood no going from the house completely housed up.

And then fell another disaster. Three or four cattle left unslaughtered strayed off in the storm; weakened by cold and hunger, they at last lay down somewhere; then they soon died and in a few hours the snow had concealed even where their bodies lay. The few remaining horses and Sutter's mules (those unlucky mules!) met the same fate. The last reserve of food was lost. Had they been mountain men, they would have known what to expect. But like so much else, a Sierran storm was unknown to them. Who would have thought that it could snow so much?

Still it continued on Wednesday. A whole week of snow! That night, however, the storm eased off, and ceased for a while. Snow fell most of Thursday again, as the storm gave a final twist to its tail. Then on Friday came a cold, dry wind from the deserts on the east. Broken clouds scudded overhead. The temperature fell far below freezing.

It was the fourth of December. The storm had lasted eight days. The oxen, the horses, and the mules were gone. The snow lay eight feet deep, almost up to the cabin roofs. On the pass, they knew, it would be much deeper, and now there was no hard crust on top. Just a month had passed since they had finally settled at the lake. Some of the less fortunate were already on the verge of collapse from the weeks of exertion and scanty food. And winter had scarcely begun.

If in this time of trial they turned to the pages of Hastings's *Guide,* once their reliance, they might have read passages thoughtlessly passed by in more careless times, which now struck with a cold chill. Just after the mention of a December as pleasant as May came the sentence:

The remarks here made, in reference to the mildness, and uniformity of the climate, are applicable only to the valleys and plains, for the mountains present but one eternal winter.

13. DEATH BIDS GOD-SPEED

MAN is a curiously hopeful animal, and among men the Irish are noted for optimism. But surely it is a high-water mark both of general human and of special Hibernian resiliency that Breen on the very next day, cheered by the mere sight of the sun, seemed restored to good spirits and even esthetic appreciation. He wrote:

Fine clear day beautiful sunshine thawing a little looks delightful after the long snow storm

Next day, on the sixth, he made a more practical note: "Stanton & Graves manufactureing snow shoes for another mountain scrabble." For once the Donner Party was lucky. Graves had spent his youth in the Green Mountains, a country of heavy snows; Stanton had lived in northern New York. Graves certainly, and Stanton most probably, had had experience with snow-shoes. All the other members of the company had lived only in countries of light snow where one expected to plunge through rather than to walk upon the surface. Had it not been for these two wanderers from the north, any further attempt to escape across the mountains would have been useless.

By another bit of what may also be called luck, material for the making of snow-shoes was at hand—the oxbows. These were long strips of tough hickory, U-shaped; with their ends passed through holes in the yoke they served to fasten the yoke upon the necks of the oxen and by pressing against their shoulders to take much of the pulling-strain. In size and shape they were close enough to snow-shoe frames, but having been designed to withstand the power of an ox, they were much too heavy for human footwear. Graves, however, managed to saw them into strips, each light enough and plentifully strong. To form the surface of the shoe, strips of rawhide were woven back and forth. The result was a very clumsy affair, lacking the turned-up toe and the tapering heel which mark the gracefully shaped snow-shoe. But a pair of them would support a man's weight upon the surface of snow, and that was the important matter.

Before a sufficient number of shoes could be prepared and the start made, another storm was threatening. Every week now was making a perceptible difference in the emigrants. Beaten upon by blizzards, half starved, they now had more and more difficulty in cutting and dragging firewood through the deep snows. They began to suffer from the cold.

About this time they must have begun to notice what afterwards seemed to them so astonishing. The women stood the strain better than the men did. Whether food was apportioned by individuals rather than by size, whether the men did more physical work and therefore expended more energy, whether the constitution of a woman is more enduring than that of a man, whether merely in these individual cases the women were hardier—these questions cannot be surely answered. Most likely several of these factors were at work, but certainly, with some exceptions, the men failed sooner.

The first one collapsed on the eighth. It was Spitzer the German. Apparently he fell in the snow outside of the Breen cabin, and was too weak to rise by himself. "Uncle Patrick" helped him into the cabin. Baylis Williams, the Reeds' hired man, was failing, too. They were suffering probably from what would be called malnutrition rather than starvation, for there was still food available. But a diet exclusively of lean meat, without even salt, is a far from balanced ration. The absence of salt in itself tends to produce extreme fatigue, and naturally some would feel this effect sooner than others.

By this time there was little communication even between the three cabins at the lake, and as for the Donners, they had not been heard from for weeks. At last, however, Milt Elliott and Noah James departed on the ninth to try to get through to the Donner camp and see what had happened. That same day toward noon a threatening storm broke.

This time it snowed for five days. Whatever melting and settling the four days of clear weather had accomplished were soon wiped out, and toward the end of the storm even Breen, who was generally conservative in his estimates, noted the snow as eight feet deep on the level.

During the storm those intending to cross the mountains continued their preparations, and when the morning of the fourteenth broke clear and cold, they were nearly ready. Fourteen pairs of crude snow-shoes were finished.

With Baylis Williams now at the point of death and starvation visibly at hand, the present attempt took on immediately an even more desperate color than either of the two previous ones. This time they dared not flinch or fail —there was nothing to which they could come back. Whether any one had to be urged or threatened into making the attempt, or whether on the contrary some had to be restrained from going, does not stand in the record. What actually happened was that practically all who were physically able made the attempt. Of the grown men at the lake cabins, Breen was sick and Keseberg's foot still crippled him; Spitzer, Williams and probably Denton were too weak. James and Elliott had left to go to the Donners; the storm had broken soon after their departure, and nothing had been heard of them since. All the other men, ten in number, were of the escaping party. To them were joined two half-grown boys and five of the young women who deemed themselves strong enough for the attempt. Those who were of the party need be considered neither heroes ready to sacrifice themselves that others might live, nor cowards running away and leaving the others in the lurch, for to go was as dangerous as to stay and not more so. The only preference lay in whether one would rather chance all to one cast, or would rather endure passively.

Among the snow-shoers we may name first of all Stanton and the two Indians. Although later the members of the Donner Party were always to call Stanton a hero, they appear to have had less appreciation for him at the time. They remembered his unfortunate advice which had kept them too long in the Truckee Meadows, as well as his stubbornness in refusing to leave the mules behind. In spite of all his services, they were not ready, except for Mrs. Reed who was herself as badly off, to share their food with him. On December 9 Breen's diary had recorded "Stanton trying to make a raise of some [beef] for his Indians & self" and had added dryly "not likely to get much."

Also among the snow-shoers was, naturally, the ever energetic Eddy. The Murphy clan was well represented with Mr. and Mrs. Foster, Mrs. Pike, and the two boys Lem and Bill. Old "Uncle Billy" Graves, the contriver of the shoes, although close to sixty, considered himself equal to the adventure, and with him went his two daughters, Mrs. Fosdick and Mary; the son-in-law Jay Fosdick was with them. The others were Mrs. McCutchen, Antonio the Mexican, Burger the German, and Patrick Dolan.

This last was the only one in whom altruistic motives may to some degree have dominated. He was a bachelor, and had got through to the lake with plenty of cattle to have supported him through the winter. His feelings, however, may not have been entirely humanitarian. He probably remembered the incident upon the desert when Eddy had threatened Breen's life rather than see his children die for lack of water. If it came to starving children, a bachelor's mere property rights might count for little. On leaving, Dolan gave instructions that Mrs. Reed and her children were to have some share of his cattle.

The constituency of the party as a whole showed the growing desperation. Four fathers left their families, and even three mothers decided that they could serve their children better by abandoning them than by remaining with them.

The proportion of men and women among the snow-shoers showed the growing dominance of the latter. The first party to attempt the pass on foot had consisted of fifteen men and two women, the second of sixteen men and six women, but of the snow-shoers five were women and only twelve men.

On the two days following the cessation of the storm they made their final preparations. The packs which they prepared were of the lightest; they took no change of clothing. Each took one blanket or quilt. They had Foster's gun; it was a heavy load for half-starved men and women, but they could take turns in carrying it, and it might save them if they found game. They had one hatchet, or light ax, and several pistols. The men had tobacco, that last solace. They assigned themselves what they called six days' rations, hoping by Stanton's guidance to get through to Bear Valley in that time, but each ration was only a strip of stringy dried beef, enough to allow each person, three times daily, a piece as big as his two fingers. This with a little coffee and loaf sugar was all.

So much one learns from the records, which like most records note only the tangible and material. What planning, what anticipations, must have filled those last two days of preparation! How often and minutely they must have figured distance and time with Stanton while the Indians looked on blankly! A man could ride it in one day from Bear Valley; it must be about thirty miles then. They ought to be able to make five miles a day, even with these crazy snow-shoes and over the mountains and half starved. Five miles wasn't much; with good conditions a man could walk that in a little over an hour; surely they could make as much as that in a whole day. But the timorous hangers-back could argue that they might freeze to death at night, or get caught in a storm, or lose their way, or even when they arrived at Bear Valley, be nowhere. No, the leaders could answer, they could keep a fire burning at night; and Stanton, even the Indians, could guide them; and as for the other things they wouldn't happen, and if they did, you couldn't do more than die, anyway. And you would do that here, starving to death in a dirty, smelling hole like a rat. Better to die on the mountains, marching with the wind in your teeth.

One imagines easily the desperation of the moment. There was perhaps another side—light-heartedness, and silly jokes which seemed funny, and even laughter as one or another took a tumble while practicing on his shoes. For men and women seldom act as the situation demands—they smother laughter at funerals and weep at weddings.

But whether or not there was laughter, one feels sure that, as the hour approached, a certain deep intoxicating exhilaration swept in upon some of them. Action and danger are never without their charm to the brave. The gambling spirit is never more enrapturing than when one puts his own life upon the cast. As they went to bed on the night before their departure, some at least must have felt the excitement and have looked forward to the next day with a feeling at least near akin to pleasurable anticipation.

When they awoke in the morning, something had happened. Baylis Williams was dead. Since they had laid Pike away in the wintry grave by Truckee River almost two months before, Death had stayed his hand. Now he was upon them again. As those who were to leave laced on their snowshoes, perhaps a certain feeling of grimness was their uppermost emotion. The body of Baylis Williams lay in the cabin. It was Death that bade them God-speed.

14. THE SNOW-SHOERS

THAT morning of Wednesday the sixteenth was clear and freezing. The wind had worked around somewhat to the east giving hope of fair weather, and the cold night had left the snow dry and feathery, so that it did not stick to the snowshoes. There was no more reason for delay. Those who were departing faced danger and bitter hardship, but as they looked into the wasted faces of those who remained they realized that, even should they themselves escape, they might never again see their wives and children. The parting was one of double sorrow.

They filed off across the snow, shuffling clumsily in the heavy foot-gear. At each step they sank a foot deep into the light snow. The women, for greater freedom of movement, had made their skirts into loose trousers, so that except where bearded faces showed from beneath the mufflings, men and women looked alike. The fourteen with snow-shoes plodded on first; then went "Dutch Charley" and the two Murphy boys stepping in the footsteps of the others. The hope of these last was that the passage of so many snow-shoes would beat down a path and allow them to walk. But the scheme did not work well, so that the three followers kept breaking through and floundering. Slowly the long line filed out of sight among the pine trees.

On the first day the party made poor progress. Three weeks before, when they had been able to walk on the crust, they had gone from the cabins and across the pass in one day, but now they were weaker, and the snow-shoes held them back. They made camp at evening not much beyond the head of the lake, about four miles, and, ironically, in full view of the smoke from the cabins. "Dutch Charley" and Bill Murphy had turned back during the day, but Lem had struggled on. It was obvious, however, that he could not keep up as he had planned; so the others improvised snow-shoes for the plucky lad out of some pack-saddles which had come with Captain Sutter's mules and had been abandoned along the road.

Camping in the snow was in itself a problem. It was too deep for them to clear out a snow-pit and build a fire on the ground, but either from their own ingenuity or from knowledge picked up from some mountaineer they hit upon the right method. They cut logs of green wood about six feet long, and with them made a platform on the snow; upon this they kindled a fire of dry wood. If the foundation logs were of good size, they would not burn through during the night. By crowding around the fire, sheltered beneath their scanty supply of blankets, the snow-shoers got through the night miserably enough.

Next day they faced the pass itself. With their snow-shoes, their wintry costumes, and the packs on their shoulders, they reminded Mary Graves, toiling in the rear, of some picture she had seen of a Norwegian fur-company on the ice pack. The climb was heart-breaking work, but sometimes they could get along without snow-shoes as they worked gingerly up the bare, slick rock-surfaces where snow would not lie. At the top some one jested, a bit grimly, that they were about as close to heaven as they could get. Nevertheless, some of them admired the magnificent scene which lay unrolled as they looked back to the east over the now frozen lake, past the smoke of the cabins, and on to the distant mountains beyond. A few steps westward, and that whole vista sank from view. That night they camped, exhausted, a little west of the pass, estimating that they had made six miles. The snow was twelve feet deep.

On the third day they had the advantage of a slightly downhill course. Nevertheless, the strain of two days of constant labor without sufficient food was beginning to tell on them. And they now faced another enemy, for as they crossed the treeless expanse of Summit Valley the white surface dazzling in the sun brought on snow-blindness. Brave little Stanton was the worst affected; he was the weakest, too, and gradually fell behind, out of sight. The emigrant trail was of course buried deep under the snow, but even though Stanton failed, the Indians knew the way. Who could miss it in any case? For the great, broad valley of the Yuba ran straight ahead toward the west. Snow flurries broke upon them with a cold wind blowing furiously. Again they estimated six miles when they camped without Stanton. An hour later he struggled in.

The fourth day repeated the third. Fierce squalls of snow swept down on them; it grew so cold that their feet started freezing. Stanton still lagged. In their weakened condition they began to fall prey to hallucinations. Mary Graves saw haze in a gorge to the right. The others assured her that it was merely mist, but she insisted that it was smoke, and even made them fire the gun for a signal. Five miles was the most that they could do. By this night they were down somewhere near Yuba Bottoms, under the high dome of Cisco Butte.

The fifth morning was clear with a cold wind from the northeast. They left the river and struggled uphill four miles to the divide. Stanton came in about an hour late, as before.

On this fifth night they were camping not far from the place at which Reed and McCutchen had turned back five weeks before, and there they were only about five miles from the cache of beef and flour which the two fathers had left at Curtis's wagon in Bear Valley. But they of course knew nothing of all that. So far they had got along well enough, and had made the five miles a day upon which they had counted. But they must now have begun to realize that even at Bear Valley they would not be out of the snow. From its depth at the place where they were, they could only suppose that the snow belt must still extend ahead of them for many miles. They saw about them, even from points of look-out, only heavily forested mountains, deep in snow. Their packs contained food for only one more day.

The morning of their sixth day broke. It was Monday, the twenty-first of December, the shortest day of the year. Christmas week! That morning Eddy dug into his little pack to see if there were not something which he could leave behind to lighten his load still further. To his amazement he found half a pound of bear's meat. To it was attached a bit of paper bearing a note written in pencil and signed "Your own dear Eleanor." She had robbed her own insufficient stores to save her husband, and in the note she urged him to cherish her gift for the last extremity; some feeling told her, she wrote, that it would be the means of saving his life.

But this sixth morning one member of the company was finished. Little Stanton, who had once been in the warm, safe valley of the Sacramento, who had come back that the women and children might be fed, who had three times led the way across the pass in the snow—Stanton was through. Fatigue, snow-blindness, and slow starvation had worn him down. He had made his mistakes, but he had lived as a hero; it remained to die as a gentleman.

That morning as his companions were setting out, he sat by the camp-fire smoking his pipe. Mary Graves approached, and asked if he was coming.

"Yes," he said, "I am coming soon."

They went on.

Stanton's chivalry had spared them any qualms about deserting him. Nevertheless his loss almost immediately brought difficulties. He had doubtless trusted to the Indians to guide them through, but to follow an unmarked trail across snow-covered mountains, especially when they had traversed it only once before and then in the opposite direction, was entirely too much of a task for these half-civilized Indians of the plains. Moreover this section of the trail followed no river course or marked ridge, but worked along and across the valleys of small streams. Each of these began by flowing west and looked as if offering the proper route, but they all soon bore off subtly to the south, leading not toward Bear Valley, only a day's march distant, but toward the canyon-scarred, tangled country along the American. It was a perfect place for getting lost.

And almost immediately they made a mistake. Instead of keeping well up on the slope and working along it, they turned off and went downhill toward the south and away from Bear Valley. On this day they used up the last of their provisions. At night Stanton did not come in.

Tuesday morning broke upon a camp without food except for Eddy's hoarded bear meat. They went on about a mile. Then snow began to fall. Starving and confused, they halted partly because they could not travel safely in the storm, partly in fear that they were already lost, and partly in faint hope that Stanton might still come up to guide them. They stayed there for the rest of the day, but he did not come.

Next day, weaker from a day and a half of fasting, they climbed to a high point for observation. Eastward rose the buttes along the Yuba whence they had just come. Northward were ugly, forbidding mountains. Westward was a high ridge blocking the way. If there was any visible choice, it was toward the south.

They camped on the height, and next day, starving, went down a valley for three miles. Then snow began to fall, not another flurry but the beginning of a real storm. This was their ninth day of travel broken only by nights spent crouching half-frozen in the snow around whatever fire they could build. Most of them had not eaten for more than two days, and in their weakened condition they could not go on much further. The situation must be faced. They halted, huddled together in the storm, and consulted as to what, if anything, could be done. All of the men except Eddy were completely dispirited and favored turning back. Eddy and the women declared that they would go forward, come what might. Then some one said that they must all die of starvation. It was not to be denied—unless they found food. Then came a pause. During the last two days, as they had marched half-mad with hunger, what strange thoughts had begun to grow in their minds? They had begun perhaps, as they looked about with maniacal cravings for food, to regard their comrades as offering certain new possibilities. Man might eat beef—good! Man might eat horse, too, as the need came, and mule. He might eat bear and dog, and even coyote and owl. He might also—and the relentless logic drove on—yes, man might also eat man.

All about lay the deep snow, and more snow was falling. They had hungered two days and more, and had no prospect for food except that which, however much they had thought of it, no one had yet put into words.

The pause lengthened, and then Patrick Dolan voiced it—they should draw lots to see who should die to furnish food for the others. Eddy seconded. But Foster objected, and of all motions such a one most surely must require unanimity. And even if they drew lots, how would they accomplish the deed? Was a man to butcher a man like an ox, or cut his throat as if he were a sheep? They had not come to that.

But another idea came to Eddy's mind. He himself was stronger than most of the others by nature, and even more by virtue of his supply of bear meat. If they struggled on blindly in the snow, some other would surely drop before he did, and might be eaten. But such a way was not Eddy's, and his own proposal shows the flame of the man. Let two of them, he said, take each a six-shooter, and fight till one or both were killed. Thus a man would have a chance for his life, and if he lost, would die in hot blood, not slaughtered like a pig. It was a man's way. But again some one objected, for the scruples of civilization were dying hard.

Eddy finally suggested all that was left to do, and a way which was in fact much safer for him—they should struggle on until some one died. It would not take long now, to judge by the looks of some of them.

They dragged themselves ahead through the storm. Death dogged their steps. Each one was to his comrade that which might perhaps be food. Whom could a man trust, or whose eyes could he meet? Could a man without hypocrisy help another through a drift, or except with ugly hope inquire how he felt? Antonio the Mexican was far gone. So was "Uncle Billy" Graves; his sixty years were telling. He was of no strength to bear up with men and women half his age, his own daughters among them. Perhaps it would be Antonio or "Uncle Billy." But they both managed to keep going, until at last all halted. The storm was blowing upon them what seemed an actual torrent of snow. In the gathering darkness, stumbling with weakness, having only one hatchet, with some of their number already collapsing, they found the task of collecting wood almost too much for them. If those who had to cut and carry the logs for the firm platform chose skimpy ones, they were scarcely to be blamed; they did what their weakness allowed. Even after the green logs were laid together, the numb-fingered men had the greatest difficulty, as the wind swirled and the snow drove, in getting the fire kindled at all. At last the flame lived; they cherished and built it up until it roared finely, their only cheer on Christmas Eve. But some of them were far gone.

Antonio the Mexican, who had followed the train as herdsman of the cattle, lay by the fire sleeping in a heavy stupor. He breathed difficultly and unnaturally. Once as he moved in his sleep, he threw out an arm so that his hand fell into the fire. Eddy, lying nearby and awake, himself exhausted, saw what had happened, but supposed that the pain would arouse the sleeper, and in any case if Antonio were not aroused—so much the better. But the hand doubled up and shriveled with the heat, and finally Eddy, arousing himself, drew it from the fire. Eddy lay down, but Antonio's breathing became a rattling sound and he flung out his arm again; the watcher, realizing that nothing mattered any longer for Antonio, saw the hand shrivel in the flame until it burned to a coal. Cold, fatigue, and hunger had done their work.

Again there was food in camp, but before any one made a move to eat, a worse crisis was upon them. Antonio had died about nine o'clock, and an hour later the storm increased in fury. Wind, hail, and snow beat down with an incredible fury upon the thirteen who still remained. The only way to save themselves from freezing was to pile more and more wood upon the fire. The unusual heat of this great fire soon ate into the too small foundation logs. Gaps opened between them, and the snow melted away. The fire, platform and all, began to settle into the hole which its own heat produced. At the same time the supply of wood which they had expected to last the night became exhausted, and some one staggered off against the weight of the storm to cut more fuel, or perhaps new foundation logs. As he worked, the head flew from the hatchet and was lost in the deep snow.

It seemed the final piling up of calamities. Even if they broke off dry wood for fuel, they could not maintain a fire without a foundation for it. And the fire was settling visibly. The snow beneath it had turned to slush and water. By midnight they found themselves about eight feet deep in a circular well in the snow with ice-cold water beginning to rise in the bottom; it was like feeling the chill of death actually creeping up toward their ankles. Several of them were almost done for. "Uncle Billy" was sinking into the stupor before death. One of the Indians sat nodding next to the snow-wall, almost frozen.

With the ingenuity of desperation the few who still maintained their wits and a little strength, set the half-wet logs on end and built up the fire on top, as if on stilts. It burned there, a precarious reliance against the power of the storm. With the icy water around their feet, they cherished their fire burning above it.

Suddenly the half-frozen Indian who sat by the snow-wall, roused himself, made a sudden clumsy push forward to get next to the fire, and upset it. The flame winked out; the embers hissed once. The poor people huddling about broke into a most pitiful wail of mixed prayer and lamentation. They were unstrung, and some no longer in their right minds. Most of them were past the point of even trying to save themselves.

At this juncture only Eddy's knowledge of woodcraft saved them. As they were, he knew all would be frozen to death in a few hours. Prodding the stupefied men and women into action he gradually aroused them, and got them to climb out of the well. Then in the full force of the storm they spread a few blankets on the snow. On these they seated themselves in a circle facing in toward the center, and over them Eddy laid other blankets forming a sort of tent-like mound. It was a device which he must have learned from some mountain-man. Apathy was already upon some of them, and so slowly did they act that before they could be herded into the shelter "Uncle Billy" Graves had died. Death came easily to him; he was past caring; but as he died he told his two daughters, it is said, to save themselves by using his body.

Once the starving wretches were crouched together beneath the blankets, Eddy himself crept in and completed the circle. They were then, as he had known, safe from freezing. The snow soon covered them, shutting off the wind better than the closest of tents. Even their starved bodies emitted still some heat, and this being conserved by the close space and by the covering of snow, soon raised the temperature.

Through the night the snow roared on, and the morning broke on Christmas Day. It scarcely brought light to the indescribable scene beneath the blankets. Jolly Patrick Dolan was the one who was going now. Instead of falling into apathy he became delirious. His words were wild and unconnected, but he was seized with the dementia of pressing ahead and reaching the settlements immediately. He began to struggle, and finally escaped from the blankets into the storm. Then he called upon Eddy to follow, saying that Eddy was the only one of the party who could be depended upon. After that, falling into complete derangement, he pulled off his boots and most of his clothing, and called upon Eddy to follow him, saying that they would be in the settlements in a few hours. Eddy went out after him, and tried to force him back, but was not able to master Dolan's delirious strength. Later, however, Dolan came back of his own accord and lay down outside the shelter; they then dragged him again beneath the blankets. For a while his agony was upon him, but as they held him tightly he gradually became quiet and submissive again. After that he fell into a calm sleep, and then toward dusk, without awakening, died.

Through Christmas night the storm still raged, and the company, now reduced to eleven, lived on as they could. Probably only the stronger ones were suffering. Most of them were half sunk in coma; after four days without food, the worst pangs of hunger had passed. Nothing human remained, but the spark of animal life glowed dully on. Madness was close upon them. They dreamed maniacal dreams of hunger, and awoke trying to sink their teeth into the hands or arms of their companions. At times they wailed and shrieked.

The youngest of them all was the next to fail. Lemuel Murphy, only a boy of thirteen, became delirious in the night, and talked wildly of food. He raged so that all of the others had to help at holding him. Still they crouched and lay beneath the blankets.

Saturday morning broke, the day after Christmas. They had now been beneath the blankets for more than thirty hours, and the situation was becoming no longer endurable. To light a fire in the brunt of the storm outside was still impossible, but in desperation Eddy attempted to get one started beneath the shelter of the blankets. He used some gun-powder for tinder, and by some accident blew up the whole powder-horn. He was badly burned about the face and hands and two of the women also suffered.

But the grim will to live still held. It outlasted the storm, and when the clouds finally broke on Saturday afternoon, Eddy, a little stronger than the others on account of his bear meat, crawled from beneath the blankets and set to making a fire. But all the wood was soaked, and even their clothing offered scarcely a dry shred. They discovered, however, that Mrs. Pike's mantle had a lining of cotton and some of this seemed fairly dry. They exposed it to the sun's rays, struck sparks into it with flint, and finally managed to blow it into a glow. After this they set fire to a large dead pine tree, and gathered weakly around rejoicing at last in the comfort of the flame.

Then they took the final step. The taboos of civilization had held against five days of starvation, but now the will to live was the stronger. Eddy held off, and strangely enough, the two Indians refused the food, and building themselves a fire at a little distance sat stoically beside it. The others cut the flesh from the arms and legs of Patrick Dolan's body, roasted it by the fire and ate it—"averting their faces from each other, and weeping."

Then they broke off boughs and laid themselves on these crude beds on top of the snow around the burning pine tree. The flames leaped up to the branches of the tree, and after a while great limbs began to burn off and fall among the men and women below. The poor creatures were too apathetic even to care, and lay among the showers of sparks; only by luck no one burned to death or was brained by a falling limb.

They offered some of the food to the plucky boy, Lemuel Murphy, but he was too far gone. The delirium had left him now, and he was quiet, sunk into a stupor. Mrs. Foster, his elder sister, sat cherishing and soothing him, his head in her lap. Night fell; the tree blazed luridly, and a quarter moon swung in the sky, casting a wan light over the deep snow. At moon-set he died.

That morning (it was Sunday the twenty-seventh) they set about the matter more systematically. They remained in camp during this and the next two days. Once the taboo was broken, things were easier. The Indians, too, joined with them. They stripped the flesh from the bodies, roasted what they needed to eat, and dried the rest for carrying with them. They observed only one last sad propriety; no member of a family touched his own dead. But the strain was scarcely the less for that. For as she sat by the fire Mrs. Foster suddenly realized that spitted upon a stick and broiling over the coals she saw the heart of her cherished younger brother.

15. THE HUNTING OF THE DEER

Thus for three days they rested in camp recruiting their strength, and drying the flesh taken from the bodies of the dead. On the thirteenth, somewhat strengthened, they prepared to move on. They had been fifteen on the first night two weeks before. Now Stanton was gone, and as for the four others the packs on the shoulders of the remaining ten told the story—that and a certain feeling in their stomachs, at once comforting and sickening.

By this time their snow-shoes had been wet and dry so often that the rawhide thongs were beginning to rot away. Their feet had suffered also from repeated frost-bite and thawing until they oozed blood from cracks. Nevertheless, wincing with the pain, they pulled on the clumsy footgear, and took the trail. Unkempt, haggard, frost-bitten, gaunt with starvation, they could scarcely drag their snow-shoes over the feathery surface.

All five who had died had been men, and white. Of the remaining ten who took the trail away from the camp of death, two were Sutter's Indian boys, and five were women. Of the eight white men only three remained, and of these Foster and Fosdick, not perhaps without reason, were beaten and despairing. It was only the fortitude of Eddy and of some of the women that kept the party moving.

Just where they now wandered, none of them knew exactly. They had no compass, and steered doubtfully by the sun, seeking the easiest route across the broken country. Even the Indians realized that they were lost; Luis admitted it in his few words of broken English. With feet aching and bloody they floundered on through the recently fallen snow, and at the end of the day estimated that they had made four or five miles. All that they could do about making a fire, now that they had lost the hatchet, was to find a dead tree, scrape away the snow at its foot, and build a fire against it. Where they now were, the snow was not so deep as it had been in the high country near the pass.

On this evening, it was Eddy who was failing. His bear meat had been long exhausted, and he had held off from touching human flesh. Now he felt no hunger, but only a sinking sensation. The others said that he was dying, but he felt too quiet and comfortable, and told them that they were wrong. But in spite of physical lethargy his mind was clear, and by sheer force of reason he at last overcame his complaisant feeling of ease, and convinced himself that his comrades were right, that his pleasant state of detachment must be the same coma which he had seen in the others before they died. Thus persuaded, he approached the only food which was available. As an honest man, he admitted that once he had begun his meal he felt no loathing or disgust. Somewhere in the back of his head a faint thought, the last vestige of those days when he had been a civilized man, informed him that he was doing something horrible. But here in the deep snow among the pine trees necessity was upon him. He was a man who must have food, and he ate what was at hand; that was all.

Next morning they went on. Every step meant pain, but nevertheless now that they had food and no more storms broke, they could make progress. All that they could do, having lost the trail, was to keep to the west, working their way laboriously across the rough canyon-seamed country. The streams fortunately were shrunken by the long-continued freezing, and were generally spanned by snow-bridges. Most often the party crossed the smaller streams, scarcely realizing what they were doing and only now and then looking down through what they called a "well" in the snow to see the water flowing five, ten, or twenty feet below. But occasionally the snow-bridge had been built up from some bush which spanned the stream; then it had merely a knife-edge at the bottom, was not more than two or three feet across at the top, and might be twenty-five feet high. It was like a "bridge perilous" of the fairy tales, and the poor refugees with their clumsy snow-shoes worked across gingerly.

On that day, the last of the year, they were following down a great ridge. The side-slope, covered with snow, was steep and dangerous, and so working gradually along and crossing side-ravines, they probably without much climbing got to the top of the ridge. On either side a great canyon lay; there was no way but straight ahead southwestward along the narrow crest.

Then suddenly they had a view. Instead of seeing only more mountains they looked ahead down a long reach of the gorge to distant ridges standing out darkly, not snow-covered, and then beyond the ridges through the clear, wintry air they saw—at last—a broad plain, stretching off green and flat. No mountain meadow that! It could be nothing but the long-sought valley of the Sacramento.

It was still discouragingly far off, and as if finally to trap them with the goal in view, the ridge which they were following came to an abrupt end. The gorge upon their left turned sharply, cut across in front of them, and joined the gorge upon their right. Directly between them and the far-off valley was this great canyon, fearfully steep, and two thousand feet deep.

That night, having made six miles, they camped at the brink of the canyon. No celebration brought in the New Year. In the morning they fell rather than walked to the bottom. On slopes which were not too dangerous they squatted on their snow-shoes and slid, but on coming to the end of the slope they usually plunged deeply into a drift. Then encumbered with pack and shoes, and faint with weakness, they had to fight their way to their feet. Getting to the bottom did not take long, and they found the stream low because of the freezing up of its headwaters. They crossed without difficulty, probably upon a snow-bridge. But going up the other side was a different tale. For fifty feet up from the river the wall was precipitous; they climbed up holding on by crevices and bushes. Then came a slope where trees could just cling. Digging their snow-shoes into the surface they had to work their way up as if ascending a stairway, each step a struggle. Blood from their feet marked the white snow. Completely exhausted after one of the hardest days which they had yet endured, they just managed to get to the top of the canyon by evening. Fosdick was the weakest, and could scarcely make it. That night they ate the last of the dried human flesh which, loathsome as it was, had been their only food for a week.

They found themselves next morning upon a sort of plateau. The country was less rugged; the sun shone more warmly; and the surface of the snow was so firmly consolidated that they found themselves able to walk without snowshoes. But to offset these advantages they were again without food, and Fosdick held them back. Their feet were worse than ever, and the toes of one of the Indian boys began dropping off at the first joints. The snow where they camped was only six feet deep.

With Fosdick a constant drag upon their progress they began to confront the problem old as the time when mankind first questioned the ethics of the wolf-pack. Should the strong delay for the weak, so that all would most likely perish, or should the strong go ahead not looking back toward those who called for help? For the time, they waited for Fosdick.

On the third they moved ahead doggedly. The encouraging signs continued. The snow was firm under foot. Oaks began to mingle with the pines and cedars. They estimated seven miles for the day, and camped at a place where the snow was only three feet deep. But Fosdick was done up, and again they had no food. Being now confident of getting along without snow-shoes they took the raw-hide thongs, crisped them over the fire, and ate them. Such fare could hardly be called nourishment, but it gave the stomach something to work on. Without food they could not go much further; their situation was the most desperate that it had been since the time when the great storm had put out the fire.

The fourth found them practically brought to a standstill. With Fosdick at the point of complete collapse they managed to advance only two miles. On this night they were able to camp for the first time on bare ground, in an open grove of oak trees. They took some boots and shoes now worn past usefulness, and having crisped them, made a pretense of an evening meal. Again, as when they had proposed drawing lots just before the great storm, the time had come for a decision. They had passed three days without any real food.

And now a new idea came to some of the starving and half-crazed refugees. The two Indians! These men and women who lay starving in the snow were westerners. Behind them lay a tradition bred by generations of warfare—rifle and long-knife against arrow and tomahawk. The Indian, that skulker by the clearing, that devil of the torture stake, was to them an enemy, a child of Satan, a lower creature. Should not an Indian be killed that a white man might live? Fosdick was dying; the others talked together.

But to Eddy, Luis and Salvador were not merely Indians. They were two men who had crossed the mountains with Stanton and had saved the lives of the company. They were men with whom he had journeyed and suffered. He was willing to cast lots as to who was to die, taking his own chances along with the Indians. But he remonstrated against coldly sacrificing them. He could not convince the others, but forestalling them he warned Luis. The Indian stood for a minute in mute amazement; then his features settled into their usual imperturbability. He and Salvador disappeared from camp.

Only the eight whites remained together. The situation now absolutely called for a decisive action. To stay longer with Fosdick was only to sacrifice every one, and he had not the grace to send the others ahead as Stanton had done. Eddy was still the strongest of the company, and he resolved that he would take the gun and go ahead, hoping to find game, now that the snow was left behind. If successful, he could return and rescue his companions; if unsuccessful, he could merely die, as they must. A mere hint of his purpose was sufficient to arouse the others; the women besought him to remain, crying that he was their only hope. But Eddy, reasonably enough, stuck to his resolution.

In the morning he prepared to set out; Mary Graves, the strongest of the others, decided to abandon her sister Mrs. Fosdick and accompany Eddy. The rest knew that they could not keep up. Mrs. Pike threw her arms about Eddy's neck imploring him to remain. The other women added tears and entreaties. But he realized that any yielding would be only useless weakness. The two companions set out. Behind them the Fosters, Mrs. Pike, and Mrs. McCutchen set out to toil along as they could. Unable even to keep up with these, the Fosdicks, husband and wife, dragged along in the rear.

Eddy and Mary Graves followed the bloody trail left by the escaping Indian boys. Eddy carried the rifle. When they had gone only about two miles, they noticed the place where a deer had lain during the preceding night. As Eddy looked, the long-enduring tension seemed to snap within him, and with the overpowering outburst of emotion, bearded man that he was, he broke into tears. Looking up, he saw Mary also weeping like a child. He was not a religious man, but with the sudden hope that he might save himself and his companions a flooding gratitude to whatever power had thus guided them moved him, and as soon as he could master himself he spoke:

"Mary, don't you feel like praying?"

"Oh, yes," she answered through her sobs, "I do, but I never prayed in my life! Do you pray?"

He had never prayed either, but nevertheless both fell upon their knees, and prayed in their own fashion. The sudden emotional outburst at least served its purpose in letting down their nervous tension, and they proceeded warily, following the trail of the animal and keeping a keen look-out.

But they toiled wearily on, seeing deer-sign, but no deer. They had come to the end of the plateau, and again as they went westward were forced to go steadily downhill. The snow lay in patches, oaks were as numerous as pines. Then at last, when they had gone almost to the foot of the plateau, they suddenly sighted a large buck. He stood quietly at the easy range of only eighty yards.

Then came the worst trial of all. They were standing at the top of a steep, high bank with a snow-drift at the bottom. With the game in full view Eddy tried to get a sight, but found himself too weak to level the heavy rifle. Panting with the exertion, he breathed a moment, changed his hold upon the gun, and tried again. Again he failed. Mary stood overcome with emotion, weeping, her head bowed and her hand upon her face. Eddy whispered for her to be quiet lest she should frighten the deer.

"O, I am afraid you will not kill it!" she exclaimed, and then managed to control herself.

Eddy, ingenious through extremity, now raised the gun vertically, placed the butt against his shoulders, and controlling the motion as well as he could, let the muzzle swing slowly in a downward arc. At the moment when the deer came into line with the sights, he pulled the trigger. The deer bounded up about three feet and then stood still. Mary burst into tears again, crying out:

"O, merciful God, you have missed it!"

But Eddy had confidence in his aim, and he had seen the deer drop its tail between its legs, sure sign that it was hit. In a moment the deer ran. Eddy leaped down the bank into the snow-drift, Mary behind him. Staggering skeletons, they pursued. The deer ran only about two hundred yards. Eddy came up while it was still alive, and seizing it by the horns cut its throat with a pocket-knife. Then he and Mary falling together upon their quarry drank the warm blood as it flowed. When the stream ceased and the deer lay still, they drew off a little and sat down, their faces covered with blood. After a little rest they were able to roll the carcass to a place where they could build a fire. They cooked and ate some of the liver and other entrails, and for the first time in many nights slept peacefully without tantalizing dreams of food.

16. THE WILL TO LIVE

SEVERAL times during the night Eddy fired the gun as a signal of hope to those behind. The Fosdicks were far back near the top of the plateau; the others somewhere between. On hearing the shots Fosdick exclaimed:

"There! Eddy has killed a deer. Now, if I can only get to him, I shall live."

But he died during the night.

His wife draped the body in their only blanket, and lay down in the bitterly cold night expecting and probably hoping to pass into the quiet coma of freezing to death. But in some way, even without fire or blanket, she lived through, and in the morning set out to reach the next camp. On the way she met two of the others returning to make use of the bodies which they expected to find, and also with ill-timed avarice to take what money and valuables the Fosdicks were known to have had. Surprised to find her coming to meet them, they turned about, and at their own camp found Eddy who had returned up the mountainside with the roasted liver and other parts of the deer.

Eddy was busy drying the venison by a fire. Mrs. Fosdick and Mrs. Foster, after eating, returned to the body of Fosdick. There, in spite of the widow's entreaties, Mrs. Foster took out the liver and heart from the body and removed the arms and legs. Again the action was justified by necessity, for the meat of one deer would not be able long to sustain seven people. The necessity, however, was little support to Mrs. Fosdick when, as if in repetition of the terrible scene following the great snow-storm, she was forced to see her husband's heart broiled over the fire.

They spent the remainder of the day in camp, resting and drying both the venison and the human flesh. On the morning of the seventh they again set forward—Eddy, Foster, and the five women. Although reprieved by the killing of the deer and by the death of Fosdick, they were still in a pitiable state of weakness and exhaustion. They had now been exposed to the hardships of the crossing for more than three weeks. They had suffered the extremes of fatigue, freezing, and mental strain, and had twice spent a period of several days without food. The effect of such trials could not help being cumulative.

On this day they were forced to follow down the mountainside, and eventually found themselves at the bottom of another canyon running north and south. Since to follow it in either of those directions would have been only lost energy, they forded the stream, and camped on the western bank.

Next morning there was nothing for it but to ascend the face of the mountain which formed the western wall of the canyon. This slope was entirely free of snow, but so steep that they often had to climb by hand and foot up the rocks and to hold on by bushes and shrubs growing in the crevices. As plains-dwellers they were appalled by the depths which gaped beneath them. Their feet were bruised, and had swollen until they burst; the pieces of blankets which served for shoes were matted with blood. But after struggling all day they reached the top. In spite of all their troubles a strange tranquillity seemed to have fallen upon them. They sat upon the ground and ate the last of their dried meat. Starvation again faced them.

For several days Foster had been failing. He had been despondent and apathetic, neglecting even to help gather wood for the fires. He began to show evidence that privation and horror had unsettled his mental balance. That evening he and Eddy, the only men remaining, were a little apart from the others. Foster spoke out—they would have to kill some one for the rest of them to get through; Mrs. McCutchen was the one, for she was nothing but a nuisance and could no longer keep up. Eddy, horrified, reminded him that Mrs. McCutchen was a wife and mother, and stoutly vetoed Foster's maniacal scheme. The latter then proposed Mary Graves and Mrs. Fosdick; neither of them was a mother, nor any longer a wife. Eddy again refused, and going back to the company warned them. Foster sullenly said that he did not care, and that he could handle Eddy. The latter, probably in scarcely a better mental state, threw a club to Foster, and telling him to defend himself, advanced upon him with drawn knife. It was an incredible scene as the two, mere shadows of men, faced each other. But Eddy was the stronger, and his knife was raised for the stroke, when four of the terrified women flung themselves upon him. They threw him to the ground and took away the knife. For a moment he was defenseless, but Foster was dazed beyond the point of action, and Eddy repeated his threats against him if a further move should be made toward sacrificing any of the company.

Next morning they stumbled on, their packs again empty of food. They were in pleasant, rolling country now, where the sun shone warmly. They saw only an occasional snowdrift. The great mountain forests had been left behind, and now they passed through open groves of live-oak and skimpy digger-pines. If they had had even half the strength which they possessed on leaving the lake, they could have advanced rapidly. But each period of starvation had worn them down the more; their feet, frozen and thawed so often, were now merely unspeakable masses of bruised and bleeding flesh.

On this day when they had gone about two miles and were crossing a patch of snow, they suddenly saw the fresh footprints of two men. Like their own, these were marked by blood. It must be the fresh trail of Luis and Salvador. The frenzied Foster immediately cried out that he would follow and kill them if he could come up with them. The whole party followed the trail, hoping doubtless to find the two dead at the end of it, for they had presumably been without food for a week and without fire for four days. The trail went on for a mile or so, and at its end Luis and Salvador lay upon the ground. They were totally spent, but they were not dead.

In the twenty-five days of suffering and starvation since leaving the lake, the snow-shoers had degenerated step by step from the level of civilized men and women. At first they had waited for a comrade who fell behind, and had flinched at drawing lots to see who should die, and had shrunk from cannibalism, even when it meant eating only a man already dead. Then they had eaten the food which centuries of civilization had forbidden them. Then as the mania of starvation worked upon them, they had plotted to kill men of another race, and then men or even women of their own race. They had gone on leaving comrades behind, and in their frenzy had tried to kill each other in open fight. Now they were ready to sink to a still lower level. Foster was no longer that gentlemanly, well-liked young fellow he had been. Now with his haggard face and matted beard and his eyes hot with frenzy he was a man out of some brutish past seeking what he could kill and devour.

Salvador lay on the ground; a little way off Luis in thirst had crawled to a small stream of water where he, too, lay helpless. Foster prepared for the deed. Eddy, although he still protested, now made no active move to prevent it. After all, every one could see that the Indians would probably not live more than a few hours at most. Eddy with Mrs. Fosdick, Mrs. McCutchen and Mary Graves went on a little way; at least they could never be called witnesses. They heard the shot—once, and then again. They camped where they were.

Later Eddy learned that Foster had first told Luis that he was to die, and had then shot him through the head. Salvador had had brief grace, and then he had gone the same way. After that no one camped with Foster except the two women of his own family. The others lay apart and kept watch. Who could tell what Foster might try as they lay asleep? He was no longer a sane man; they traveled with a scheming maniac.

Eddy and the three women who kept with him had now nothing at all to eat except the grass with which they managed to stay their stomachs. Deer were plentiful, and sometimes were seen grazing close by, but no one was strong enough to take accurate aim. As they traveled, all staggered as if far gone in drink. They could not go more than a quarter mile without resting. The slightest obstacle caused them to stumble and fall. They were like infants learning to walk, and the women when they fell would weep like infants, and then, rising, totter on again. Even the tough-sinewed Eddy, when he came to a fallen tree-trunk no more than a foot in height, could not step across it, but had to stoop, rest his hand upon the log, and get over it with a sort of roll.

They passed now across a country of grassy and thinly-wooded hills with gentle slopes. For two weeks they had had fair weather, but now a storm broke upon them. They were low enough down to escape the snow, but the cold rain sluiced down and muddy torrents began to boil in the ravines. Nevertheless on the tenth and eleventh they made, as they thought, about seventeen miles, and toward the close of the latter day came upon an Indian trail, which they decided to follow.

On the twelfth, rain still beat upon them, and they continued at their crawling pace. Finally near the close of the day, one of them suddenly called out:

"Here are tracks!"

"What kind of tracks—human?"

"Yes—human!"

With a new flood of hope they staggered forward. They turned the point of a clump of chapparal, and came into view of an Indian village.

They took no thought as to whether the Indians might be hostile. The Indians for their part were amazed at these haggard, bloody wraiths which suddenly descended upon them, and being mere timorous Diggers, they ran for the woods. Soon they returned, and seeing the terrible plight of the newcomers, they even seemed stirred to pity. But in this village the men were no noble hunters of the woods in whose lodges hung venison and bear-meat; the best that they could offer was their own poor fare of raw acorns and later some acorns ground and baked into a loaf. It was not a food to which the starving whites were adjusted, and Eddy in particular seemed unable to digest it.

In the morning the Indians put them upon the trail westward. The rain still beat down, and after going on a few miles and arriving at the next village, the refugees were glad to halt for the rest of that day and for the next. They were not improving much in strength, and it still seemed possible that they might fail even now when so close to the end. On the fifteenth and sixteenth, however, with the sun shining brightly they managed to reach still other villages, making a distance which they again estimated at seventeen miles. Some Indians generally accompanied and aided them from village to village, and at each halt other Indians received them kindly and gave them acorn bread. Although the others ate this, Eddy could not, and was reduced to his diet of grass.

On the morning of January 17 the chief of the village managed with great difficulty to gather a large handful of pine-nuts, which he gave to Eddy. These seemed to supply some deficiency in his body, so that on eating them he felt wonderfully refreshed. His courage and energy revived, and he became the leader instead of the laggard. He was again able to proceed without help.

On this same morning the others seemed correspondingly exhausted and despondent. After advancing only a mile or two, Foster and the five women gave up. Their feet had grown steadily worse since the time of their frost-bite, and the agony of walking added to mere exhaustion at last caused their spirits to fail. They lay down by the side of the trail, prepared to die.

But Eddy on the contrary was filled with a new determination to push on. He left his comrades and with one Indian went ahead. For five miles he got along with little aid, and as his strength finally began to fail, he and his guide met another Indian, who for a gift of tobacco consented to join them. With some assistance, his strength gradually failing, Eddy made another five miles, and then with an Indian aiding

him on either side, he half walked, half was dragged along.
Grimly the will-to-live still held.

Around Johnson's ranch, the first settlement at the edge of
the Sacramento Valley, several of the emigrants who had
arrived late in the year had put up rude houses in which to
pass the winter before settling permanently in the spring. In
the one of these farthest up the river lived Mr. and Mrs.
Ritchie with their daughter Harriet. An hour before sunset
Harriet, going to the door, was thunder-struck to be con-
fronted by two Indians supporting between them something
which might be human. It spoke, asking for bread. Harriet
stared a moment blankly and burst into tears; then realizing
that the thing was a white man, she took hold of him, helped
him into the house and to the bed.

Eddy sank into the blankets too weak even to turn himself
over. The little community sprang into action. Mrs. Ritchie
prepared food for the sufferer, and Harriet ran to rouse the
neighbors. Horsemen spurred off to carry the news to those
farther away. The wives of the poor emigrants, having for
themselves only the remnants of what their wagons had
brought through, ransacked their last reserves of tea, coffee,
and sugar, and contributed whatever bread was available. A
California settlement always had beef to spare.

In a short time four men with packs, guided by the
Indians, were following the back-trail by the light of the new
moon. At midnight they came to the five starving women and
Foster. One man spent the rest of the night preparing food,
and in spite of cautions the refugees ate to the point of en-
dangering their lives. All became sick, but managed to survive. Next morning other men went out from Johnson's with
horses. As they rode along, they traced Eddy's path for six
miles by the blood which he had left in his tracks. That night
the six survivors were brought in—starved, blood-smeared,
unkempt, almost naked, but still living.

Of the ten men and five women who had camped at the
head of Truckee Lake on the night of December 16, eight
men had died, and two men and all five of the women had
come through. They had been thirty-three days upon the way.

17. CALIFORNIA RESPONDS

At Johnson's ranch the morning of January 19 broke fair and beautiful, and as Eddy after thirty-six hours in bed felt the warm sun and looked out over the plains deep in green grass, indescribable harmony, gratitude, and hope possessed his spirit. Even the thought of his wife and babies far off among the mountains seemed to lose its grimness. Nevertheless something must be done, although just what was harder to say. In the little group of settlers at Johnson's were neither men, nor provisions, nor knowledge of mountaineering sufficient for a rescue-party. The nearest settlement of any size was at Sutter's Fort, forty miles southward; and even there, as Reed had discovered two months before, the war had drawn off the able-bodied men. Beyond Sutter's was long and dangerous journeying over marshy plains, across rivers swollen by winter rains, and through rough and lonely hill country before a rider could make the ranches of Napa Valley or the little town of Sonoma. To Yerba Buena or the pueblo of San José was still farther, and even these slightly larger settlements might not be able to spare men and money. Central California was at best only a frontier, and now it was all confusion with native Californians and immigrant Americans at each other's throats. The only government was a make-shift of the Americans, half-military, half-civil, uncertainly grafted upon the broken stem of the Mexican system.

Still something must be done, and on the advice of those at Johnson's, Eddy from his bed dictated a letter to John Sinclair, an American with a ranch near Sutter's, who held the old Mexican title of alcalde and whose jurisdiction covered in a shadowy way all of northern California. An Indian runner took the letter, for the recent rains had made the valley half lake and half quagmire, and a horse would have bogged down in the first sink-hole.

At the ranch the Indian found the Alcalde gone to Yerba Buena, but he gave his message to Mrs. Sinclair. Her first response was to send him back with a load of underclothing for the five women of the snow-shoe party who had arrived almost in a state of nudity. Then she appealed to Captain Kern, commanding officer at the Fort.

The Captain called a meeting, and the few men still remaining at the settlement gathered in the armory. Most of them were newcomers, farmers from the Mississippi Valley, like the men of the Donner Party; the others were in the main ex-sailors, who had taken French leave from their ships at Yerba Buena and escaped inland to take Sutter's pay. Captain Kern explained the plight of the party at Truckee Lake, and called for volunteers. He offered wages of three dollars a day, the charges to be assumed by the government. Three dollars was princely pay, but the farmers and sailors gathered in the adobe-walled room hung back. To go into those mountains in snow as deep as that! Even a mountain-man wouldn't do it! And besides you couldn't count on an army officer; he might be all right himself, but back in Washington, they maybe wouldn't allow the bill. Only three men volunteered, and they offered themselves rather for the love of adventure and the hope of aiding the starving women and children than for the lure of high wages.

Of these three, one was Aquilla Glover, an emigrant of the past year who had known the Donners on the plains. He was a man of some standing, so that his name in the records reads generally as "Mr. Glover." Another of the volunteers was also a recent emigrant. His name was Moultry, and parents with leanings toward the grandiloquent had christened him Riley Septimus. But the West played havoc with such bombast, and he was known usually as "Sept Mootry." The third volunteer was Joseph Sels, who had been a sailor and so was probably a deserter, a fact which may account for his having an *alias* of Joe Foster. But may his sins, like Moultry's name, be forgiven him! They were gallant spirits, all three who stepped forward ready to face death in the snow.

Three, however, was not a sufficient number, and so the enterprise hung fire until Alcalde Sinclair returned from Yerba Buena in a day or two. Then he and Sutter offered to become personally responsible for the wages. This was a different story, and four more men volunteered. Sutter and Sinclair supplied food and horses, and preparations for leaving commenced.

But all realized that these few even with what reinforcements they might pick up at Johnson's would not be enough to accomplish much, and Sutter decided to send his launch down the river to Yerba Buena with an appeal for further aid. Thus some connection might also be established with Reed and McCutchen, who had tried so valiantly to get across through the snow in November and who had then ridden south to raise help. They would be needed now, and before this something might have been heard of them.

But those at Sutter's Fort would not have been surprised at Reed's failure to reappear, if they had known all his ridings and counter-ridings, his disappointments and his various adventures of the past three months. Certainly as he had headed south in November, the bitterness of his failure still upon him, he must have expected to be back in no great time. But again he had not prospered. At San José everything was in confusion. In addition to the trouble in the far south, the Californians had risen in revolt close at hand, and an armed force under Sanchez blocked the road to Yerba Buena.

So Reed during most of December had to cool his heels in San José waiting for something to be settled. He found there many emigrants whom he had known on the road, and some others of earlier years who had been caught in the snow in '44. There was no lack of sympathizing, but with war at the doorsteps no one would do more than sympathize. Reed realized that for the moment the best that he could do would be to help the people of San José in their difficulties, hoping that they might later help him in his. He accordingly accepted, under Captain Weber, the lieutenancy of a company of mounted riflemen, a motley band, thirty-three in number, described as "sailors, whalers, and landsmen."

They marched through to Yerba Buena, and then toward the end of December advanced against the enemy in a column composed of volunteers, a detachment of marines, and ten seamen with a six-pounder pulled by two yoke of oxen. The whole army, commanded by a captain of marines, numbered one hundred and one. On January 2 near Santa Clara the Californians showed fight, at least to the extent of hovering around just beyond rifle range; they trusted to their horsemanship, and tried to provoke the Americans to an attack. A year earlier the Americans would probably have obliged at once with a pell-mell charge in utter contempt of all "Greasers" as fighting-men. But lately Natividad and San Pasqual had somewhat bloodily taught them that the native

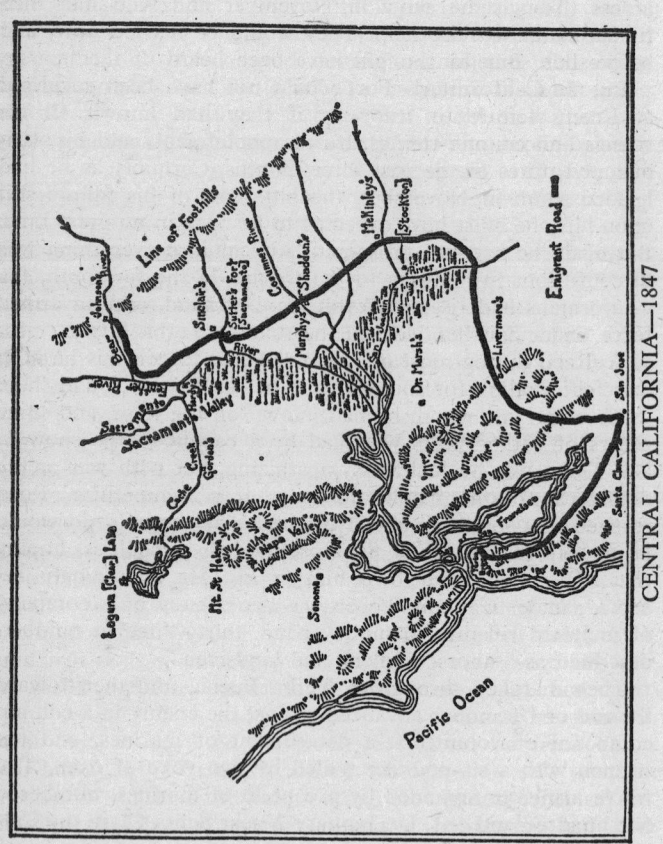

CENTRAL CALIFORNIA—1847

Californian like the ancient Parthian was most dangerous when he seemed to be running away. On this day therefore the Americans declined to throw themselves into a hand-to-hand combat with the better mounted Californians armed with lances. They marched along stolidly, and the sailors, unlimbering the six-pounder, kept the enemy at a distance with grape-shot. But as the cannon bogged down in a marshy place, the Californians swooped in closer; bullets whistled and two men were hit in the American ranks. Then the lancers wheeled about, and the "Battle of Santa Clara" ended as they galloped off to the shelter of the hills.

That evening an embassy came in, asking terms for a truce. The Californians, it transpired, were fighting not so much for the sacred cause of freedom as to protect their ranches from indiscriminate plundering in the name of military requisitions. A treaty was then arranged, and the volunteers disbanded. But all this took time, and it was close to February 1 before Reed got to Yerba Buena prepared to start efforts for relief.

The little village scattered about the cove at the end of the peninsula, although it was just at the point of assuming its greater name of San Francisco, was as yet a very minor settlement. It was more famous for its harbor than for anything else; the naval officers, busy during these months at changing Manifest Destiny into history, appreciated the safety of the bay's sheltering hills and mud bottom. In February 1847, the *Warren,* sloop-of-war, and the *Savannah,* frigate, were lying there at anchor. On the latter, Captain Mervine and his crew were still fresh from the unexpected drubbing they had taken from the Californian cavalry-artillery at Dominguez Rancho.

As soon as possible Reed made his plea to the naval officers, who were also the civilian authorities. He found that his residence in San José had not been fruitless, for its citizens had just forwarded a petition urging a relief expedition. Nevertheless the officers agreed that nothing could be done on governmental authority; personally, they would do all that they could. Lieutenant Bartlett, who was acting as alcalde, offered to call a public meeting for subscription of funds, and the Governor, Captain Hull, set the ball rolling with fifty dollars. Captain Mervine and Mr. Richardson, Collector of the Port, each matched the governor's subscription.

On the evening of February 3 the meeting assembled in one of the chief saloons. The officers of the navy and "nearly every male citizen" were present. One need not imagine, even so, a vast throng. Probably fewer than two hundred heard His Honor the Alcalde call the meeting to order. Nevertheless there was a certain weight of significance about the occasion, for Yerba Buena was just beginning to think of itself as a future metropolis, even if no one had yet composed a slogan about "knowing how." So the alcalde made a clever political move when he read the petition from San José, and then remarking that this was the first occasion on which the citizens of Yerba Buena had been called upon for a collective charity, added his hope that they would do something better than a *petition*.

The meeting once organized, Reed was called upon to speak, but the attempt to picture to his hearers the probable plight of his family at that very moment was too much for him, and he sat down overwhelmed with tears. His friend, the Reverend Mr. Dunleavy, who also had crossed the plains during the last summer, then took the floor. He spoke eloquently of the trials which the unfortunate company had encountered during the overland journey. As to where they were now located, he gave as his opinion that they would have been able to reach Truckee Lake before being caught by the snow. He spoke of their probable fate unless relief arrived. Perhaps already, he feared, it was too late. But, he hoped, the company might with prudence hold out until March.

As he sat down, so moving was his speech, a sudden rush of people with money came from all parts of the room so rapidly that the chairman had to ask for a moment's respite until he could appoint a committee to take charge of all that was being offered. Seven hundred dollars was raised then and there, and later by the aid of the sailors and marines the total was run up to thirteen hundred. As the editor of the village newspaper commented three days later, an early manifestation of California local pride: "This speaks well for Yerba Buena."

A few volunteers also offered themselves. Chief of these was Selim E. Woodworth, Passed Midshipman, U.S.N., thirty-one years old, who for the time being was upon an extended leave of absence. He was, we may note for the curious-minded, a son of the author of "The Old Oaken Bucket." During the summer he had out of sheer adventure crossed the continent to Oregon, and had thence made his way to California. To him was given official charge of the funds, under instructions from the governor and the committee.

The fourth and fifth of February were busy days. Supplies were purchased and loaded into a small schooner donated for the purpose. All was ready for a start on the evening tide of the fifth, when Captain Sutter's launch appeared off the town. The horrible situation of the Donner Party, and their exact location, at which Mr. Dunleavy had so shrewdly guessed, were now actually revealed, and the committee at Yerba Buena decided that what was most needed was not a mere hasty dash across the mountains but a sustained effort supported by a half-way camp for the sustenance of both refugees and relief parties. Accordingly they held up the schooner for another day, and set out to work all night collecting and preparing supplies.

Later that very evening more news came in. Old Caleb Greenwood, the trapper, arrived from Sonoma where McCutchen had been stirring up efforts for relief. Lieutenant Maury of the Navy, and General Vallejo, the open-handed Californian ex-governor, had promised Greenwood five hundred dollars as a reward, if he could get a relief party organized and started; he had come to Yerba Buena to buy warm clothing. Horses for the expedition were already collected at his camp near the head of Napa Valley.

Now for the first time the committee had found a man who could really tell what the chances of success were. Greenwood was eighty-three years old, he said; he had been in the mountains since the Sierra Nevadas were nothing but little hills. He had been with the Astoria fur traders in 1810. He knew the mountain country like his own backyard, which was just about what it was. He claimed he had come overland to California twenty years ago, and had been the first white man ever to see the big lake in the mountains north of Sonoma, and it was twenty years since he first saw it. (If so, he must have come overland with Jed Smith.) He had lived with Indians, and had a flock of sons by a Crow squaw. Like any good mountain-man he hated Blackfeet, and despised "Spaniards." Lately he had been guiding "emigrators," as he called them; Greenwood's cut-off on the overland trail bore his name. He was still active of foot, and except for rheumy eyes did not look his age. He was clothed in a suit of tanned buckskin so ancient that it led Edwin Bryant to the suggestion that perhaps, like great-grand-dad in the song, "He wore the same suit all his life."

But buckskin or no buckskin, old Greenwood's word about the mountains was worth having. Yes, he could get through to the camp, he thought; he had crossed the mountains over the snow in April last year and could do it again. But he had to have money to buy supplies and get men. It would take ten or a dozen good men who could be counted on in the snow, not just greenhorn emigrants and sailors. He would take his own son Brit, and John Turner, and a few of the hunters who could be picked up around Laguna Lake and Mount Saint Helena. Maybe they could drive horses ahead of them over the snow, and kill them for food when they got to camp. At the very least he and some of the others could get over on snow-shoes.

So the committee added Greenwood as another lieutenant, and the plans became more complicated. Governor Hull advanced four hundred dollars of government money. Wood-worth, it was decided, was to take the schooner with its supplies and a crew to work it as far as Hardy's ranch on Feather River, not more than twenty miles from John-son's. Reed was to join the new expedition with Greenwood; the two of them would cross to the north side of the Bay and then ride overland, enlisting men on the way, and taking along the horses from the camp in Napa Valley. They would rejoin Woodworth at Hardy's. On February 7, both parties left Yerba Buena.

With Woodworth in the schooner went a letter to Sheriff McKinstry at Sutter's Fort written by the Reverend Mr. Dunleavy, and expressing that gentleman's hopes and prayers for the success of the expedition:

Yours of the first inst. came to hand, on last evening at 9 o'clock and since that time until this moment, now 10 o'clock this morning, we have had no time to write, eat, drink, or sleep —our time has been employed in making the best preparation for the relief of our suffering countrymen, and women, now in the mountains. Oh! *God,* It is shocking to hear of their suffering—

may he that *thunders* when he pleases, and holds the storms,
O may *he* save *them* from perishing in the wilderness.

As to what could be accomplished by the men who had
been scraped together and sent ahead by Sutter and Sinclair,
probably not even Mr. Dunleavy with all his trust in God had
much confidence. As for old Greenwood, he offered to bet
that when such people, farmers and sailors, went into the
snow, not one of them would come back alive. He had no
takers. . . .

With the arrival of the snow-shoers at Johnson's and the
events following upon it, the story of the Donner Party thus
enters upon a new and more complicated phase. Before this
time the emigrants had been an isolated party struggling
ahead by their own powers. But from now on, new actors,
new motives, and new problems enter the story. Relief
parties push ahead, halt, divide, rejoin, become themselves
the objectives of still more relief parties. The threads of narrative multiply. Nevertheless the life of the emigrants in the
snow-leaguered camps remains one of the chief interests, and
there we must now return to pick up the thread left behind
when we followed the snow-shoers upon their departure on
December 16.

18. YULE-TIDE BY THE LAKE

To Reed riding through various adventures and to the
snow-shoers fighting their way ahead through storms and
across canyons, the months of December and January had at
least offered much of change and excitement. But those poor
creatures huddling in the cabins by the lake had known during those months only a time of monotony and gradually increasing despair.

One might think that Breen's diary for those hard weeks
would at least be a record of Promethean endurance, but
actually he found little which seemed worthy of record.
The changes were too slight; he could not be expected to
note a daily variation of pallor and emaciation. The weather

was always with him, and he recorded it faithfully—direction of wind, sky cloudy or clear, rain or snow, depth of snow, frost or thaw. Often such notes constituted the whole entry. He even permitted himself commonplaces as to the state of the moon, and once, like a man trying to pad out a letter, he even recorded the fact of the full moon twice for the same day.

As an Irishman he was of course a Roman Catholic, but for the first month of the diary he might have been an atheist. As conditions grew more pressing, his mind very humanly turned to religion, and four days after the departure of the snow-shoers the Greater Power suddenly made his appearance in the terse ejaculation: "Tough times, but not discouraged   our hopes are in God. Amen." After this entry religious phrases were frequent.

A consistent optimism was the diarist's most notable trait. There is no indication that he ever had any real fear that he or his family might not survive. This optimism, along with intense desire to escape, led him of course to much wishful thinking. He clutched at straws. One day, for instance, he noted that in spite of a north wind the snow was melting, and added hopefully "may continue." Again, in the dead of winter he declared: "looks some like spring weather birds chirping qu[i]te lively."

Because of its obtuseness and lack of introspection the diary is not, one would say, a source-book for a psychological novelist. It is for that very reason the better testimony, for it is thoroughly genuine, simple and direct. If it is lacking in analysis, it much more than compensates by being also lacking in egotism, heroics, sentimentality, and dramatization. It contains very few passages which raise the suspicion that they were written for a reader, and equally few which seem written in justification of the writer's own deeds.

Perhaps the judgment is wrong, and Breen's diary is actually the best possible psychological record. For behind its uninterpretative record of wind and changes of the moon we can sense the thoroughly healthy mind of an average man, numbed by long suffering and privation. He has supped too full of horrors for one horror more or less to make much difference.

Breen's preoccupation with the weather has fortunately preserved for us an accurate day-by-day record. The winter progressed in an almost regular cycle. If the wind was from the south or west, great masses of cloud moved in across the peaks, and snow, often mixed with rain or sleet, descended upon the flat-roofed cabins. A storm generally lasted for several days, and might run on to a week or more, until the snow around the cabins deepened by a foot or several feet. Finally the storm ceased, and a spell of bitterly cold weather followed. Then from day to day the sun seemed to gain strength in the clear winter sky. The white surface grew wet and soggy; the snow settled and consolidated, sometimes decreasing two or three feet in depth. Then the wind shifted again, and another storm broke over the cabins.

Breen's estimates of the depth of the snow during the early part of the winter make plain the piling-up with each storm. On November 27 he reported: "the ground not covered," but five days later, "snow must be over six feet deep." On December 13 it was "8 feet deep on the level." On the twenty-seventh, "Snow very deep say 9 feet."

Buried beneath the snow, the cabins were dim and damp caves. The flickering fires lighted them uncertainly. The kettles where hides and bones were boiling steamed almost without ceasing. With the departure of the snow-shoers the congestion had eased a little, but still in each of the small cabins were crowded from five to eleven men, women, and children. All were unkempt and unbathed. Every one spent much of the time in bed, wrapped in blankets and quilts which had not been sunned in months. Even the cold weather failed to keep down the vermin. The sick looked haggardly at those who could still move about. The starved babies were too weak to cry. The smells mingled—boiling hides, babies, sickness, unwashed bodies, filth.

In December the Breens and probably most of the other families still had a little reserve of beef. Most of the dogs had by this time gone into the kettles, but Breen's Towser and the Reed children's pet, little Cash, still remained. A few cupfuls of flour were hoarded as the basis of gruel for the babies. But even before Christmas hides had become the staff of life.

Their preparation was a matter of some length. They were taken from the piles where they had been stored, dirty and unwashed. They were cut into conveniently sized strips, and held over a fire until the hair was singed off. Next they were scraped clean, put into a kettle, and boiled. The boiling continued for hours. Finally the hide became soft and pulpy, and then the kettle with its boiled-down mass was taken from the fire and allowed to cool. It stiffened into a glue-like jelly, slightly nutritious, but nauseous. There was no salt for its seasoning, and it had to be eaten straight or at best with a little pepper. Even in the pangs of starvation some found it almost impossible to stomach.

As the pinch grew worse, they went about retrieving bones which, stripped of all flesh, had previously been thrown aside to the dogs. These bones, if boiled a long time, would exude enough juice to flavor the water into a suggestion of soup. This, if drunk hot, was a little comforting, but hardly nourishing. But the boiling might be continued still longer, and finally, they discovered, the bones would actually soften until they could be crumbled between the teeth. At other times the bones were charred brown, and then eaten.

In the Murphy cabin some kind of skin served as hearth-rug. The children lying before the fire began to cut off little pieces, toast them crisp over the coals, and eat them. In this way, almost before any one became conscious of what was happening, the fire-rug was consumed.

Such fare, and even that in insufficient amounts, soon weakened every one's knees. Wood for the fires became more and more a problem. The snow-blanket was a good covering, and no one seems to have suffered much from actual cold. Still, fires were necessary both for heat and for the long process of boiling hides and bones, and the men as they sallied forth into the deep snow often found that the task overtaxed their powers. Even when the tree had been felled it sometimes buried itself in the soft snow so deeply as to make doubly difficult the work of getting the logs cut and carried to the cabins.

But these incidents were only often-repeated bits of the daily life. They were a part of the monotony. Long-suffering endurance was really the chief virtue. As every one grew weaker, the life became so circumscribed that each of the cabins lived to itself. A visitor from one of the others was an occurrence of certain note, and Breen lapsed into calling them strangers—"saw no strangers to day from any of the other shantys." As for the Donners in their camp by the creek—they seemed almost as far away as California, and news from them was a first-rate event.

In fact nothing at all was heard from them for more than a month. On December 9 the two teamsters Milt Elliott and Noah James had started off across the snow for the other camp, but a storm had closed down behind; since nothing further was heard of them, they had been given up for lost. But on the evening of December 20 Milt came struggling back to camp through the drifts. His story was the worst news yet.

Yes, he and Noah had got through to Donners' all right. Things were pretty bad there. "Uncle Jake" Donner was dead. So were Sam Shoemaker and James Smith and the Dutchman Reinhardt. No, they hadn't starved, not just that. They still had hides in camp. But Uncle Jake had been sickly all the way across the plains—he died the first. The others just seemed to lose hope and sicken. They couldn't live on the sort of stuff they had to eat. Things were worse there even than they were here at the lake. They didn't have log cabins, but just tents and brush shelters that let the water in. You were wet most of the time; you had to keep shoveling the snow off the top of the tent to keep it from caving in. Then, some days, you couldn't keep a fire going. They seemed to be in a place too where there was more snow. They were in a worse way for food than the ones at the lake. A lot of their cattle had strayed away in the storm and been lost. They were eating wood-mice—when they could catch them. They had even tried to eat a moldy buffalo-robe, but it had proved too tough. Hides might keep them going for a month; that was about the limit. "Uncle George" was in a bad way. His hand that he cut when he was chiseling the axle hadn't ever healed. He was in bed all the time, and the hand seemed to be festered. That left them with only Noah James to do the man's work about camp besides Uncle Jake's young step-sons and Jean Baptiste.

Milt with his story of the Donner camp got back just ahead of the big storm of Christmas week, the same storm which had put out the snow-shoers' fire and brought death to four of them. The season brought little cheer, except perhaps the grim comfort that they were not so badly off as the Donners. Some of the children talked of Santa Claus but without confidence. Two days before Christmas Patrick Breen, feeling that the situation called for religion more urgently, began to read the Thirty Days' Prayer.

Mrs. Reed and her children probably felt more than the others the desolation of this Christmas season, for they had been used to more luxuries than the poorer emigrants. But Mrs. Reed had a surprise in store; on other days a "pot of glue" might suffice, but on Christmas they would dine as a respectable family ought. From hoarding-places she drew forth the materials for a feast. The children were in ecstasy as they looked upon some tripe, a cupful of white beans, half a cup of rice, a few dried apples, and a piece of bacon two inches square. The tripe and bacon were cut into small pieces and went into the kettle along with the beans and rice. The children stood about close to the fire watching the kettle boil, and as occasionally a bean or a piece of tripe was thrown to the surface of the liquid, they hailed it with a shout. It was a real Christmas dinner to the children, almost wastefully profuse, and there was a fine dignity with almost a wistful pride in the mother's injunction as they commenced the meal:

"Children, eat slowly, there is plenty for all."

Four days after Christmas the insufficient diet of hides claimed another victim. This one was the German Burger— "Dutch Charley." Breen's entry for the thirtieth ran:

Fine clear morning froze hard last night Charley died last night about 10 o clock. had with him in money $1.50 two good loking silver watches one razor 3 boxes caps Keysburg tok them into his possession Spitzer took his coat & waistcoat Keysburg all his other little effects gold pin one shirt and tools for shaveing.

This inventory of Burger's effects suggests that Breen felt a certain doubt about the way these Germans behaved. There were a lot of things about Keseberg which nobody liked. A man who would steal blankets from a dead Indian! There was that matter of old man Hardkoop also when Keseberg back on the Humboldt had put him out of the wagon to die. Such suspicions and memories may account for a note in the diary standing entirely without context as if a memorandum for future reference—"Keysburg has Wolfings Rifle gun." "Wolfings" of course stood for "Wolfinger's," the German

who had never been heard of since he had been left behind
at Humboldt Sink to cache his goods, along with Reinhardt
and Spitzer. These two had said that the Indians came down
and killed him, and it had sounded reasonable. But now Milt
must have brought back from Donners' the story which was
known there. It was that as Reinhardt was dying he had confessed to George Donner his own part in the murder of
Wolfinger. Wolfinger was said to be rich and there may
have been hope for booty. The desolate sink of the Humboldt must have seen some ugly work after the last wagons
had sunk out of sight behind the sand hills. But now the
whole matter had an ironic twist—Wolfinger had died
quickly; his murderer had saved him the weeks of starving
in the snow which he himself had had to endure.

Thus the year ended. To the snow-shoers its last day had
brought a view of the Valley and hope for the future. To
the diarist it reinforced the sense of need for divine assistance, although the gathering of the clouds inspired no hope:

Thursday 31st Last of the year, may we with Gods help spend
the comeing year better than the past which we purpose to do if
Almighty God will deliver us from our present dredful situation
which is our prayer if the will of God sees it fiting for us Amen.
morning fair now cloudy wind E by S for three days past
freezing hard every night looks like another snow storm Snow
Storms are dredful to us snow very deep crust on the snow.

19. "PROVISIONS SCARCE"

DURING the first week of the new year Eddy had shot the
deer and Fosdick had died. In that same week Reed had
fought in the skirmish by Santa Clara.

At the lake, that week brought a crisis for Mrs. Reed. The
oxen which she had been able to purchase from other emigrants in November and whatever meat and hides Dolan
had left to her, had long been consumed, and she and the
children had lived from hand to mouth on anything they
could procure. The time had come for sacrifice, and little

Cash, the children's pet, went into the kettle. The family lived on him for a week; they ate flesh, feet, hide, entrails, everything. Then they faced starvation again.

When in November the men had built the double cabins which housed the Graveses and Reeds, they had roofed the Reeds' end entirely with hides. Now nothing was left for food except those hides. It was literally a case of eating yourself out of house and home.

Poor Mrs. Reed had had to endure almost more than seemed possible. She was only thirty-two, but she had lived a life that makes her seem older. She had been married, a mother, widowed, and married again at the age of twenty-two. Since that time she had borne three more children, and had failed in health so as to be considered a confirmed invalid. She suffered from terrible headaches which incapacitated her three or four days at a time. Then had come this journey, planned to include so many luxuries as to be merely a pleasure excursion. But everything seemed to have conspired against Mrs. Reed. First of all her mother Mrs. Keyes had died. Then had come loss of cattle and wagons and property in the desert. Three weeks later she had witnessed that horrible scene by the Humboldt, Snyder staggering to his death and her husband holding the bloody knife. Then had come hatred and ugly looks, and even worse times. Now she was among strangers, some of them enemies. Household and friends had scattered—her husband was banished, the Donners were far away, the teamsters were gone, Baylis Williams was dead, Eddy and Stanton had disappeared beyond the pass, to life or death, no one knew which. She had left only the helpless children, the faithful Milt, and Eliza Williams. And Eliza was no help. She had grown rattle-brained in the emergency, and did childish things. She was as much trouble as a child.

But Milt was staunch. He was only twenty-eight, but like Mrs. Reed he gives the impression of greater age. One senses in him that type beloved of the novelist—the faithful servitor. So much a member of the family was he that he always called Mrs. Reed "Ma." He had driven the four yoke which pulled the great family wagon, and had been proud to see to it that the oxen hit each bridge safely and did not jolt his mistress and the family too much. He had given faithful service, but bad luck had dogged him. His mistake had caused the loss of his master's oxen on the desert, and the anger which he had innocently aroused in Snyder had caused Snyder's death and Reed's banishment. But in return he had stuck manfully by his mistress, and even now when the hides had to be taken from the roof, he stood with her in an enterprise which might be called quixotic, if it were not better described as simply desperate.

Mrs. Reed had decided to leave the three smaller children, and with Milt, Eliza, and young Virginia to attempt the crossing of the mountains. She left little Tommy, only three years old, with the Breens; Patty went to the Kesebergs' cabin; the Graveses took Jim. As if to make the mother's task impossible, the children cried and pled not to be left behind. She quieted them finally only by telling them that she was going in order to bring back bread. Even the unobservant Breen noticed the strain of parting: "It was difficult for Mrs. Reid to get away from the children."

On January 4, just before noon, Mrs. Reed, Virginia, Milt, and Eliza left the cabins. They took with them a little dried meat. It was the sort of ridiculously valiant attempt which one wishes to succeed, if only to prove that reason and reasonable people are not always right. But "Fortune favors the bold" is a delusive proverb, and Mrs. Reed had nothing except boldness to count on. She may perhaps have had in mind little except a heroic death, to die facing to the front and leaving more food for the children who remained behind. Certainly the mad attempt was doomed from the beginning. After only one night of freezing in the snow Eliza's spirit failed, and she turned back. The other three—mother, daughter, and faithful servant—went ahead. Virginia was so weak that on the steeper slopes she had to climb on hands and knees. In this fashion they actually scaled the pass. On the other side they had to pause to improvise snow-shoes. They went on for another day. Milt had a compass, but it did not seem to be working properly. Thus misled, they wandered to the north, and struggled through a bewildering confusion of rocks and hummocks around the shores of a frozen mountain lake. At the height of over seven thousand feet the cold of the winter nights was terrible; even so, they were sometimes so exhausted that they slept soundly. But on the third night Virginia's feet were frost-bitten. Then finally they turned back. As long as they had been going ahead, Virginia had kept up valiantly, but the turning back took all the heart out of her, and she could scarcely get along at all. Milt was so weak that he could no longer carry her, as he had sometimes done. In some way they managed to get down over the pass and arrived at the cabins on the morning of January 8, having spent four nights in the snow. The following day brought the fifth great storm of the winter, which, if it had caught them in the open, would have meant sure death to them all.

With this storm and the daily shrinking of what poor supply of food still remained, life by the lake settled down into an even more bitter struggle. From the ninth to the thirteenth the storm howled through the pines. Breen's notes during this time in their very brevity suggest the snowed-in cabin, the absolute lack of contact with anything outside, and the failure of to-day to differ from yesterday. Only on the last day of the storm does the entry rise to a slight climax:

Snowing fast   wind N.W   snow higher than the shanty must be 13 feet deep   dont know how to get wood this morning   it is dredful to look at.

In the emergency with the cold creeping in upon them and the cabin roof buried five feet deep under snow, they had to split pieces from the logs on the inside of the cabin to keep the fire going. By this time the Reeds had begun to stay with the Breens, who of all the emigrants were best supplied with food and were a little more charitable. But aside from their hides, about all that the Reeds got to eat were the leavings. Bones which the Breens had already boiled two or three times the Reeds would take and boil for several days more. Virginia was in a bad way; her feet had been frost-bitten upon the mountain, and she was failing. But Peggy Breen had a soft spot for the girl, and occasionally when her husband was not looking, she would slip Virginia little pieces of meat and watch to see that she ate them.

For the Breens with good foresight had commenced to eat hides early, and so had still some meat left. They seemed able to digest the "glue," and to suffer less nausea than the other emigrants did. "Murphys folks and Keysburgs say they cant eat hides," Breen noted once, and added the comment: "I wish we had enough of them."

With the addition of the Reeds, fifteen people were crowded into the cabin. Half of them stayed in bed all the time. Often "Uncle Patrick" prayed aloud, the others kneeling with him while one held a burning pine splinter for a candle. So impressed was Virginia Reed with his piety that she swore to become a Catholic if rescued, in childish lack of logic forgetting that her own mother and many others were praying just as fervently and probably just as efficaciously in their Protestant fashion.

Strangely enough Virginia remembered some pleasant times. Now and then they all talked together, and they had a few books. She read again and again the life of Daniel Boone, losing herself in the story of one who like themselves had suffered and endured greatly in the wilderness.

Uncle Patrick had his big Bible too, from which they could gain comfort. Like them, the prophets and the patriarchs had known hunger and thirst and cold, and one wonders whether in the noisome cabins the readers ever stumbled upon those verses which might almost seem written to suggest their own troubles. As when Job tells of those:

Barren with want and hunger, who gnawed in the wilderness, disfigured with calamity and misery.

And they ate grass, and bark of trees, and the root of junipers was their food.

Then they might have read that passage in Psalms, discomforting at first with its assurance that God sent the very storm which raged outside, comforting in the end with promise that He would yet send the spring:

Who giveth snow like wool; scattereth mists like ashes.

He sendeth his crystal like morsels: who shall stand before the face of his cold?

He shall send out his word, and shall melt them: his wind shall blow and the waters shall run.

"Hail, snow, ice, stormy winds, which fulfill his word"— the emigrants had had plenty of such fulfillment.

After this storm of the middle of January, the news from the other cabins was worse than ever. Old Mrs. Murphy had gone blind. Young Landrum Murphy was failing; at times he went out of his head.

On the seventeenth the entry ran:

Fine morning sun shineing clear wind S.S.E Eliza came here this morning, sent her back again to Graves Lanthrom crazy last night so Bill says, Keyburg sent Bill to get hides off his shanty & carry thim home this morning, provisions scarce hides are the only article we depend on, we have a little meat yet, may God send us help.

(God was indeed working in his own slow way, for on this same day the two Indians dragged the half-dead Eddy to the door of Ritchie's cabin.)

The nineteenth was a fine day at the lake, just as it was for Eddy dictating his letter to Sinclair and looking out peacefully upon the grassy plain.

Clear & pleasant [wrote Breen] thawing a little in the sun wind S. W Peggy and Edward sick last night by eating some meat that Dolan threw his tobacco on, pretty well to day (praise God for his blessings,) Lanthrom very low in danger if relief dont soon come hides are all the go, not much of any other in camp.

For the next week the diarist gave an account rather more detailed than usual:

Wed. 20th Fine morning wind N froze hard last night. Expecting some person across the mountain this week.

Thursd. 21 Fine morning wind W did not freeze quite so hard last night as it has done, John Battice & Denton came this morning with Eliza she wont eat hides Mrs Reid sent her back to live or die on them. Milt. got his toes froze the Donoghs [Breen regularly gave Donner an Irish form] are all well.

Frid. 22nd Began to snow a little after sunrise likely to snow a good dale wind W came up very suddenly, now 10 o'clock

Satd. 23rd Blew hard & snowd. all night the most severe storm we experienced this winter wind W sun now 12 oclock peeps out.

Sund. 24th Some cloudy this morning ceased snowing yesterday about 2 oclock. Wind about S.E all in good health thanks be to God for his mercies endureth for ever, heard nothing from Murphys camp since the storm expet to hear they suffered some.

Mod 25th Began to snow yesterday evening & still continues wind W.

Tuesd 26 Cleared up yesterday to day fine & pleasant, wind S. in hopes we are done with snow storms, thos that went to Suitors [Sutter's] not yet returned provisions geting very scant people geting weak liveing on short allowance of hides.

On the next day Mrs. Keseberg, whose cabin shared one wall with that of the Breens, managed to get around to see her neighbors. Still the news was worse. Her baby, Lewis, had died three days before. Her husband was sick. In the other cabin the three Murphy boys, Landrum, William, and Simon, all were sick. Landrum was the worst, and had to stay in bed all the time.

But even under such conditions the old hatreds did not die out altogether, or perhaps they even smoldered the hotter under the fear of starvation. On the thirtieth Breen had to record:

The Graves seized on Mrs. Reids goods untill they would be paid also took the hides that she & family had to live on, she got two peices of hides from there & the ballance they have taken you may know from these proceedings what our fare is in camp there is nothing to be got by hunting yet perhaps there soon will. God send it *Amen*.

The *you* in this entry is one of the few indications that Breen ever consciously thought that he was composing his record for a reader.

Again a full moon swung through the sky at night. Thursday, Friday, and Saturday were warm; "like spring weather," wrote Breen. At the camp the snow high above the cabin roofs was wet. Far off in the Sacramento Valley the treacherous adobe mud along the emigrant road was hardening beneath the sun.

Early on the morning of January 31 Landrum Murphy died. Breen's entry for the day recorded that fact, and added no note in his usual optimistic manner. Even the weather was depressing. "The sun dont shine out brilliant this morning froze pr[e]tty hard last night."

But for once Breen should have permitted himself more optimism than he did. In spite of the death of Landrum and in spite of the dim sun, January 31 should have been recorded in red letters. For on this day seven horsemen driving pack-animals took the road north from Sutter's. With the long-continued rains the American must have been a swirling torrent, but whether they were ferried across or merely swam their horses at the ford, no one has troubled to note. This was an insignificant detail in comparison with the greater trials to follow. In any case, with the passage of the river they made only a short day's journey, and camped on Dry Creek. Relief had started.

20. THE SEVEN AGAINST DEATH

ON Monday, the first day of February, those same seven riders and their pack-train plugged on across the pl in, and that night they camped only three miles below Johnson's. On the same day Breen's eldest son lay sick, and a more worried tone sounded in the father's record:

Sun shines dimly the snow has not settled much John is unwell to day with the help of God he will be well by night Amen.

Next morning, Tuesday, Glover and his relief party rode into Johnson's early, and set about gathering additional recruits and making preparations. So far they had traveled light, and at Johnson's they made ready their supplies for the push across the snow. They slaughtered cattle, cut the meat into strips, and dried it over fires. From the hides they s! ced long strips of rawhide to be used in making snow-shoes. Johnson had no mill, and so for a small supply of flour they pounded wheat in Indian stone mortars and ground it in coffee-mills. They knew that time pressed, and they wor .ed with only a few hours off for sleep, but even so they spent two days and two nights at this labor.

Starvation also worked day and night, and did not stop

for sleep. Mrs. McCutchen when she had left with the snow-shoers had entrusted her baby to Mrs. Graves. The little waif had lingered on, but it died on Tuesday, while at Johnson's the fires blazed and the men looked out toward the mountains.

On the morning of Thursday, February 4, the relief party mustered for departure. With recruits picked up at Johnson's they numbered fourteen, although some of these were only going in with the animals and would not attempt the snow. They were a drab-looking crew, the men mostly bearded after the fashion of the time, dressed in the nondescript clothing of the frontier, and mounted either on horses or mules. Alcalde Sinclair had come up from his ranch, and made a little speech to spur them on.

The names of the band are worthy of record, and also what type of men they were. They included, first of all, Glover, Moultry and Sels, the original volunteers. The greater number of the others, like Glover and Moultry, had been emigrants of the past year, farmers not frontiersmen. Among these were the Rhoads boys, John and his younger brother Daniel, both of whom were Mormons. M. D. Ritchie, another emigrant, was known as "Captain" or "Colonel" for having served through the Black Hawk campaign; it was to his house that the Indians had dragged Eddy. The two Tuckers were also emigrants. George, the son, was a mere boy of sixteen; the father was called "Dan" and is generally noted as Daniel in the records, but his real name was Reasin, and the other only a nickname derived probably from the popular song, "Old Dan Tucker." Jotham Curtis was the emigrant whom Reed and McCutchen had brought back from Bear Valley.

Of those who were not emigrants, Joseph Sels (*alias* Foster) had been one of the three original recruits. Like him, "Ned" Coffeemeyer was a sailor, and may quite likely have been a deserter from some whaler or hide-drogher. Adolph Brueheim, a German, had also come to California by sea; he had been a passenger's servant and had been permitted to remain in California. He went by the fine nickname of "Greasy Jim." Joseph Verrot, whose name was generally spelled by sound as Varro, had come to California with Frémont in '44. Of William Coon nothing is known except that he was a harmless half-wit of little account.

The last man of the fourteen was William Eddy, he who had frozen and starved with the snow-shoers. After only two and a half weeks for recuperation he was again venturing into the snow.

The leader was Aquilla Glover, but the title has also been given to "Dan" Tucker and to John Rhoads. The doubt is characteristic, for like most enterprises of the early West, this one was merely an association of equals. Glover might hold the purse-strings, and on his word Sutter and Sinclair would distribute the pay, but in the mountains the men would follow whatever leader dominated the situation.

With fourteen riders and a string of pack-animals the relief party headed out of Johnson's under heavy skies. It was slow going, for more rain had fallen, and the ground was soft. The animals sank deeply at every step, and after two or three miles among the foothills a pack-horse went into a mud-hole up to his belly. He struggled about, turned his pack, and finally getting out of the hole bucked and plunged until he got himself clean of saddle and everything, and took the back road to the ranch. Disgruntled, they gathered up the pack, lashed it on Eddy's horse, and sent Eddy and young Tucker back after the runaway. The others went on, and made ten miles for the day.

Had they known what they were riding into, they all might well have turned back to Johnson's to wait better weather. For in the higher mountains the seventh great storm of the year was already well started:

Thurd. 4th Snowed hard all night & still continues with a strong S: W. wind untill now abated looks as if it would snow all day snowed about 2 feet deep now.

On Friday the horsemen rode on. The animals slipped and slithered in the mud, and now and then bogged down. The morning was gloomy and overcast, and rain was threatening. It struck them about noon, and sluiced down in torrents, cold and unceasing. The men were soaked and half-frozen. The trail became a morass. Brought to a standstill, they halted on a little flat, and managed to get a fire going where two big pine trees had fallen one on the other. They laid down pine bark and branches, piled the packs upon these to keep them out of the water, and laid the saddles on top to keep the rain off. There was no hope of sleep, for the water stood two or three inches deep on the ground and the torrent of rain never ceased. Eddy came up driving the runaway ahead of him, having left young Tucker on the road with a jaded horse. Every one had to stand up all night; they got what comfort they could out of the fire.

Morning brought no relief. The rain still poured down like Noah's Flood. Soon after daybreak Tucker came in; he had lost the road in the darkness, and spent the night without a fire or blanket or any shelter except a pine-tree. He was done up with cold and exhaustion, and when he began to get warm at the fire his arms and legs swelled until he could hardly move. All that day and the next night the rain never ceased. Drenched and stiff, they crouched and stood around the fire. The storm was holding them back a good two days at a time when every hour counted, and even more than they knew, they were striving against death.

At the lake the situation was more tense; the end even of the hides was near. Relief must come soon now, if it came at all. On Friday Breen wrote:

Peggy very uneasy for fear we shall all perrish with hunger we have but a little meat left & only part of 3 hides has to support Mrs. Reid she has nothing left but one hide & it is on Graves shanty Milt is livi[n]g there & likely will keep that hide.

He paused, and then scrawled as an afterthought, crowded at the bottom of the page, a sentence which would have been a blow in the face to one of the men who crouched that evening in the rain beside the fire: "Eddys child died last night." And for the next day:

Satd. 6th It snowed faster last night & to day than it has done this winter & still continues without an intermission.

Again came an isolated sentence at the end: "Mrs. Eddy very weak."

To the draggled and discouraged men about the fire no relief came until daylight of Sunday. Then after nearly forty-eight hours of downpour the rain ceased, and a good warm California sun came out. They found that in spite of their efforts to keep the packs dry, the unceasing deluge had wet everything—clothing, blankets, flour, jerked beef. There was nothing for it but to halt for another day to dry things out; otherwise the food would spoil, and besides there was a limit to what the men could stand. They hung blankets and clothing on lines, and built fires. The sun shone all day; by evening everything was dry, and the men had a chance to rest and pick up a little sleep.

On the same day Breen wrote:

Sund. 7th Ceased to snow last [night] after one of the most severe storms we experienced this winter the snow fell about 4 feet deep. I had to shovel the snow off our shanty this morning it thawd so fast & thawd. during the whole storm. to day it is quite pleasant wind S. W. Milt here to day says Mrs. Reid has to get a hide from Mrs. Murphy . . .

On Monday morning the relief party packed up again and moved on. They made good progress until about noon; then they came to Steep Hollow, and stopped, appalled. Usually an insignificant stream flowed there, but after two days of sluicing rain a torrent filled the canyon—a hundred feet wide, twenty feet deep, and too fast for man or horse to dare. But the fourteen men, already gaunt from hardship and lack of sleep, were not to be foiled by any mountain stream. They found a convenient pine-tree, and felled it across the torrent. Even so, it sagged, and in the middle a foot of water flowed over it. Some one ventured across, and rigged up ropes as a safety-guard. Then they carried the precious packs of meat and flour across. The horses and mules were the worst problem, for they could not walk the tree-trunk, and they balked at swimming. Finally the men forced two horses into the water above the tree. One managed to reach the other bank and scrambled ashore, but the force of the current sucked the other down under the tree. He disappeared completely for a few moments and then bobbed up, feet first, twenty yards below. The current whirled him a hundred yards downstream, and finally flung him into a shallow, half drowned.

After that the men tied ropes together until they had a length sufficient to span the stream. Then some of them crossed the tree-trunk with one end of the rope. The men remaining tied the other end to a horse and forced him into the water. Thus half swimming, half dragged, each animal was got across. The passage of Steep Hollow used up half a day; it could ill be spared. . . .

"Fine clear morning," wrote Breen this same day, "wind S. W. froze hard last [night]. Spitzer died last night about 3 o clock . . . we will bury him in the snow." He dipped his pen again, and, curiously, for the third time in four days brought his entry to a close with mention of the same family: "Mrs. Eddy died on the night of the 7th."

She had lived until the baby died, and then flickered out. Of the three to whom Eddy had said good-by, only his little son Jimmy remained, and he was left to the charge of old and failing Mrs. Murphy in the death-haunted cabin beside the great rock. . . .

But on Tuesday Eddy rode on with the others. They began working along the ridge between the Bear and Steep Hollow, and after four miles came to snow. It grew deeper rapidly, and the animals floundered about in drifts. At last after four miles more they came about noon to Mule Springs, and camped. The snow was three or four feet deep; the animals could find no food, and could not be taken further. This was discouraging, for on leaving Johnson's they had hoped to get as far as Bear Valley before having to start in on foot; the great storm had brought the snow-line much further down than usual.

During the rest of the day they made ready a sort of advanced supply-base at Mule Springs. They cut two branches with forks in them, set them in the ground at convenient heights and distances, and laid a ridge pole from fork to fork. Against this they leaned other poles, and then covered them with cedar boughs to shed rain. Inside this brush tent they stored all the extra provisions, and assigned young Tucker and the half-wit Billy Coon to stay and watch them. Since it was impossible for the animals to remain at Mule Springs, Eddy and Verrot were assigned to take them back to Johnson's. Eddy had been weak at starting, and every one now saw that he could not possibly attempt the snow. What he had been through already was enough to finish most men. . . .

And as if his turning back were to mark the end, Breen wrote: "John went down to day to bury Mrs. Eddy & child." The entry for that Tuesday was little but a chronicle of disaster. The baby Catherine Pike was all but dead. Faithful Milt Elliott lay at the Murphy cabin unable to rise from his bed. No one had heard from the Graveses for several days. "Keyburg," wrote Breen, "never gets up says he is not able." . . .

Next morning Eddy and Verrot started back, and the ten who were to go forward prepared their packs. Each man took a blanket, a tin cup, and a hatchet, but most of the pack consisted of dried beef and flour. They had no scales and the weight was determined simply by the amount that a man could carry. The estimates ran from fifty to seventy-five pounds for each, in any case a killing load for men who had to break their own path through snow and up and down gullies and canyons. Curtis carried only half weight.

The snow was hard enough for them to get along without snow-shoes. They walked in single file, each stepping in the foot-prints of the preceding one. The leader had the worst time, for at each step he plunged in knee-deep. After a few minutes of this he became exhausted, and fell to the rear, the next in line taking his place.

As they struggled ahead, death again outraced them. Fifty miles away across mountains and snow-fields, Breen took up his pen again, all unconscious of the ten men who fought the drifts:

Beautiful morning wind W: froze hard last night, to day thawing in the sun Milt Elliot died las[t] night at Murphys shanty about 9 o'clock P: M: Mrs. Reid went there this morning to see after his effects. J Denton trying to borrow meat for Graves had none to give they have nothing but hides all are entirely out of meat but a little we have our hides are nearly all eat up but with Gods help spring will soon smile upon us.

So the faithful Milt died. On Sunday he had been at the Breen cabin in concern about how Mrs. Reed was to get another hide; by Tuesday night, he himself was dead. Virginia and her mother dragged the body up from the cabin to the top of the snow, and buried it there, patting the surface down until it looked like a fresh grave mound. They had lost, as they knew, their best friend. . . .

Knee-deep, in single file, bent beneath their packs, the ten men plunged ahead. For some reason, perhaps the almost instinctive tendency of overladen men to flinch at going up-hill, they worked down from the ridge. Evening found them at the bottom of Bear River Canyon, having made a distance of only six miles. They were exhausted by a day of constant struggle, and night offered little chance for rest. The snow was so deep that to dig to the ground was impracticable, and so they built a platform as the snow-shoers had done. Warned by the others' experience, they took care that their green logs were both large and long enough. Even so, to spend the night each man could only throw his blanket over his shoulders and crawl up as close to the fire as he could. All ten sat huddled together unable to lie down, dozing as they could. When from time to time the fire burned down and the frost of the winter night grew more biting, one of them had to crawl out and pile on fuel.

On Thursday the rescuers, much as they were needed at the lake, found themselves brought almost to a standstill. Their descent into the canyon proved to have been a mistake, for its walls were so precipitous that they could not advance up it, and had to climb toward the ridge again. After only two miles they were forced to halt to make snow-shoes. They cut pine boughs, stripped them of bark and then bent them into shape as they heated them over a fire. They strung rawhide strips for the lattice work. But after all this work the shoes turned out to be useless. In the lower parts of the Sierra the warm sun soon makes the snow-surface soft and wet, so that the snow sticks to the snow-shoe and makes it unmanageable. The men found that they could do better by merely plunging ahead knee-deep. They abandoned the shoes, and after a day during which they made little progress, they camped and spent another miserable night huddled upon a platform.

For this day Breen had little to report. Actually matters at the camp were so bad that a delay of a week might see few remaining for the relief party to save. Virginia Reed was close to death, kept alive only by the scraps of meat which kind-hearted Mrs. Breen gave her surreptitiously from her own stores. The Englishman John Denton, who was living with the Graveses, was in a bad state. The men and boys were so weak now that they hacked pitifully as they strove to fell trees for firewood. Patrick Breen's voice rose almost continuously in prayer; the others knelt beside him. Once in a pause they all heard from far above the faint honking of wild geese. It was a sign of spring, but the deep snow all about gave it the lie.

Next day, Friday, the relief party made Bear Valley. They were about thirty miles from the lake, no more than a strong man might walk in a summer day. But this was not summer; on the expanse of Bear Valley the snow lay ten feet deep. At the upper end of the valley the rescuers dug for the cache left by Reed and McCutchen in November, but when at last they uncovered the remains of Curtis's wagon, they found it rifled by bears. That night rain and snow fell, and the ten men cowered comfortless upon their platform.

At the lake the storm was not severe, but the words of the diary ring with a certain poignancy:

A warm thawey morning wind S.E. we hope with the assistance of Almighty God to be able to live to see the bare surface of the earth once more. O God of Mercy grant it if it be thy holy will *Amen*.

The rain which descended upon Bear Valley during Friday night meant another delay, and the relief party had to spend Saturday drying out. They also made a cache of some of their provisions in order to lighten their packs and to ensure supplies on the return trip. To do this they tied the provisions into bales, and suspended them from the branches of trees high enough from the ground to foil marauding animals.

On this day also they girded themselves for the final ordeal. They had spent ten days in getting from Johnson's to Bear Valley, and in that time had seldom been dry, warm, or rested. They had already exhibited courage and stamina nothing short of heroic. But what they had so far experienced, bad as it was, was only the preliminary. The really dangerous part lay ahead in the high mountains and deep snow. With luck they could make it. But if they were caught in a storm, or if they lost their way as the snow-shoers had, or if luck broke against them in any of a dozen other ways, they would probably never be heard of again. Right ahead of them stood the steep wall rising to Emigant Gap. (Breen reported fair weather, and added: "Mrs Reed has headacke the rest in health.")

In the morning came mutiny. Three of the men—"Colonel" Ritchie, Jotham Curtis, and "Greasy Jim"—refused flatly to go further. There was no way to force them, and their desertion discouraged the others. For a moment it looked as if the whole expedition might fail. But "Dan" Tucker rose to the emergency, taking it upon himself to promise every man who kept on to the end five dollars a day from the time they entered the snow. Five dollars was pay for a lord, but it did not look so lordly when a man sat cold and sleepless upon a plaform of pine logs laid upon ten feet of snow, and gazed out one way toward the great snow-swept gorge of the Yuba, and the other toward the wall up to Emigrant Gap. Deep in snow except where crags stuck through like black teeth, those great hard mountains were cold and white like death.

Nevertheless the seven stuck. It was not so much love of money, one can well imagine, or even pure desire to rescue starving women and children; more likely it was stubborn male courage and that deep-seated sense of honor that a man should not flinch in a task to which he has set himself.

So the three went back, and the seven kept on. They were now three times sifted; the young, the weak, and the cowardly had been left behind. The seven who remained should be re-membered and like bluff Sheriff McKinstry, "I will again give you a list of their names, as I think they ought to be recorded in letters of gold": Glover, "Dan" Tucker, Sept Moultry, Ned Coffeemeyer, Joe Sels, and the two Rhoads brothers.

Of these seven not one was an experienced mountaineer. The two sailors, Coffeemeyer and Sels, had presumably never before been in the mountains or had any knowledge of the route. The other five had crossed only by the emigrant road in the autumn. All had probably, however, gathered as much information as they could at Sutter's and Johnson's, and knowledge which they had gained about the geography of the mountains now served them well. For as they looked from Bear Valley at the precipitous slope up to the Gap, it was a discouraging sight, and they decided boldly to attempt another route, which was known to have been followed once by some emigrants. This would lead them up the Bear and over to the Yuba with scarcely any divide to cross. Then they would follow up the canyon of the Yuba until they re-joined the main route. It had proved a bad way for wagons, but it was possible, and perhaps better for footmen.

They now had to be careful about their course, for they were passing through unknown country. Nevertheless they moved ahead, and on the whole had a surprisingly good day which fully justified their change of route. They crossed successfully the few miles from the headwaters of the Bear to the Yuba, leaving a sinuous trail across the broken country as they wound in single file about hummocks and climbed up and down ravines. Regularly the leader fell to the rear, and the second man took his turn at breaking trail. Even to follow the Yuba once they had reached it was not an easy task, for now the river was completely bridged by snow, and indistinguishable from its tributaries. There was always the chance that they might turn aside up the wrong gorge. Whenever they came to a convenient dead pine they stopped long enough to set fire to it so that the charred trunk might be a guide-post on the return journey, if snow should have covered their footprints. That night they camped somewhere along Yuba Bottoms, having made a dozen miles.

This day was Sunday the fourteenth. "John Denton not well," Breen recorded. Virginia Reed was failing; it did not look as if she could last more than a few days.

The seven pushed on. Now on Monday they were around the bend of the Yuba, and had less fear of getting lost. The buttes formed a landmark behind, and ahead they could sight now and then the upstanding peaks above the pass. But the going was much worse. A storm had blown up, and the snow which was falling was light and feathery. After only three miles it became impossible to advance further, and they had to stop again to make snow-shoes. They then struggled on for two miles more, and camped after making only five miles for the day. Hardship and lack of sleep were wearing them down. If the storm lasted, they might be done for.

At the lake the struggle for life was growing fiercer. Mrs. Graves, desperate for her own children, was willing to let the Reeds starve:

Mrs. Graves [wrote Breen] refused to give Mrs Reid any hides put Suitors pack hides on her shanty would not let her have them says if I say it will thaw it then will not, she is a case.

Luck held for the relief party, for in the morning the snow-fall ceased. They toiled on again, still on snow-shoes except where some steep hillside was clear. The peaks at the pass grew nearer, but for the whole day they made only five miles.

Breen noted wind and weather, and added: "we all feel very weakly to day   snow not getting much less in quantity."

Next day was Wednesday, ending the second week since the seven had left Johnson's. They had a little easier going as they crossed the open expanse of Summit Valley, and after struggling ahead eight miles they camped that night at what they called the head of the Yuba. They made another cache of provisions to be picked up on the way back. The snow they estimated at close to thirty feet. The peaks were close overhead, and the gap between them was clear. The seven were not more than what would have been, in the summer, two hours' walk from the cabins, but the hump of the pass sticking up shut them off as well as if they had been a hundred miles away.

At the lake Breen, with no sense of help close at hand, recorded the weather.

21. "OLD DAN TUCKER'S COME TO TOWN"

On Thursday, the eighteenth of February, the seven at last faced the pass. A mile away and five hundred feet above them they could see the gap between the jagged peaks. But even with lightened packs five hundred feet was a hard climb for men exhausted by a week of almost sleepless struggle against the snow. And now the altitude began to tell against them. Glover and young Daniel Rhoads were failing badly, and had to be relieved of their packs by the others. But doggedly all seven worked their way upward through the light snow which made triple work of every foot of climbing. Then finally the slope eased off, and a narrow passage of level ground with high slopes on either hand led them, floundering through the snow, to where the view toward the east suddenly opened out before them. Down the face of the pass and across the frozen lake they could look out over forest-covered valleys toward distant mountains. They saw no trace of life. Then they began the descent—easier but more dangerous. It was midday, and past.

As they clung like flies against the white wall working their way downwards, a keen-sighted watcher from the lower end of the lake might have made them out as black specks. But no one saw them; as week on week had passed since the departure of the snow-shoers, hope of rescue had failed, so that the emigrants were no longer likely to stand dully in the cold gazing toward the west. As the day passed in the noisome cabins, Breen at some time made the entry in his diary:

Froze hard last night to day clear & warm in the sun cold in the shanty or in the shade wind S. E all in good health Thanks be to Almighty God *Amen.*

As the sun was down behind the pass, the seven came working their way across the snow which covered the frozen lake. Dusk was falling, and they came into the trees to the place where Eddy had told them they would find the cabins. They saw only snow, and a sudden fear fell upon them that they had struggled so hard only to arrive too late. Spontaneously they hallooed together. At the sound they saw a woman emerge, like some kind of animal, from a hole in the snow. They floundered toward her, and she, tottering weakly, came toward them. She spoke, crying out in a hollow voice, unnerved and agitated:

"Are you men from California, or do you come from heaven?"

Other human figures, ghastly and horrible sights, began to appear. It was as if the rescuers' halloo had been Gabriel's horn raising the dead from their graves. Their flesh was wasted from their bodies. They wept and laughed hysterically. They cried out as well as they could in hoarse and death-like voices, confusedly:

"Relief, thank God, relief!"

"Have you brought anything for me?"

From the lightened packs the seven distributed food in such quantities as they thought safe. Tucker pressed on to the Graveses' cabin half a mile down the stream. There was little time for more rejoicing, for even the seven rescuers were as completely exhausted as men can well be, and the comparatively warm and dry cabins offered them their first ch ce for a real sleep in more than a week. They turned in, prudently setting a guard to prevent any of the famished and half-crazed emigrants from rifling the supplies.

Morning brought the rescuers a chance to see more fully the terrible conditions at the cabins. The snow was high above the roofs. Inclined planes led up from the c b s o the top of the snow, and up these slopes the dead bodies had been dragged with ropes since the starving p ople had not been able to lift them. Some bodies now lay upon the snow wrapped in quilts. Some of the hides which were being used for food were putrefied from having served as roofs of cabins and thus been kept warm on the inside. The emigrants were overwrought emotionally, and many seemed mentally unbalanced. Expectation of death had made religious feeling dominate the minds of some; these prayed constantly so that Biblical imagery filled their minds, as with the woman who had first seen the rescuers and cried out asking if they were sent from heaven. But others reacted in the opposite direction, and lavished their curses equally upon God and Hastings. Some were so broken by long suffering that they seemed to have lost all sense of self-respect, pride, or principle.

On this day three of the strongest from the rescue party— Tucker, Moultry and John Rhoads—set out for the Donner tents, taking with them a small amount of beef. The four others rested and prepared for the return, which was set for Monday. By this delay they ran the risk of being trapped by another storm, but the rest was imperative.

Breen's entry for this day was curiously unemotional and matter-of-fact:

Froze hard last night 7 men arrived from Colifornia yesterday evening with som provisions but left the greater part on the way to day clear & warm for this region some of the men are gone to day to Donnos Camp will start back on Monday.

It will be noticed that, once aided, Breen with genuinely human forgetfulness neglected to record his thanks to the God to whom he had so often called in time of trouble.

His notes for the remaining two days of the rescuers' stay

were also curious. Apparently he thought that with the time of stress passed the keeping of a record was less important. The entry for Saturday was the shortest of the whole diary, merely the two words: "Pleasant weather." But this was rivaled by that of Sunday: "Thawey warm day." In his brevity he did not mention the death on Saturday of the baby Catherine Pike; for her, relief had come, but not from over the pass.

By this time Tucker, Moultry, and Rhoads had returned from the Donner tents, bringing with them six refugees. These were the teamster Noah James, Mrs. Wolfinger, and four of the older children. All of them were in bad condition, especially Leanna Donner, who had barely been able to drag herself as far as the first cabin. The story from the Donner tents was, as usual, bad. No one had died, but George Donner's arm was worse; he could not last long. Both of the Donner women were in fair condition and would have been able to make the crossing, but Tamsen would not abandon her sick husband and smaller children, and Elizabeth also stuck to her post. The only man left to do the work of the camp was the little mongrel Jean Baptiste. He had wanted to come away with the rescuers, and had been sullen and ugly when they told him that he must remain and take care of the women and children. Nevertheless he had had to stay. Tucker and the two others had felled a tree, and had left a little food, but not enough to do much good. Jean Baptiste was still trying to find the bodies of some of the cattle which had been buried in the big storm. He had a long pole with an iron point on the end which he thrust down into the snow, hoping to bring up a bit of flesh or some hair. But since the snow was so deep and since the cattle might have wandered anywhere over a long distance, his chances were not very good. In the meantime only one hide was left to support the twelve people still remaining. A day or two would see the end of this, and the Donners said firmly that then, unless Jean Baptiste should find cattle, they had determined to dig up the bodies of those who had died of starvation. George Donner and Jean Baptiste, Tamsen and Elizabeth Donner, and eight of the younger children still remained at that camp.

On Sunday the weather still held fair, and at the lake cabins, the relief party completed its plans. Besides the six brought from the Donner tents, they gathered seventeen from the cabins. Various reasons determined who was to go and who to stay. The Reeds along with Eliza Williams must certainly go, for lately they had been entirely without supplies of their own. The Breens, who still had some meat and part of a hide or two, were to stay, except for two of the older boys. Two of the Graves girls, of fifteen and thirteen, were picked for the crossing. Then Billy Graves of eighteen pled hard to go for his chance to escape, but his mother said that he was the only one who could cut wood for her and the younger children. Finally she agreed that if he would cut enough to last for a while he might go. He was a tough-grained farmer's boy, and in spite of his starving condition he managed to get the wood cut and ready before Monday morning.

Keseberg lay on his back unable to get about much, but Mrs. Keseberg was able to travel, and she took her little Ada, only three years old. Keseberg thus left alone, the last remaining of all the Germans, moved into the Murphy cabin.

Mary and William Murphy of twelve and eleven years were also selected for the crossing. This left old Mrs. Murphy, who was blind part of the time, to care for her two small grandchildren and for Eddy's only remaining child with no one to help her but her boy Simon, who was only ten, and Keseberg, if in his condition he could be called a help. This was too much; so John Rhoads agreed to carry little Naomi Pike in a blanket. He was the readier to do so, because he had seen her mother at Johnson's and been moved by the story of her sufferings with the snow-shoers.

The Englishman John Denton also joined the party. He had been in a bad state for some time, but he at least could make the effort to escape.

Seventeen, altogether, were to be left at the lake—two men, three women, and twelve children. At the Breen cabin were "Uncle Patrick" and Peggy with four of their boys, and the baby Isabella. At the Murphy cabin beside the great rock Keseberg was left with old Mrs. Murphy, Simon, and the two little boys. At the downstream cabin remained Mrs. Graves with her baby and three other children. The Reeds' end of the cabin was now deserted, roofless, and half full of snow. Glover was able to leave almost no food at the camp, so that after his departure conditions would be as bad as they had been before.

The twenty-three who were selected to go with the relief party on Monday comprised three men, four women, and seventeen children. Of the last, three were three years old, one five, and one eight; the rest were nine years and upwards.

John Rhoads was to pack Naomi Pike. Probably Mrs. Keseberg was attempting to carry three-year-old Ada. But all the others, young as they were, must walk. To have loaded a child upon many of the men of the relief party would have destroyed all chance of success. They would have work enough as it was in breaking trail, carrying packs, and helping in emergencies. Besides, any one could predict that before they got to Bear Valley some of the children would be giving out entirely.

It was now more than two months since Stanton, Eddy and the other snow-shoers had left the camp. Glover and his men had carefully concealed the fate of that party in fear that if it were known, no one from the mountain camps would have the courage to start. The relief party had merely said that Stanton and the other men had had their feet frost-bitten and so could not return.

Any one comparing the situation of the party which was now leaving with that of the snow-shoers would have had difficulty in deciding which one had the better chance. In the earlier one all the members had been adults, and they had been for a shorter time on starvation rations. But the present party had the advantage of a snow-surface consolidated by two weeks of generally thawing weather; they had also seven guides who knew the route even in the snow, and guides who were, in spite of their weakened condition, very giants of strength compared with Stanton and his starving companions. But for this party as for the other the real turn of fortune must depend upon the weather—if a storm broke! And already it had been generally fair weather for more than two weeks. How long would it hold?

On the twenty-second, Washington's Birthday, they got under way. As in the song, "Old Dan Tucker" had come to town, and things had happened.

22. THE CHILDREN WALK

Late that Monday morning they filed off through the pine-trees. Since no snow had fallen, they could follow the trail which the seven had made when coming in. This made trail-breaking easier. A man with snow-shoes went ahead, and the others followed, stepping in his tracks where the snow was pressed hard. Even so, it was killing work. The little fellows like Jimmy and Tommy Reed could not reach from one footprint to the next, but had to rest a knee on the hill of snow between and scramble over each time. The line soon lengthened. The stronger ones like Billy Graves kept up with the leader; far behind lagged the weaker ones—the Reed children, Leanna Donner, and poor John Denton.

The men of the relief party encouraged the stragglers, but they soon saw that Tommy Reed simply could not make it. And there was no one to carry him. He struggled on for two miles, a truly heroic distance for a three-year-old, and then gave out. Patty, his sister of eight, was in little better condition. Glover had to break the news to Mrs. Reed that the two children must be taken back to the cabins. This was practically a death-sentence, but the safety of the whole party could not be jeopardized for the sake of two.

Mrs. Reed was faced with the most terrible of dilemmas. Should she struggle onwards to save herself for the sake of her husband and two children, or should she go back with the other two? Glover promised that once he had got the party safely through he would return to rescue Patty and Tommy; he pledged his honor. But a man's honor seemed a small thing compared with sending her two children back among the crazed inmates of the cabins, and Mrs. Reed was almost too prostrated for a decision. Suddenly she grasped at a straw; her husband was a Mason; this man might be.

"Are you a Mason?" she asked.

As the luck fell, he was.

"Do you promise me," she went on, "upon the word of a Mason, that when you arrive at Bear River Valley, you will return and bring out my children, if we shall not, in the meantime, meet their father going for them?"

"I thus do promise."

Then Mrs. Reed, Virginia, and Jimmy said their good-byes to Patty and Tommy. Little Tommy was too small to realize what was happening, but experience had already aged Patty far beyond her eight years, and her clear-eyed stoical acceptance of the situation was more moving than childish tears would have been.

"Well, mother," she said, "if you never see me again, do the best you can."

Even the hardy men of the rescue party were at the point of weeping when Glover and the indefatigable Moultry started back with the two children. On the way to the cabins Patty with her matter-of-fact, childish disillusion informed the two men that she was willing to go back and take care of her little brother but that she never expected to see her mother again.

At the cabins they had an ugly reception. The Breens at first absolutely refused to take in two more children to feed, and they would not even let them come into the cabin. Glover promised that another relief party would soon be on the way and that he could leave a little food for the children's support. So finally the Breens yielded, and received the children with a very ill grace.

Glover and Moultry got back to the others when a camp had been made for the night after a march of only about three miles. They carefully kept from Mrs. Reed the news of what reception Patty and Tommy had been accorded.

At the camp, since twenty-eight persons must be accommodated, the men were forced to build several platforms. Food was scarce, for the relief party was counting upon the caches which they had made on the way over. Until they should reach the first of these at the head of the Yuba, the allowance for each person was only one ounce of smoked beef and a spoonful of flour twice a day. On the first night some of the famished emigrants who were past all moral control, stole and ate the rawhide thongs from Ned Coffeemeyer's snow-shoes to the great disgust of that stalwart rescuer.

Next morning they began the ascent of the pass. On the march little Ada Keseberg gave out completely, and her mother was unable to carry her. Mrs. Keseberg frantically offered twenty-five dollars and a gold watch to any one who would carry Ada. The child was taken along, and the march progressed over the pass and approached the cache at the head of the Yuba. Some one finally noticed that poor John Denton was missing. Two men hurried back along the trail, and found him sleeping in the snow, deep in the coma which precedes death. They labored an hour at arousing him, and finally with the greatest difficulty urged him forward to camp.

Here they arrived only to find that disaster had preceded them. The bale which constituted the cache lay scattered about, and the provisions were devoured. Some animal had probably gnawed the thong by which the bundle of food was suspended, and once the pack lay upon the snow, had made short work of it. Some said it was a mountain-lion, some a fisher, some a marten; most likely the tracks of all three were to be seen. But no matter who the culprit, the relief party with its train of failing children was left without food four days' journey from the next cache, which also for all they knew might be plundered. It was a situation which might have justified the seven men in abandoning the greater number of the refugees and pushing ahead for their lives with only a child or two who could be carried and a few of the strongest boys who might stand the pace. But these seven had already been sifted; no cowards were left among them, and their courage only blazed up the brighter as it was tested. Was there not still rawhide to be eaten?

Next morning four of them set out to advance as rapidly as they could over the snow, reach the next cache and, if it still contained food, to bring it back to the emigrants. These four included Moultry and Coffeemeyer, two of the strongest, along with Glover and Daniel Rhoads who were weakening and had best be got out of the snow before they too became a burden on their companions. The four disappeared ahead, and left to Sels, John Rhoads, and Tucker the even harder task of helping along the train of weakening women and children, and of starving with them. The morning was cloudy and a storm seemed at hand; the wind blew from the west, hard in their faces.

When they had gone not more than a mile, Denton failed again. He was snow-blind as well as exhausted; this time he was through, and knew it. Like Stanton the American, Denton the Englishman died true to the best traditions of the common race. He did not whine or funk. He merely told the others that he could go no further, that they could be of no use to him, and had best press on to save themselves. He asked only that they should, if possible, send back relief to him. His heroism impressed the three who had tried to rescue him, for ill as it could be spared, they left with him nearly all the food which they had remaining. They built a fire for him and gathered a pile of wood. Tucker left his own quilt. In the end, wrapped warmly and seated by his own fire, Denton looked so comfortable that some of the others almost envied him, and little Jimmy Reed, tired of the freezing labor of the snow-trail, wanted to stay with Mr. Denton. Then they went ahead, leaving their comrade in the comfort which could have only one end.

Hungering, weak, and rapidly becoming frost-bitten, they labored on, and that day even with the down-grade to help them the most that they could make was eight miles. They camped probably at the same place where the seven had camped eight nights previously. The three rescuers built platforms and heaped wood on the fires, but during the night little Ada Keseberg died. Her mother had lost one baby already; now she was childless, and not to be consoled.

In the morning, still weaker, they went on. Of the hardships of the next forty-eight hours no one has left a detailed record. Twenty-two remained in the party, all told. John Rhoads still carried little Naomi Pike. Tucker and Sels shepherded the other children. The storm still held off. At night it froze hard; the days were sunny and warm. The going was best in the early morning; in fact then they made most of their distance, for the snow was frozen hard on top and they could walk on the crust. After the sun got up, the men started breaking through. The children (and this was something that no one had probably counted on) actually went along better than the men because their lighter weight enabled them to skid over places where the men floundered. On account of the wetness of the surface snow-shoes were a doubtful aid. The leaders had at least no fear of being lost, for they still followed the old trail through the snow, and they passed every now and then one of the charred pine trees left as markers.

When each morning the sun had softened the crust, the children began to have a hard time. Jimmy Reed, only five years old, had the worst of it. There was no one to carry him, and often his mother and sister were afraid that he could not keep going, and wondered what they would do if he failed. They encouraged him by saying that every step took him nearer his father. The men, too, jollied him along, telling him that they would buy him a horse in California and he would not have to walk any more.

In the afternoons they camped early, for the soft snow-surface wore them out and the men needed much time for the building of platforms. At night they ate a little toasted rawhide, and then huddled around the fires, their clothing wet from having dragged through the snow all day. At times in the mornings they found their clothes frozen stiff. Would they ever get through? Had the martens robbed the cache in Bear Valley? Would the others get there, and if they did, would they come back?

Eight miles was all that they could make in a day. They had left the cabins on Monday, and Friday afternoon found them, they thought, within a day's journey of Bear Valley. They halted and built their platforms. And there at last Moultry and Coffeemeyer struggled into camp with food in their packs. Those two men of iron had, practically without food, gone through the snow from the head of the Yuba to Bear Valley and eight miles back under packs in three days.

The two brought a little beef, enough to relieve the immediate need, but their news was not encouraging. They had found the cache in Bear Valley, but no second relief party was waiting for them there. Glover and Rhoads had gone ahead toward Mule Springs, two more days' journey, where at a time which must have seemed years before, they had built a brush hut and left supplies under guard of young Tucker and half-witted Billy Coon.

The children were giving out. Four of them had to be carried now, but nothing was left but to press ahead for Mule Springs. In the early morning they left camp on a hard crust. They strung out a long distance on the trail, but had made four miles when the leaders caught sight of something ahead, men winding in single file through the trees. It might be Indians, they thought for a moment. Then they knew it was another relief party! A quavering cry of "Bread! Bread!" went up from the straggled line of starving children.

As the leading men of the new relief party came struggling up through the snow, one spoke out, "Is Mrs. Reed with you?—Tell her Mr. Reed is here." Both Mrs. Reed and Virginia were close enough to hear. At the word, the wife, overcome by the sudden news, slumped down upon the snow. Virginia leapt forward, trying to run but tripping and falling in the snow from weakness. She struggled on, and then came to her father, who caught her in his arms.

"Your mother, my child, your mother!" he cried. "Where is *she?*"

Virginia pointed to where she lay upon the snow. This was the meeting that they had after months of separation, tortured by fear and uncertainty and by the memory of that blood-stained moment of parting by the Humboldt.

But it was still no perfect reunion; Patty and Tommy were starving beyond the pass. There was much to be done.

Reed had not been surprised at meeting the company, as they had been at meeting him, for he had passed Glover and Rhoads at the lower end of Bear Valley, and they had spurred him on. He had camped at the upper end of the valley, and spent most of the night baking bread in preparation, and even making some sweet cakes for the children. In the morning he had left much of his food in Bear Valley with a man to guard it, and had hastened on with nine others.

This was encouraging to the refugees, but what lay beyond was even more so. At Mule Springs they would find supplies and horses and there, if not sooner, they would meet Mr. Woodworth and old Caleb Greenwood with their men. Beyond Woodworth was Captain Kern who had moved up from the Fort to establish a relay camp. Beyond Kern was Johnson's ranch and beyond Johnson's was Sutter's where Sutter, Sinclair and McKinstry were forwarding supplies. Finally, beyond Sutter's was Yerba Buena where Alcalde Bartlett and Governor Hull were backing up the relief work with money and necessaries. There was something heart-moving in the way that California, war-harried and thinly peopled, had rallied to the cause of humanity. It was as if a strong chain were extending itself link by link across the mountains, finally to reach the camps and draw out the sufferers. The seven had merely gone ahead in the strength of their own stout bodies and stouter hearts, but the next relief would have the organized strength of many men behind it. . . .

But Reed hardly told much of this during the brief halt by the snow-trail. His men passed out small quantities of bread, and promised that more was waiting in Bear Valley. Then the two companies parted. The one was just commencing the dangerous part of the journey; the other was finishing it.

Before noon Billy Graves and some of the stronger refugees scrambled into the camp at Bear Valley. The others kept straggling in as they could, and it was night before all had arrived. Here at last they had enough food, and the problem was to keep them away from it. Young William Hook, Jacob Donner's step-son, ate too much and fell deathly sick. They made him swallow tobacco-juice so that he vomited and felt much better. But his fate pursued him. That night, uncontrollably ravenous, he sneaked out to the tree where provisions were stored, gorged himself, and when found in the morning was too far gone for tobacco-juice.

The others went ahead leaving him with a camp-keeper. Young William Murphy stayed also, for his feet had become so badly frost-bitten that they had swelled past the point of walking. Hook died quietly about ten o'clock. The two others carefully removed some food from his pockets, and then buried him just under the ground at a place where a fire had melted the snow away. The camp-keeper and young Murphy' then moved off for Mule Springs, the latter having decided that it was a case of walk or die and that of the two he preferred walking even with frost-bitten feet.

Two more days brought the refugees, now only eighteen in number, to Mule Springs. Here they found Woodworth encamped on bare ground, with snow lying about merely in patches. Green grass was growing and the pack-animals grazed upon it. Bare ground, green grass, and horses, the emaciated and frozen people regarded almost in the nature of miracles.

Woodworth himself they did not regard so favorably. When they arrived, they found that he had men rubbing his feet for fear they might be frost-bitten. In this there was something curiously effete to the eyes of people who had just come out of the real snow. In disgust Mrs. Reed remarked to Virginia, "We had better take care of him, reverse the order of things." A keg of fourth-proof brandy was also in evidence about camp, for the son of the author of "The Old Oaken Bucket" did not confine himself to the beverage celebrated in that song.

After resting for a night the refugees were supplied with horses and sent on. The sun shone warmly; every mile of road brought them to lower altitudes. In a few hours they passed from winter to spring. The road wound through pines and chapparal; bare ground, that wonderful thing, was all around them. Their weary bodies rested as the horses jogged along. And with the sudden let-down of tension the resiliency of human nature asserted itself, and life shifted from the tragic to the comic vein.

Mrs. Keseberg, a few days previous, had been a Rachel weeping for her children, not to be comforted. Now she was only a German woman speaking broken English and getting into funny sorts of trouble with her horse. There had not been a full supply of saddles and bridles; most of the refugees were riding with only one or the other, and Mrs. Keseberg had been given merely a saddle in the hope that her horse would follow along after the others. But the horse liked to pick up grass under trees and threatened to brush Mrs. Keseberg from the saddle; whereupon she called out: "Mrs. Reed, I will kill *mine self* before I get through!" It seemed very funny to Virginia Reed.

Even funnier was Virginia's own experience, for a gallant swain who attended the horses took the occasion to press a suit. He had never seen her before, but women were scarce in California, and he decided that he had better get a word in before some one else had a chance to snap Virginia up. She was only thirteen and was half starved, but time would correct both those faults, and he might at least get a promise, even if he had to wait a few years for its fulfillment. But to Virginia, being only thirteen and not greatly struck by her admirer, the proposal was only very funny, and although he kept returning she put him off with childish delight. Thus with warm sun and laughter the afternoon wore away.

Three days later, on March 4, they were at Sutter's. The refugees were distributed variously, but the Reeds, as became their aristocracy, were taken in by Alcalde Sinclair. Kind little Mrs. Sinclair, she who had forwarded underwear to the women of the snow-shoe party, did everything she could to make them comfortable.

And they were comfortable for a day; then the long-deferred storm broke at last. The Sinclairs did their best to supply hopeful thoughts, but Mrs. Reed knew too much to be deceived. If it was rain in the valley, it would be snow higher up. She did not sleep at night. She stood for hours, it seemed, in the doorway looking out toward the mountains.

Strangely enough, her husband four months before had stood at almost the same place looking out in the same direction and questioning as she was now—what was happening out of sight behind the veil of rain and beyond the line of the foothills.

23. REED TRIES AGAIN

BY this time twenty-six of the Donner Party were safely across the mountains. Of the others twenty-eight were dead; and two, Reed and McCutchen, pushed on a second time through the snow for the rescue of the thirty-one who still starved in the mountain camps.

Reed, who had turned up a day's journey beyond Bear Valley so unexpectedly and providentially with bread for the starving, had not got even as far as that without hardship and struggle. The three weeks which had passed between his departure from Yerba Buena on February 7 and his meeting with the refugees on February 27 had been filled with action. He had crossed the bay by boat along with old Greenwood, and then hurried on through Sonoma and Napa picking up contributions in money, horses, and recruits along the way. He had rejoined his old comrade, big McCutchen. Then with forty horses and a dozen men he had ridden hard through the hills for Gordon's ranch in the Sacramento Valley. The trails were rugged and muddy; the streams rushed bank-full; beyond Gordon's the tule-lands were under water. He added peril of drowning to the many he had endured in the last half-year. Thirst, hunger, lynching, freezing, war, flood—he had known them all.

But it took time to get across the hills and through the floods. The middle of the month had passed when the muddy *caballada* splashed into Hardy's ranch where Feather River flowed into the Sacramento. There they expected to find Woodworth with the schooner to ferry them across, but to every one's disgust Woodworth was not yet there. Here was a pickle! In front a great river (and even in summer the Sacramento was no trout stream) swirled by at flood-height, and Woodworth who should have been here to ferry them across and furnish supplies for the expedition was taking his time somewhere.

But trust an old trapper like Greenwood to know a trick for that. His men scattered back from the river, shot some elk, flayed them, and made ready the skins to build a "bull-boat" for the crossing. Next morning, however, a little schooner owned by Perry McCoon, one of the Americans at Sutter's, appeared in the river, and on it Reed and McCutchen joyfully ferried over with their horses. Leaving word for the others to follow, the two galloped for Johnson's, arriving there while it was still early in the day.

Johnson drove up a herd of cattle; Reed and McCutchen shot down five and soon had the meat drying. Johnson's Indians were set to work grinding wheat in a handmill. By morning they had two hundred pounds of flour, together with plenty of jerked beef, and when Greenwood and his men arrived everything was ready for the start. They left word for Woodworth to hurry on, and rode for the mountains. It was February 22, by coincidence the same day on which the relief party started back from the camp by the lake.

Reed had better luck than Glover, for the streams had fallen and the snow receded. In three days he and his men camped at Mule Springs where they left some supplies with Greenwood and some others to watch them. The old man, for all his high talk in Yerba Buena, had decided not to try the snow; the infection in his eyes might well bring on snow-blindness.

Next day Reed and the others went ahead on foot, forcing along eleven lightly loaded pack animals through the snow. The day after, they had to send back the animals—so much for Greenwood's plan of driving them all the way to the lake! They settled down glumly to the work of floundering on through the snow under heavy packs. That night they made the upper end of Bear Valley, passing Glover and Rhoads on the way. Next morning they met the relief party with the refugees struggling along the snow-trail. . . .

From this point their really difficult and dangerous work commenced. They numbered ten in all, a picked lot, much superior, any one would have said, to Glover's seven. First of all was Reed; his hardihood was beyond question, and he was whipped on by the thought of his two children waiting for him by the lake. Another man, Hiram Miller, was a staunch fellow and an old friend of Reed's from Springfield. Then there was big McCutchen, a giant in strength; he had no hopes, for his wife had come out with the snow-shoers, and he knew now that his child had died. But his honor still required that he should do as much as he could for those who had shared their food with his family.

The other seven seem to have been Greenwood's recruits, not farmers or emigrants, but trappers, hunters, and mountain-men. The chief among them was none less than John Turner who had been with Jed Smith on that famous first overland journey to California in '26. He was as good an exemplar as might be found of that famous breed, the mountain-man of the twenties and thirties. He loomed up a man of immense frame and muscular power, and as for his swearing —well, as Edwin Bryant remarked, "I had heard mountain swearing before, but this went far beyond former examples. He could do all the swearing for our army in Mexico and then have a surplus." With Turner and McCutchen together the second relief might almost have melted the snow ahead of it by mere heat of language.

The other trappers in the party were able seconds to Turner. As usual, some were of the French breed, with probably an Indian cross, such as Gendreau whose name usually got into writing as Jondro. Dofar also was French. "Brit" Greenwood was the half-breed son of old Greenwood by his Crow squaw. Nicholas Clark seems to have been associated with the trappers, although he had deserted from a ship at Yerba Buena a few years previous. With Cady and Stone he formed a trio of hardy young men (Reed called them "the boys") who overflowed with the surplus energy of youth.

With such a group of real frontiersmen piloted by Turner the second relief had every chance for a speedier and more successful journey than that of Glover and his men. They had moreover several other advantages. They were off to a good start, and were not at the very beginning drenched, half frozen, and worn down by lack of sleep. They had the advantage of traveling over snow consolidated by a fortnight of fair weather. They had moreover a trail beaten down, and camps located and left partially in readiness by the preceding party. Most of all they had the heartening confidence that they were not entirely on their own, that Woodworth was close behind ready to stretch out a hand on their return, or to relieve them if they fell into difficulties. They were under only one disadvantage: that after such a long period of fair weather the rhythm of nature might be expected to reassert itself in a storm.

With all their advantages they pushed ahead rapidly. Thoughts of Patty and Tommy spurred Reed on, and he set the pace. The others had all that they could do to keep up with him. Some miles beyond where they had met the refugees they cached some food. Warned by the robbing of the other cache, the trappers used another device. One of them climbed to the top of a small pine tree, secured the provisions there, and then as he descended cut off smoothly all the branches so that an animal could not ascend.

As the afternoon advanced, the snow grew softer under the heat of the sun, and progress became more difficult. They camped along Yuba Bottoms, probably at the same place where the other relief party had already twice spent a night.

They made scarcely more than a halt, for at midnight they pressed on. Turner did not fear losing his way in the darkness, and hoped to get the advantage of the hard-frozen crust. A stretch of soft snow forced them to halt again from two to four, but after that time they went on rapidly in the bitter cold of early morning across a hard-frozen surface. They camped early as the snow again grew soft, but during the night and morning had covered as much ground as the first relief under worse weather conditions had labored over in two and a half days. They estimated the snow where they camped as being thirty feet deep. Somewhere they made a second cache.

As soon as the snow began to harden again the next night, the three "boys," Cady, Clark and Stone, set out to push ahead as an advance party. They became confused as to the route and even considered turning back, but were suddenly put at rest by discovering a sure sign-post. Sitting against a snow-bank, head bowed upon breast, was the body of poor John Denton as he had been left four days previous. Being thus assured, the three went ahead rapidly over the pass and came to within two miles of the cabins. At that point they saw ten Indians, and at once supposed that these might have killed the helpless people at the cabins. They themselves were without arms, and accordingly they went into hiding and spent the rest of the night fireless.

In the morning they advanced cautiously, and soon saw—so great had been the melting in the last ten days—the top of a cabin just sticking out of the snow. The three paused long enough to distribute a little food, and then Clark and Cady pressed on to the Donner tents where they had reason to believe that need was even more urgent. About noon, it was March 1, the rest of the party arrived at the lake cabins.

The first sight which greeted Reed was his little daughter Patty sitting upon the corner of the cabin roof with her feet upon the snow. She sprang to meet him, but fell in her weakness. Raising her in his arms, the father asked fearfully of Tommy, but Patty, sobbing, told him that Tommy was inside sleeping. Reed descended through the snow-hole to the cabin, and found the boy a mere skeleton. On being aroused, the child could not at first recognize his father, but asked time and again of Patty, whom he had come to regard as a mother, if this really were his father.

In the Breen cabin, where his children were, Reed found conditions not so bad as might have been feared, but at the Murphy cabin conditions passed the limits of description and almost of imagination. In the noisome huddle of filth and unspeakable things deep below the surface of the snow, Keseberg lay almost helpless. Old Mrs. Murphy was even worse; she had become childish, and laughed and wept by turns. Her boy Simon was old enough to take care of himself a little, but the two small children, the sons of Eddy and Foster, lay helplessly in bed crying weakly and incessantly for food. Reed and McCutchen on their arrival at the cabin found Stone, the rough frontiersman, busily engaged in the domestic task of washing out some of the children's clothes. The condition of the two little boys was past telling, for they had lain in bed for days, unwashed and unchanged. Al-

though Stone had already given them something, Reed was so
moved that he even risked their lives by giving them more.

Then he and McCutchen warmed water and began a
clean-up. First they took off their own clothes and laid them
on the snow outside to avoid danger of infection with the
vermin which now swarmed in the cabin. They then took
up the children, soaped, washed, and oiled them, and wrap-
ping them in flannel returned them to bed in a fairly comfortable state. Afterwards the two comrades washed Keseberg, the man who had once raised up his wagon-tongue for
Reed's hanging. The irony of the situation was not lost upon
the German, and unnerved he even pled that some one other
than Reed should wash him. Such a returning of good for
evil was more, he said, than he could bear.

As they worked, Reed and McCutchen could not remain
insensible to what had recently been happening in the cabin.
Only a week had passed since the departure of the first relief party. No one had died at the lake cabins, and yet (so
close was the contest between starvation and rescue) that
brief period had seen the bitter struggle for existence pass to
another stage. Perhaps the feeling that relief was so close
at hand had made life seem at once dearer and more precarious. A certain tone of desperation seems to run through
the last entries of Breen's diary.

On the day following the departure of Glover's party, he
had at last shot his dog Towser, and dressed the flesh. Mrs.
Graves had come after the sound of the shot to beg meat,
and had been refused. Then at nights they began to hear
a grim sound of howling. The wolves came up close to the
cabins now, sniffing about and digging in the snow after
the bodies of the dead. The wolves themselves might have
been eaten, but none of the starving people dared risk freezing to death in the bitter nights to get a shot at them.

Ever hopeful, Breen recorded a few signs of spring. The
snow was melting and consolidating in the long spell of sunny
weather; the level of the surface had fallen by five feet. And
he had heard wild geese honking overhead at night.

Then one day he was amazed to see a solitary Indian walking along from the direction of the lake, carrying a heavy
pack. He seemed not to feel the slightest curiosity, but as he
caught sight of the white man merely gave a sign for him
to keep distance. Then he took from the pack half a dozen

fibrous roots, laid them on the snow, and went on his way. When he had gone as mysteriously as he had come, Breen went up and took the roots. They were shaped like onions, and tasted to him somewhat like a sweet potato, but full of tough little fibers.

The entry of February 26 was the only indication of the final crisis:

Mrs. Murphy said here yesterday that [she] thought she would commence on Milt. & eat him. I dont think that she has done so yet, it is distressing.

Only three days later, as Reed and McCutchen labored in the Murphy cabin, they saw lying at the door the mutilated body of the faithful Milt. The head and face were untouched, but elsewhere most of the flesh had been torn away. Bones and half-consumed parts were in the cabin. Tufts of human hair, of different colors, lay about the fireplace.

Breen recorded nothing of this in his diary. He seldom left his own cabin, and most likely after her visit of the twenty-fifth Mrs. Murphy never ventured to attempt the two hundred yards of snow which separated her from the Breens.

The entry for March 1 was the diarist's last. He felt apparently that he was going to survive, could tell his own story, and so need not bother to record it.

Mond. March the 1st To fine & pleasant froze hard last night there has 10 men arrived this morning from Bear Valley with provisions we are to start in two or three days & cash our goods here there is amongst them some old [mountaineers?] they say the snow will be here untill June.

Two pages of the crude little homemade notebook are blank; then a blot, and the word *Journal* scrawled on the last page.

24. REED VISITS THE DONNERS

THAT night the relief party camped upon the snow, preferring the cold to the vermin and stench of the buried cabins.

Next day was Tuesday, March 2. Four of the men remained at the lake to make preparations for the return, but Reed with three others went on to the Donner tents along the tracks left by Cady and Stone.

The story which the two "boys" told and the sights which Reed and his comrades saw with their own eyes go far in horror and yet rouse admiration at the grim courage and clear-eyed determination with which gentle-hearted people like the Donners sacrificed their own most deeply grounded conventions and violated the final taboo of society, to save their children.

As Cady and Clark told their story, they had on approaching the tents first caught sight of Jean Baptiste carrying across the snow the leg of a man cut off at the thigh. He had been sent from the George Donners to "borrow" (the housewife's word) this supply of food which was in some sense the property of the other family. It had been granted, but with the word that nothing more could be given to them.

On seeing the two rescuers approaching, Jean Baptiste threw back the leg into a hole in the snow where lay what was left of the body of Jacob Donner. The head was cut off, but was preserved by the cold, the features unaltered. The arms and legs had been removed, the trunk cut open, and the heart and liver taken out.

Cady and Clark pressed on toward the Jacob Donners' tent, and came next to some of the children seated upon a log. So far had starvation sunk the little ones into apathy that they paid no attention to the men as they approached or even when they stood close by. The two men gazed upon the children sitting upon the log, their chins and breasts smeared bloodily as they innocently tore and ate the half-roasted heart and liver.

By the time of Reed's arrival Cady and Clark had distributed food, but otherwise had effected little change. The tent of the Jacob Donners stood huddled among the snow-banks. Around the fire were bits of human hair, many bones, and half-consumed fragments of limbs. Within the tent lay Elizabeth Donner already far gone. For the sake of her children's preservation she had allowed them to eat the only food which remained. For herself she declared that she would die before she ate of her own husband's body, and she was already close to making good her word.

With her were her four youngest children, all under eight, and her older boy, Solomon Hook. This last youngster of fourteen had once tried to escape across the snow by himself, but had been forced back, snow-blind and demented. At times he was difficult to control and for this reason Jean Baptiste was living in the tent along with the family.

Reed's first move was to relocate the tent and to make every one as comfortable as possible. He and his comrades, half-sickened, then withdrew into the snow to escape for a moment from the sights which they had been forced to witness, but by bad luck they stumbled right upon the four open graves. Reed gazed again upon the features of Jacob Donner. The severed head of the old man still lay there, the bearded face upwards. In the other graves nothing remained but a few fragments.

Reed then went on to the tent of the George Donners. There he found Tamsen Donner still healthy and apparently strong. Her three little daughters, the oldest only six, still survived. There also Reed saw again his old friend, kind-hearted "Uncle George."

Only a year ago they had both been in safe and settled Springfield, planning their trip to California. They had last met when Reed, a fugitive, had ridden into the Donners' camp on the Humboldt. Since that day Reed's life had been tense with action; there would have been much which he would have liked to tell his friend.

But as George Donner lay there, emaciated and prostrate, he on his side could have had little to tell except of grim endurance. His wounded hand had made him a cripple all through the winter, and now the infection was eating fever-ishly far up toward his shoulder. He and the family had eaten whatever they could—meat and tallow, hides, bones, mice. They had had other troubles also as the winter deepened. Daily they had to fight cold and dampness. Once the children had been in wet clothes for two weeks; in the colder weather they stayed in bed most of the time. Yet in some way they had lived through. Then when they had been down to the last hide, the first relief had got through. It had brought little food, only a mouthful, and once that was gone they had been forced to the last extremity.

Still, since the first relief, things had been a little better in some ways. There was hope again. And when people themselves were decent, conditions could never be entirely bad. Aunt Betsy and Tamsen were good women. They helped each other, visited back and forth when they could, and prayed together.

Jean Baptiste? Well, he had been surly after the relief had left him behind, but after a talking to and some promises for the future, he had settled down. He was a tough little fellow, kept his strength for cutting wood, and was kind to the children. He took them up on the snow for exercise and air. He had a big Navajo blanket brought all the way from New Mexico. When the weather was coldest he would lay it on the snow, then put a child at each end and roll them up until they met in the middle and lay there like two papooses. Then he propped them against a stump and let them watch while he worked cutting branches off the big tree which the men of the first relief had felled for him.

On good days after Tamsen had dressed her husband's wound and he had fallen asleep, she would go up to the snow and sit by the children. Sometimes she brought her diary and wrote; sometimes she sketched the mountains all covered with snow and the pine-trees sticking up out of it. Sometimes she told the children stories—of Joseph, and Daniel, and Elijah, and of little Samuel who said, "Speak, Lord, for thy servant heareth." And she taught them to say by rote that they were the children of Mr. and Mrs. George Donner. This was just in case—well, in case things didn't turn out as well as they might.

And thus the last week had worn through. Now it was March, and the snow was sinking. The sun was warm again, high in the south. Wild geese went honking northward. There was even hope of food, for Tamsen had seen bear tracks. But it would all make very little difference probably for George Donner. The arm and shoulder were bad; death's mark was on him.

But there was much to be done these few hours while Reed was with them. Most of all, they must decide who was to go back with him. Reed would leave Cady and Clark to take care of those who stayed, and Jean Baptiste, now that the danger was over and Woodworth was expected any day, was willing enough to remain too. George Donner and Elizabeth could not cross the snow; that was certain. Tamsen was strong enough, but she would not leave her husband even with Cady and Clark to care for him. Reed urged her to go, but she refused. As for the younger children, it seemed best to let them all remain for a few days until Woodworth with his larger party should arrive. So only "Sol" Hook, and Mary and Isaac Donner, all from the Jacob Donner tent and all big enough to walk for themselves, started back with Reed that afternoon.

Cady and Clark remained to care for the camp and its nine survivors. They had food enough for a week, and before that time was up, Woodworth would have got through to them.

25. AT THE HEAD OF THE YUBA

WHEN Reed with his companions and the three children arrived again at the lake that same day, he found preparations well along for the departure. During the day McCutchen, Turner and Brit Greenwood had cached some of the emigrants' goods so that they could be found and brought out in the summer. After all, they represented everything that the poor refugees possessed in the world, and so even in the face of death were not to be lightly left behind to the mercy of thieving Indians and spring freshets.

McCutchen had a good story of Mrs. Graves. She had them remove an innocent-looking cleat from the bottom of a wagon-bed. This cleat had been nailed there as if to support the extra weight of a table carried in the rear of the wagon, but on being taken off it was found to have auger-holes bored part way through it. In these holes the Graveses had piled coins to the amount of several hundred dollars.

Besides this money Mrs. Graves decided to take along a violin, an object of considerable value on the frontier. This had belonged to her son-in-law Jay Fosdick, whose death, along with the other gruesome details of the snow-shoers' escape, had been so carefully concealed by the relief parties.

Reed had hoped for an early start in the morning, but there was no hurrying the emaciated refugees. Every one in the camp who could possibly move or be carried was to go. This meant besides Reed's own children all the Breens and Graveses who had not already escaped. With the addition of the three children from the other camp they totaled seventeen. Only three were adults—Patrick Breen, his wife Peggy, and Mrs. Graves. Of the children, two were boys of fourteen and the rest ranged from eleven down to infancy. Mrs. Graves had her Elizabeth, only about a year old, and Mrs. Breen carried little Isabella of the same age.

At the camp all the cabins were left deserted except the one which Eddy and Foster had built against the great rock; in it were left Keseberg, old Mrs. Murphy, her boy Simon, and the two little waifs, James Eddy and George Foster. Stone of the relief party remained to care for them. The story of the camp by the lake seemed to be almost at an end; only five of the Donner Party remained there to await Woodworth's arrival.

At midday on March 3, ten days after the departure of the previous party, they finally left the cabins. The refugees were extremely weak and many of the children had to be carried or helped along constantly. The straggling line reached the frozen lake, and struck out across its smooth white surface. The snow was hard enough, but the rate of advance was painfully slow. Reed must soon have begun to doubt whether he had not attempted too much in burdening his men with so many children who were unable to get along by themselves. But it must be all right, for they would soon be meeting Woodworth; already it was high time that his men should appear, black specks on the white wall of the pass ahead. But in any case there was no prodding these people along any faster. It was not only their bodies; their minds as well seemed to have lost all vigor. They could not be made even to realize that there was any reason why they should try to hurry.

The plan had probably been to do as the first relief had

done, that is, to camp at the end of the lake and scale the pass in the morning. But progress was so slow that by evening they were only halfway along the lake, and had to come in from the ice and made a camp among the trees back from its margin. Experience or perhaps the old-time knowledge of the mountain-men had taught them how to spend the nights more comfortably than Glover's party had been able to do. Now they made a foundation for the fire by cutting two pairs of green logs, laying them upon the snow in the shape of a cross, and building the fire at their intersection. In the angles between the arms of the cross they spread pine-branches upon the snow, so that every one could lie down and with the heat of the fire even rest in some degree of comfort.

The behavior of the refugees during this first evening seemed to indicate that they hardly realized themselves still under the shadow of death. They were in fine spirits and joked heartily. Breen took the violin, and played gayly upon it for two hours. In the morning, continuing the spirit of pleasantry, some of the men of the relief party began to joke about Mrs. Graves's money, which one of them was carrying. How about a game of euchre to see which of them should keep it? Mrs. Graves took the matter seriously and became alarmed. She got her money back, and remaining behind after the others had left camp, she concealed it to her own satisfaction.

The second day was the same as the first. They straggled across the surface of the lake again, made a few miles, and encamped at the foot of the pass. Again the strains of the violin sounded over the snowy solitudes. To the men of the relief party it must have been a little irritating. Why couldn't Breen put some more energy into helping push the children along, and not scrape so much on that damned fiddle? Reed was getting nervous. This good weather had lasted nearly a month now, and it wouldn't last forever. Clouds were starting to pile up over the pass, and the wind was blowing. Food was getting low, for he had left at the camps every ounce he could. All that remained now was rations for a day and a half, and it was a long way ahead, fifteen miles he supposed, to the nearest cache.

Next morning he decided that, Woodworth or no Woodworth, something must be done. He called Turner, Dofar,

and Gendreau, good mountaineers all, and told them to go
ahead to the next cache and send one man back with food.
The other two, or all three, if that first cache had been
robbed, should push on to the next cache. If they met Woodworth anywhere, they should join him, but in any case they
should make all haste that they could with provisions. The
three men had to be sent ahead with absolutely no food for
themselves.

Step by step what had been a carefully planned expedition
of relief was degenerating into a precarious and desperate
adventure. Something had happened somewhere. Some link
in the chain had snapped. Where was Woodworth? They
would soon be as badly off as Glover and his men—worse
off, if that wind kept on blowing from the south. They were
almost out of food now, and they were still in sight of the
lake.

That morning they must scale the pass. The three mountain-men went ahead; strong and unencumbered they worked
up over the great snow-banks on the heights and disappeared.
Far behind, scarcely seeming to move, the others toiled along
foot by foot. Only four really able-bodied men remained to
prod and carry the seventeen refugees across the pass. This
day they would have to make the full distance, for the treeless, wind-swept summit offered no camping places. It was a
killing struggle, but probably the refugees realized at last that
it was cross or die, and so labored more for themselves than
they had on the two preceding days. They had enough to
spur them on, for the clouds hung heavy. About noon they
reached the summit, and by three o'clock they arrived at
the "head of the Yuba" where the men of the first relief had
already twice made a camp. The spot was a bleak one among
the trees just to the north of an open valley which let the
wind have a clear sweep. Nevertheless piles of wood and the
remains of platforms made this the easiest place to camp.
Soon the cross of logs was cut and placed, the pine-branches
spread, and the fire kindled.

The short afternoon wore away, but as they looked westward along the snow trail, no man came back bearing food.
Turner, Dofar, and Gendreau, strong men and skilled in mountain ways—surely Turner at least, that giant for strength,
could have made the fifteen miles ahead to the cache and
the five miles back in one day. Had the cache been robbed?

Or had the three mountain-men, seeing the clouds piling up from the south and knowing what that meant, merely gone ahead on their own? These were chilling questions for a man to ask himself as he sat watching the fire burn on the cross of logs, while the children huddled upon their boughs, and the wind blew coldly from the open sweep of the snow-covered valley, and the darkness of the winter evening deepened among the pine-trees.

That night the storm broke.

Winter had still a twist left to its tail. First came a fierce wind with snow, as it seemed, in torrents. With the night and the clouds and the thick-driving snow, the darkness shut down like a solid wall. And it was cold—an icy, bitter cold made all the more cutting by the gale and the hard-blown snow, the merciless cold of an elevation of seven thousand feet.

From the children shivering beneath their poor blankets rose a steady wailing, and from the older refugees a mingled sound of praying, weeping, and lamentation. The four men of the relief party, already worn down by a hard day's march, had to labor almost continuously. They stuck pine-branches into the snow upon the windward side of the camp, and the snow drifting up behind these made a rude wind-break. The fire took constant labor. It had to be kept blazing high, or else the people might have frozen where they lay, and the higher it blazed the faster it consumed wood. From the heat and the falling embers the snow rapidly melted out from beneath the cross, and the logs themselves tended to shift, with the danger of throwing the whole fire into the snow and extinguishing it. By the same process the logs themselves were gradually sinking lower and lower into a hole in the snow.

Hourly the wind seemed to blow harder; the driving snow fairly cut the face. The constant labor in the cold wore the men down. At intervals the flying snow-particles actually blinded them. Once Reed could not even see where the fire was or tell whether it was burning.

Morning brought no improvement. The cold, the wind, and the snow continued. Even the darkness was scarcely relieved, for in the storm the men could not see more than twenty feet to windward. Reed divided what was left of the food—only a spoonful of flour for each person. The children cried dismally, and kept saying they were hungry. The older people were more afraid of freezing. Brit Greenwood, the half-breed, began to funk, and joined Patrick Breen at praying. Reed, Miller, and McCutchen worked heroically. The wind was so cold, and they were so exhausted now, that when they went away from the fire to cut wood, they could not stay more than ten minutes without returning to warm themselves.

Reed had been keeping a diary during his expedition, and toward the end of this terrible day, crouched somewhere beneath the snow-wall he made his entry for March 6. He must have written in the spirit of the shipwrecked seaman who commits his last words to a corked bottle; death was very close, and with that sense of the importance of the final moment which the imminence of the end brings to most people he recorded the details of the last twenty-four hours. As a courageous and self-contained man he allowed himself only one expression of his emotions, the simple statement— "I dread the coming night." At the end, perhaps with the feeling that it might be the last entry, he wrote ominously: "Night closing fast, and with it the hurricane increases."

The next few hours justified his fears. Reed himself, apparently, had the first watch while the others rested. But the labor of the fire was too much for him. He became exhausted and was again blinded; the cold chilled him through, and he sank into a deathly coma. The untended fire died down. Drifting snow began to sift over the whole party. The continual pelting of the flakes told against the fire, and besides, snow now and then slid from the overhanging branches. Then the foundation logs shifted, and embers hissed in the pool of snow-water beneath. The camp lay in ominous quiet.

It could not have been more than a few minutes before the cold awakened some of the sleepers, and suddenly confusion succeeded to the treacherous stillness. The children wailed all together. The women wept or prayed. Breen prayed, and the demoralized Greenwood joined with him. Reed lay helpless. Only Miller and McCutchen sprang into action.

And even Miller was in bad shape. His hands were so frozen that as he seized an ax to cut some kindling the skin split open upon his fingers. But the gigantic McCutchen labored furiously, at the same time sparing some breath to curse the scared half-breed who prayed womanishly when he should be carrying wood. It was nip and tuck with the fire to save the remaining embers in the teeth of the storm. The frantic refugees were even a hindrance. Mrs. Breen had suddenly become an enraged Irish virago. With a torrent of cries upon the saints and the "Vargin" she overwhelmed the desperate men working at the embers and piling up dry sticks. They were getting three dollars a day, she shrieked above the storm, and was it just to "murther" people?—her children were freezing, or fallen into the fire-pit, or dead. She raged on until McCutchen finally loosed a salvo of oaths against her, ordering her out of the way.

But Miller and McCutchen conquered, and the cheering flame again began to stab upward into the night. It was time, for most of the children could not long have existed in the cold. Then the two men dragged Reed to the fire, chafed his hands and feet, and labored until finally they brought him back to consciousness and some degree of activity. McCutchen himself was so chilled that as he sat by the fire he gradually charred through the four shirts that he was wearing, and did not know that he was getting warm until he felt the scorching of his skin.

The crackle and glowing warmth of the blazing logs brought back hope. The children drew up close, talking in little ejaculations of pleasure: "I'm glad we've got some fire! . . . Oh, how good it feels! . . . It's good our fire didn't go out!"

Morning came at last, and the storm continued. The force of the wind even increased. Overhead, the great pines swayed; their branches lashed about, until Reed feared that the trees might be blown down upon the poor people crouching around the fire. Nevertheless the horrors of that second night were not quite equaled again. The men kept the fire going steadily, and there was no longer any immediate fear of freezing to death. But every one was getting weaker from starvation and exhaustion.

On the morning after the third night of storm they found that little Isaac Donner was dead. He had passed away sometime during the night as he lay between Patty Reed and his sister Mary, and had gone so quietly that neither of them realized until morning that anything had happened to him. His sister was in little better condition, for her feet were frozen and had become insensible; during the night she had lain too close to the fire so that one of her feet had become badly burned without her knowing it.

Finally about noon of this third day, March 8, the storm ceased. Most of the party had now been without food for more than twenty-four hours. The only thing to be done was for those who could to press on, and for those who could not to remain where they were upon whatever chance there was of being rescued by Woodworth or by some one else.

The four men of the relief party, although badly worn down, were still able to travel. Miller was now in better condition than McCutchen, and he undertook to carry Tommy Reed. Heroic little Patty refused to let her exhausted father carry her, and pluckily decided that she could walk for herself. Solomon Hook also felt strong enough to attempt the march. In spite of her burned foot Mary Donner also decided to try, for to stay behind seemed merely to accept death. Mrs. Graves and her children were too weak, but Breen and his family in the judgment of both Reed and McCutchen were able to make the attempt. Mentally, however, they were too far gone. When urged to move, Breen merely replied that he would rather die in camp than upon the way. Reed remonstrated and argued, saying that they should all stick together as long as they could, and at least die in the act of attempting to save themselves. Finally Reed called his men together, told them to witness what Breen was saying, and solemnly declared that if the children died, their blood would be upon Breen's own head. To rely on Woodworth any longer, he said "was leaning upon a broken stick."

The relief party piled up three days' supply of fuel. They had no food to leave. Probably unknown to the rest, however, Mrs. Breen still kept a few seeds which she had somewhere collected, a little tea, and about a pound of a sugar-loaf. This sense of their own resources may have had something to do with the Breens' willingness to stay by themselves instead of going on with the others. The fire had now melted out a great hole. On the sides of this pit and around its edge, actually above the fire, the seven Breens and five Graveses remained, and the others set out across the snow. Those who were attempting to go ahead had absolutely no food except for about a spoonful of crumbs which Reed had procured by scraping the seams of the food-bags. It was so small an amount that he carried it in the thumb of his woolen mitten. To call it a supply of food or to attempt to dole it out seemed foolish, and he hoarded it for some emergency or perhaps to avoid the feeling of being absolutely without resources, just as a man down-and-out on the city streets hoards his last nickel.

Mary Donner with her burned foot soon fell helpless in the snow; she was brought back and left again by the fire. The four men and three children continued. They were starving. The new-fallen snow was so light that at each step they sank deep. Moreover, extremely cold weather had as usual followed the storm, so that they rapidly became frost-bitten.

Little Patty was the weakest, but she steadily refused to allow her father to carry her. Finally, however, her physical exhaustion grew too much, and she became the prey of hallucination. Thoughts of death and heaven had for months been part of the precocious child's daily life. Now her subconscious mind suddenly asserted itself, and she cried out happily to her father that she saw a beautiful sight of stars and angels. Every one realized that Patty was at the point of death, and they gathered round to do what they could for the gallant child whose example had already, in their extremity, led them on. They wrapped her in a blanket, and chafed her hands and feet. Her father, taking the last pitiful treasure of crumbs from his mitten-thumb, warmed and moistened them between his own lips, and then pressed them into the child's mouth. Gradually she revived from the death-like and treacherously pleasant sleep into which she had fallen; her first thoughts were only regrets at having left behind the comforting dream of the stars and angels.

Then Reed keeping her still wrapped in the blanket carried her forward on his back where the heat from his own body kept her revived. She was still dangerously close to death, but her spirit had revived, and throughout the rest of the short afternoon while the starving, grim-faced men gritted their teeth and plunged on yard by yard, the child's confident courage and faith bore them up and heartened them. As big McCutchen said, with an oath to make it stronger, Patty was surely an angel on earth.

Somewhere along the Yuba they made camp. Most of the men found that their toes had lost all sensation, and knowing this sign of frost-bite they thrust their feet into the snow to let them thaw out. It was a dismal camp. They were still without food. They had no confidence that they could make the distance which lay ahead of them through the snow. They had no real hope of being saved except by their own exertions. Turner, Dofar, and Gendreau had perhaps found the caches robbed, or perhaps those three had themselves been overtaken in the storm without a fire, and frozen stiff. Even old mountain-men sometimes were caught. As for Woodworth—their state of mind about him had got to the point of best being expressed by spitting into the fire. They had looked for him too long already.

26. CADY AND STONE

REED and his men were not the only ones who during the last few days had looked in vain for Woodworth. During that time while the relief party had labored over the pass and endured the storm, the few emigrants remaining at the lake and by the creek had waited also, clinging on grimly to existence. But a new and disturbing factor had entered into the life of those at the camps.

Upon his departure Reed had left Stone at the lake, and Cady and Clark at the Donner tents. They were willing to remain ostensibly to care for the emigrants, but on second thought one begins to wonder why as many as three had to stay. Jean Baptiste was still with the Donners, and surely he along with one other man could have cared for that camp, and thus left another man free, instead of eating up the slight supply of food, to carry a child across the snow. But we must remember that the Donners were known to be wealthy, and the events of the next few days leave the impression that some of the men of Reed's party crossed not so much for love of humanity as in the hope that they might find some pickings.

The very first happening raises suspicion. Almost as soon as Reed was well away from the lake camp, so soon indeed as to suggest a preconceived plan, Stone deserted his post there, and with no valid reason that one can imagine struck out across the snow for the Donner tents. Arriving there, he found that Clark had been gone since morning on the track of a bear. It was a black bear, a she with her cub. On the preceding day he had sighted them, and had put a shot into the old one, but she had got away. Now he was out following the blood-trail. If he could get another shot, it would mean food in camp. So much the better that he was away, Stone may have considered, for one possible competitor was thus removed.

Mystery, naturally enough, veils just what happened next, but certainly Stone joined Cady and the two of them talked with Tamsen Donner. Perhaps the men bargained with her or threatened; perhaps she merely pled with them to rescue her children. In the end she seems to have offered them five hundred dollars to take Frances, Georgia, and little Eliza, and deliver them to their older half-sisters at Sutter's Fort. She must have paid the money in cash, for she had no way of arranging credit. She added, to send along with the children, a few keepsakes and other light articles, such as some silver spoons, which, as the little girls noticed, the men seemed willing enough to add to the weight of their packs.

The mother combed the children's hair, a loving last touch. Then she dressed them for the journey. There might be no food in camp, but still the children of George Donner would not go off to face the world as ragamuffins. They had quilted petticoats, and linsey dresses, and woolen stockings. The two smaller girls had cloaks of a fine garnet-red, twilled, with a white thread interwoven. And like little girls of a fairy story they had red hoods, of knitted stuff, to match. Frances had a warm shawl instead of a cloak, and her hood was blue.

Then the mother brought the three little ones to the bed where their father lay helpless, and they said good-by to him. The two men led them up the steps to the top of the snow. The mother came, and bundled them in their cloaks and hoods. She spoke; it seemed to the children as if she were talking to herself, as she said good-by and entrusted them to God.

They were small to face the snow-trail. Frances was under seven; Georgia was five; Eliza was a mere tot, lacking a week of being four. The two younger ones soon had to be carried. They had traveled only a little way when the men stopped, laid a blanket on the snow, and set the children down upon it. Then Cady and Stone went a little distance ahead. They stopped, still within view, and talked together. The children sat watching, tiny spots of red and blue in the great whiteness of the winter forest. Their little faces pinched with starvation peered out, big-eyed and frightened, from beneath the hoods. The three little girls shivered, but not with the cold. They were old with the experiences of the last few months, and they guessed too well what the men might be discussing. Frances comforted the little ones; she could lead them back to their mother, she said, just by following the footprints in the snow. It seemed a long time that the two men stood there talking.

What arguments of greed, expediency, fear, or compassion passed back and forth, no one can know. In fact the two men may not ever have considered such a devilish proposition. But their actions suggest a compromise. For they came back to the children, took them to Mrs. Murphy's cabin by the lake, and left them. Cady and Stone themselves probably took refuge in the deserted Breen cabin.

Just what those two may have been planning can never be known, for before any plan could be put into action the storm broke. It was that same blast which had appalled Reed and his companions in their camp at the head of the Yuba. As it struck, winter again closed down upon the cabins.

Life for the three little Donner girls seemed suddenly to have become a hideous dream. In their tents by the creek they had at least had the light of day; family love had never failed, and in some way living had kept a little touch of dignity. Had not their mother combed their hair before she sent them away?

But here the cabin was a foul, dark cave. Only a flickering fire lighted it uncertainly. No one even greeted them or tried to comfort them after their hard journey. They had just a heap of pine-branches to lie on in a cold place by the doorway, and a blanket to huddle under. They made out other people lying also upon beds of branches. A child cried, wanting food. Another joined, and then little Eliza began to weep sympathetically. A terrifying voice cried out gruffly to be quiet or he would shoot them.

After the storm broke, it was even worse. The snow sifted in, and lay upon their bed. The others had the best places, and the three children could not get close to the fire which burned against the great rock forming one side of the cabin. Poor old Mrs. Murphy blundered about, half-blind always, and sometimes not able to see at all. She was weak in body and childish in mind. She did what she could for the children in a kindly, fumbling way. But then there was Keseberg with his great shock of overgrown hair and his bushy beard. He went limping by on his bad foot like some ugly gnome or ogre of the underworld. The children feared him vaguely, and probably Frances, who was old enough to notice what was going on, could have told just why she feared him. Once as Eliza lay sleeping, he stopped by the bed and made some remark about her which set the two older children into a frenzy of fear. Outside the storm howled.

It beat as heavily upon the Donner tents as upon the cabin. That evening after Cady and Stone had gone off with the three little girls, Clark had returned from his all-day fruitless trailing of the bear. Already the storm was threatening as, worn-out, he stumbled back through the snow. His pals had sneaked out. It was night and with a storm threatening he had no chance of following them even if he had wished. Next morning he found the storm at full blast, and the new-fallen snow deep around the Jacob Donners' tent where he was sleeping.

There was nothing to do but to stick it out. They had been caught short on wood, and Clark preferred to endure the cold rather than to sally forth with an ax. Food failed, and in the icy chill of the tents hunger bit cruelly. The wind blew so hard that now and then they could hear trees break and come down with a crashing of branches. After two days of storm little Lewis Donner died, and Elizabeth the mother became half-frantic with grief. Then the storm finally ceased.

Its ending at last freed Cady and Stone, storm-bound at the lake. Whether or not they had ever planned to carry the three little girls through to safety, they now, as the sky cleared toward noon of March 8, abandoned the children to whatever fate offered and without even revisiting the Murphy cabin fled by themselves across the snow. They did not, however, neglect to take with them the pack of silver spoons, silk dresses, and the other valuables which Mrs. Donner had given them.

They were strong, comparatively well fed, and unhindered

by children or starving refugees. Even across the new snow they ate up the distance. They crossed the pass, hurried down by the camp where the Breens and Graveses still shivered about the fire burning in the snow-pit, and that same evening came up with Reed and the others where they were trying to thaw out their frost-bitten feet.

Of what greetings were spoken and of what suspicious glances were cast askance at the packs, no one has left record. Probably not much was said. After all, the expedition was not under military discipline, and if Cady and Clark chose to put their own interests first, no one could well say them nay. Moreover with gentry like them, it was a word and a blow, or perhaps a shot. The sheriff's writ did not run in the mountains of California. Probably Reed and the others kept quiet.

They had plenty on their minds, anyway. Freezing in the snow, you couldn't think so much about what other people did. Next morning, as they tried to walk, their frozen feet burst wide open; they left a blood-trail behind. Even Cady was frost-bitten and half-crippled; there would be no racing across the snow for him this second day. They all set out, carrying Patty and Tommy. They could not hope to make Bear Valley that night, and it would be a touch-and-go thing, unless they should meet with Turner or one of the others bringing back food, or else come upon the long-delayed Woodworth.

27. EDDY AND FOSTER

By that morning of March 9 the well-planned organized attempt at the relief of the Donner Party, which had shortly before seemed so close to full success, had on account of the great storm broken down completely. Rescuers and refugees alike were scattered in small isolated groups, each as helpless and in as precarious a position as another. Farthest away were Clark and the few survivors by the creek; then came the unfortunates at the lake, now augmented by the three Donner children. In the grim camp at the head of the Yuba were those who remained of the Graveses and Breens. Somewhere along the snow-trail were Reed and his companions, and still somewhere else were the three mountain-men, Turner, Gendreau, and Dofar. But *where* was Woodworth, he who by a single decisive move might have prevented the whole disaster? Where had *he* been during this week of terror while others were dying of cold and hunger, suffering untellable agonies, and in their despair turning to gaze upon the bodies of the dead?

On March 2, the day when Reed was visiting the Donner camp, Mrs. Reed and the other refugees who had come out with the first relief party had seen Woodworth comfortably encamped at Mule Springs on the edge of the snow, having his feet rubbed. Even there he was within striking distance of the pass, and if he had gone ahead, could have made contact with Reed or reached the cabins before the breaking of the storm. Thus indeed he had been planning, for he had just written to Sheriff McKinstry that he intended to start in with four men and three mules carrying four hundred pounds of flour; and he had added grandiloquently: "I shall not return until all the people are in camp." But either his courage had oozed away or something else had delayed him. In any case he weathered the storm snugly with plenty of food available, in Bear Valley.

The storm over, he was still sitting there comfortably, when on the evening of the eighth two men came plowing up through the new snow from the lower end of the valley, and entered his camp. They were Eddy and Foster, the survivors of the snow-shoe party, and a queer pair for traveling companions. Only two months before they had stood, knife against club, each ready to kill the other. But now the madness of that frightful time had passed by, and trouble had drawn them together.

Both had been waiting and building up their strength at Johnson's. Eddy had gone in with Glover's party, but had been forced to return from Mule Springs. Then had followed more anxious waiting until the two of them should hear on the return of the relief party what fate had overtaken their families at the cabins, for Eddy had been forced to leave there his wife and two small children, and Foster his little son. On March 3 the refugees had come to Johnson's, but there was nothing but bad news for the two men who had waited. Mrs. Eddy and the baby Margaret were dead. James Eddy and Georgie Foster were still living—if it could be called living. But they had been left at the camp. There was hope of course that Reed and Woodworth might bring them in.

Then two days later came the storm. Like Mrs. Reed standing in the doorway at Sinclair's looking out at the mountains, the two fathers knew what a storm meant. They remembered Christmas night in the driving snow when they sat crouched in a circle beneath the blankets with Antonio and Uncle Billy Graves dead and Dolan raging in his frenzy. Such scenes might now be happening on the mountains, with their own children the sufferers. They could calculate about where Reed must be, and could guess how badly he might need help. The strain of waiting became too much, and like brave men, they acted. They obtained some of the horses which had been collected for the relief work, and on the seventh in the teeth of the storm they clumped out of Johnson's, headed east, nerved again to endure the freezing and starvation of the snow-trail. They were in no mood for sparing horses, and made good time. Fifty miles that day, over the miry mountain road, they flogged their horses on, and camped at Mule Springs. Next day under clearing skies they slogged ahead through the snow on foot, and thus came to Woodworth's camp.

It must have been a blow to find him in Bear Valley, and to learn that he had never been any farther into the mountains. Their respect for him began to ooze away. His actual rank was only Passed Midshipman, but he obviously considered himself General-of-the-Army. Enough for him to establish advanced headquarters at Bear Valley, and thence send forward his lieutenants to the firing-line. As befitted a commanding officer, he kept his hands clean, by having a man to carry water, make the fires, and cook. Half-a-dozen other men, who beneath the clear sky might have been pushing on to make contact with Reed, sat about the camp in Bear Valley as a sort of headquarters guard.

To the fathers' inquiry as to why he was not already over the mountains, Woodworth pointed out that the trappers, his guides, had gone on with Reed. Eddy countered shortly that until the storm he had had the best possible guide in the snow-trail which the preceding parties had left. Woodworth finally agreed to go forward a certain distance further, but he would not attempt a crossing and he advised the two fathers not to try it. The scorn of their reply carries on even at second or third hand—"that they had passed over under vastly more difficult circumstances, and that they would certainly attempt it again."

Next morning the two fathers, Woodworth, and five of his men set out. When they had gone only a short distance, they met three half-frozen and exhausted men hauling themselves along through the snow. They were Turner, Gendreau, and Dofar, whom Reed had sent ahead to bring back food. The story which they told did not tend to allay anyone's fears for what might have happened to Reed and to those still left beyond the pass. The three had pushed forward to the first cache, only to find it robbed by martens. Before they could arrive at the next cache the storm had broken. They were without food, and probably had been caught without even the supplies of wood which Reed's party had been lucky enough to find. As a result, in spite of all their training in the craft of the mountains, they had suffered almost as badly as greenhorns. The redoubtable John Turner had been frozen so badly that after the storm had ceased, the others had to help him forward. Traveling thus they had managed to get to the second cache, a part of which was still intact. Dofar had taken some of it back a short way and hung it on a tree for Reed to find.

This story only spurred Eddy and Foster on, but to their great disgust Woodworth by three o'clock "had become tired from carrying his blanket," and the party camped. Then at last toward evening as they sat around their fire, they became aware that something was disturbing the deep silence of the snow. Was it the faint, distant scream of a mountain lion? But it sounded more like some one hallooing, and they hallooed in return, and sent a man forward. What they had heard turned out to be the advance-guard of Reed's party who had located a place to camp, and were calling to those farther back on the trail.

Aided by the food which Dofar had left for them, Reed and all his company had won through. Even little Patty had survived. But that last day's march had been made upon frozen and bleeding feet. Blood-stains on the white snow marked the trail.

With contact once established, the rest seemed easy for those who were emerging from the snow. They had food now, and soon would come to the horses and go out along the emigrant road dropping down along the easy ridges until the flowers bloomed all around, and birds sang, and they finally found the spring full-blown at Johnson's.

For Reed the time of terror was past. He and his family had had more bad luck than most; they had suffered as much as any, and had taken as many chances. He himself had faced the desert and the rope; he had starved on his terrible journey with Herron; he had heard the hum of Mexican bullets, and dared the Sacramento in flood, and twice gone into the snow with McCutchen. No one could say that he had failed to bear himself like a man. But all that he had done was as little compared with the extremities which Mrs. Reed and the children had known—when they had starved so long, and when Mrs. Reed and Virginia had wandered desperately among the peaks with faithful Milt Elliott, and when Tommy and plucky little Patty had gone back to the cabin to face starvation the second time. And yet as it came about so strangely, the whole family had come through safely where so many had perished on every side. In a few days now, he and Patty and Tommy would join the others at Sinclair's. He had something to be happy about, even through the torture of his frost-bitten feet.

But not every one camping in the snow by the Yuba could have Reed's comforting thoughts, and even he had on his mind the memory of the Breens and Graveses and little Mary Donner, left helplessly lying about the fire in the snow-pit. In the morning they held a council. What should be done to bring out the rest? Woodworth asked for volunteers, but his men held back and he himself made no offer to lead them. He and they had learned too much of what happened to men in the snow; the pain that they had read in other men's faces sufficed; they had seen the blood-marks by the trail. Glover and his men had come through well enough, but all that had happened to these others, hardy and skilled mountain-men that they were, showed what the snow and cold could do—big Turner being helped along like a child, Cady and Brit Greenwood with toes ready to drop off and leave them crippled for life.

The two fathers stood ready to lead the way, and they

offered to become responsible for almost any sum to any-one who would follow them. But the others shrugged their shoulders. Eddy and Foster were paupers, weren't they? Hadn't they lost everything they had? Their word wasn't worth a thing. Then Reed and Miller added their promises to those of Eddy and Foster, but still the men held back. Only one volunteered, and he stood ready to go merely out of his own courage and a good heart. He was a young giant, John Starks by name, who had come up from Johnson's with Woodworth. But his very size was against him, for he weighed two hundred twenty-four pounds, and if a man like that got into soft snow, he floundered like a stallion in quick-sand. Eddy and Foster were ready to set out by themselves, but this was highly dangerous, and Reed managed to per-suade them to return to Bear Valley, and there to have an-other try with Woodworth and his men.

So the united parties worked their way back a day's journey to Woodworth's camp, and only after they had all arrived safely in Bear Valley did the courageous little Patty reveal the secret which she had cherished through all those days. For with a child's shrewd intuition she had probably realized that these silly men would have thrown her treasures away as so much useless weight. But when everything at last seemed safe, she calmly drew from her bosom a lock of her grandmother's hair tied up in a piece of lace, a tiny glass salt-cellar, and a little wooden doll with black eyes and hair. There by the campfire she soberly set out to tell the doll what had been happening in the last few days.

But there was more serious business afoot too that day in Bear Valley, and Woodworth finally agreed to assume finan-cial responsibility and offer from the relief funds three dollars a day to each volunteer and fifty dollars bonus to each one who would carry out a child not his own. Even so, Howard Oakley, a Mormon emigrant who had come up from Yerba Buena with Woodworth, was the only one of his men besides Starks who took up the offer. The only two who had come out with Reed unfrozen and in fair condition were Miller and Stone. Both of these volunteered to return, and although Stone had proved himself far from trustworthy, this was no time to be squeamish about his motives. Another man named Thompson finally engaged himself to accept Foster's personal promise of fifty dollars. In the end the party was organized in two sections with Miller attaching himself to Eddy upon the same terms as Thompson had to Foster. These four were to press on to the lake camp for the rescue of James Eddy, George Foster and the other children. Starks, Oakley, and Stone, in Woodworth's pay, were to bring out the Breens and Graveses, if any of them remained alive.

As the seven men set out along the snow-trail on the morning of the eleventh, they must have been far from hopeful. Reed, sure enough, had said that the little boys were still alive when he left camp. But that was a week ago, wasn't it? You couldn't look for little codgers like that to hang on forever. And the Breens and Graveses were as good as gone when Reed left them. Uncle Patrick and Peggy his wife didn't have the sand then to get up and walk. All they'd be likely to find there was a lot of corpses around a dead fire, unless maybe the ones that held on longest had eaten the ones that died first.

Nevertheless they pressed on as fast as they could, and camped that night halfway up the Yuba. Next day they went ahead making good time. The only incident which marked their progress was their coming upon the body of Denton. Eddy stopped to examine it more closely than the previous parties had. Beside the body he found a little journal, a pocket pencil, a piece of rubber, and a slip of paper. On the last were lines of verse written in pencil, in places smudged out with the rubber and rewritten. In his last moments the Englishman had been composing poetry. There deep in the Sierran snow-fields his mind had reverted sentimentally to the stately homes and pleasant countryside of England. His first stanza ran:

> O! after many roving years,
>   How sweet it is to come
> Back to the dwelling-place of youth,
>   Our first and dearest home;
> To turn away our wearied eyes
>   From proud ambition's towers,
> And wander in those summer fields,
>   The scenes of boyhood's hours.

Summer fields—and the snow where they had camped last night Eddy had found fifteen feet deep!

That afternoon about four o'clock under a bright sun they approached the place where Reed had left the refugees. Suddenly they stood upon the brink of a great cup, twenty-five feet deep, melted into the snow. At the bottom, the fire burned upon a space of bare ground as large as an ordinary room, and about it was a jumble of blankets and children and hideous things. Patrick Breen and Peggy lay in that strange apathy which seemed to affect them, sunning themselves comfortably with no apparent thought of the future. The body of Mrs. Graves lay there with flesh nearly all stripped from arms and legs. Her breasts were cut off and her heart and liver taken out, and all of these were boiling together in a pot upon the fire. Her year-old baby sat wailing, with one arm resting upon the mangled body of its mother. Little remained to be seen of the corpses of two children.

By means of steps which the refugees had cut into the snow, the relief party descended to the fire. Eddy, with thoughts of his own child in his heart, took up the weeping infant, hushed and stilled it. The others distributed food, and soon even the baby was soothed by a little thin soup.

It was not pleasant telling—what had happened in those six days. Mrs. Graves, the story ran, had lost control of herself, and wildly urged that they should kill her own baby. But in the bitter cold of the first night after Reed had left, the mother herself had died and along with her Franklin Graves, her five-year-old son. Only eleven miserable creatures were still alive on the morning of the ninth. The fire now burned in a deep hole far below them, and they got little heat from it. At last, however, they saw that it had actually melted clear through the snow and was burning on bare ground. One of the boys climbed down by a branch of a tree, and finding it much more comfortable to be in the hole close to the heat and sheltered from the wind, he encouraged the others, and they made steps down the steep walls of snow which ringed the fire.

Mrs. Breen doled out her scanty supplies, trying to keep the family alive as long as possible. Once she thought that her eldest son John was dying, but with a little sugar pressed between his lips he managed to revive. Finally on the fourth day something had to be done, and, as Mrs. Breen told the story, Mary Donner—poor little waif, frozen, burned, and starved—said that they should eat the dead bodies. Patrick Breen with a knife climbed up to the surface of the snow. They ate the children first, and then Mrs. Graves. Thus in their strange shelter, a snow-pit twenty-five feet deep with a fire burning at the bottom, eleven of them had lived through.

The relief party had not expected to find nearly so many, and the result was embarrassing. Starks, Oakley and Stone had come with the idea of taking back to Bear Valley all who remained alive, but to start through the snow with eleven nearly helpless people seemed merely to be inviting disaster. No one, moreover, had much sympathy for Breen, who by refusing to travel with Reed when he was still strong enough seemed to have forfeited his right to further consideration. If the three men should carry little Mary Donner, helpless with her burned foot, and the three orphans of the Graves family, this would seem to be all that could be expected of them.

But gigantic John Starks flatly vetoed the proposition. He had come into the snow, he said, to take out the people who had been left there; the others could do what they pleased, but he would stick by his charges, all of them. The result was a split. Oakley took charge of Mary Donner, and Stone of the Graveses' baby. Starks was to carry Jonathan Graves, and to assume the task of guiding and helping the seven Breens and Nancy Graves.

With these arrangements completed, the relief party early the next morning divided, and left the camp at the head of the Yuba deserted at last. Oakley and Stone with two children pushed ahead for Bear Valley; Starks and his charges followed laboriously; Eddy, Foster, Miller, and Thompson set out eastward across the pass.

28. BEFORE THE LAST PLUNGE

WHEN men abandon a sinking ship, so the stories go, they at first conduct themselves with some degree of steadiness and order. But as the ship lurches more heavily, they feel the tension, and the rhythm quickens until the last moments are a wild running about the decks. Then the boats go down with a run; men leap overboard; and the vessel dips to the final plunge. So the rhythm seems to quicken in the rescue of the Donner Party. Glover's men had doggedly pushed ahead in a spirit of calculated audacity; Reed's party had been more hurried; and now Eddy and Foster with their two aids seem by comparison to run, as if they felt the ship settling beneath them.

They had reason to feel panic, for now all felt that no leader was behind backing them up. Woodworth was a broken stick, and Reed, crippled and half-frozen, was good for no more dashes into the snow. Besides, all knew what a storm could do; they had seen Reed's men, and the things about the fire in the snow-pit. Eddy, Foster, and Miller all had been through storms in the open, and nothing but sheer courage could have taken them over the mountains again.

It was four o'clock in the morning, and the dawn was only breaking. The four men left the snow-pit, and faced the climb to the pass. Suspense lay heavily upon them, for the two fathers knew that this day they would reach the cabins and learn—whether they were still fathers.

The sun had risen before they were sliding down the snow walls of the eastern slope, and as it came toward ten o'clock they were close to the cabins. The two fathers, spurred on by their suspense, left the others behind. They came to the great rock, and by it, still deep in snow, the cabin which they themselves had built in those bitter times of November. About it they saw the same sights from which Reed had recoiled, that confusion of filth and mutilated bodies. They pressed on, down the snow-steps, and into the noisome, dark cabin. They asked their one question, and had one answer.

For Death, too, was quickening his rhythm. The poor children had starved too long, and the scant supplies which the relief parties had brought were not enough. And starvation had perhaps an ally.

That story is confused and doubtful, but as the little Donners remembered, one night Keseberg took Georgie Foster to bed with him. In the morning the child was dead. For three months, since its mother had gone out with the snow-shoers, Grandmother Murphy had fought starvation for that child's life. Now he was dead. She took the body, half blind as she was, and sat down with it in her lap. Wildly, with a bitterness which welled up from the months of unavailing self-sacrifice, she broke out into accusations against Keseberg —he had killed the baby, strangled it while it was in bed with him. Then Keseberg came and took the body from her. He hung it up, said Georgia Donner, "in sight, inside the cabin, on the wall." But it did not stay there long.

As for James Eddy, Keseberg had eaten that body, too. In a sort of perverted bravado he quite openly told as much to the almost frenzied father. And by such a confession he was taking more of a chance than he knew, for Eddy suddenly chilled with the conviction that such a man should not live. Whether he had killed the child or not, he had at least forfeited the rights of a human being. There were axes at hand, or even a club would do. But then as Eddy looked upon the horrible and emaciated figure before him, weak with months of starving, he realized that much as Keseberg might deserve to die, he could not bring himself to strike down such a defenseless, helpless, and withal pitiable creature. The most that he could do was to resolve soberly that if Keseberg should ever get through to California, then he would kill him.

Now, however, first thoughts of grief, and second thoughts of retribution had to give way to the work of rescue. So far, Eddy and Foster had hardly had a chance to consider the situation, but now it was time to begin planning. At the cabins were Keseberg, Mrs. Murphy, her son Simon, the three little Donner girls, and also Tamsen Donner.

The presence of the last was easily enough explained. She had worried constantly for fear that her children had been caught in the storm, and finally had sent Clark to the cabins to bring word of them. His report—of Keseberg and Georgie Foster and of things in general—had caused her to leave her husband to the care of Clark and Jean Baptiste and to come struggling through the snow the day before Eddy's arrival, to see for herself what could be done and what protection she could offer the children.

But the question now, as it neared noonday, was not how she had got here, but what she was to do next. She had, she confided to Eddy, fifteen hundred dollars in silver which she would give him for taking the children out. He told her that he would not burden himself with even a hundred dollars of that weight, but that he would take the children out or die with them on the trail.

So the children were to go. But what about herself? She was remarkably strong, and even in good flesh. There was no doubt of her being able to make the crossing. But still she faced that dilemma of husband against children. Little indeed was left to take her back to the other camp, now that both love of life and love of children beckoned her on across the pass. By the creek, Elizabeth was dead, gentle sister Elizabeth with whom she had labored and prayed through the long winter. After her death little Sammie, the youngest of all her children, had been the only one left, and Tamsen had carried him to her own tent. There to keep him warm she had put him into the same bed with his Uncle George. A ray of hope had come when Clark had gone out and killed a half-grown bear, boldly following the animal into a cave at the risk of a hand-to-hand fight. As for her husband the infection was eating at his shoulder now. A few more days might see the end. But still her duty to him in his last hours drew her back to the camp by the creek. Besides, there was little Sammie, although he, too, would probably not live long. And finally, if she did not return, she would be leaving Clark and Jean Baptiste in the lurch. And now there was no great hope that another relief party would be coming through.

But on the other hand, as Eddy waited for her decision, it was a fearful thought to abandon her children and to let them go out into a strange land to meet the future without either father or mother. Once she asked the men to wait while she returned to the tent—then she could relieve Clark and Jean Baptiste, send Sammie Donner out with them, and perhaps, it was possible, she might find George Donner dead and her dilemma already solved.

But at the suggestion that they should wait—it would mean a whole day—Eddy and Foster shook their heads. They were willing to risk their lives by carrying out the children, but they had brought no extra food, and, even had they themselves been willing, they could not have held their men for an hour's delay, with the chance of a storm.

So she made her decision. For the second time she said good-by to the children; Elitha and Leanna, she knew now, had got safe through, and though they were scarcely more than children themselves, they would take care of the little ones. Then through the wilderness of snow and forest she set out for her place at her husband's death-bed. As she walked off through the trees, so the story is told, she did not once look back.

The relief party had traveled light, and brought no supply of food to be left at the cabins. They cut some wood, and did what they could to make Mrs. Murphy comfortable. As for Keseberg, no one cared much, and in any case he seemed to have a way of looking out for himself.

It was noon by this time, and the men had been at the cabins only two hours. They were ready to return, however, and the less delay the better. Only four children were left alive, one for each man. Foster took charge of Simon Murphy, his wife's little brother; Thompson took Frances Donner. These were larger children and heavier to carry, but in compensation could walk part of the time. Eddy took Georgia Donner, and Miller took Eliza. Georgia could walk a little now and then, but Eliza had to be swung in a blanket and carried like an Indian child. The men had left their camp at four in the morning, and had been working hard all day. Nevertheless, without a rest and now still further burdened with the children, they took the back-trail at noon. They wanted to be ready for the pass early in the morning, and their precipitancy was such as to suggest panic, had it not been so obviously based upon mere prudence. For three of the men knew what it was to be caught in a storm, and they had no intention to be so caught again. Toward evening they came to the foot of the pass.

There they were surprised and disgusted to find Clark and Jean Baptiste. These two had deserted the dying George Donner and little Sammie, and fled to save themselves. And they had not gone away empty-handed, either; for Clark, content to leave the child to perish, carried a pack of forty pounds in booty and two guns.

Next morning they worked their way up the ascent. Each of the four men with a child, Clark laboring under his even heavier load of loot, and Jean Baptiste, weak from his winter of starvation, getting along as he could. As they stood at the top of the pass, we can well believe that they cast a look back across the snow-covered lake. Perhaps they saw a wisp of smoke rising from the cabin hidden among the pine-trees. Then as they went ahead, lake, valley, snow-covered forests, and far-stretching ranges toward the east disappeared from view behind the hump of granite and snow. The day was March 14. Not until another month had gone would any one cross that pass again, or ask the mountains to reveal more secrets.

29. INTERLUDE

IN a sense, it was finished. The days to follow were to see some suffering and some heroism, but at least so far as the story is known, the great crises were passed. Tragedy had yielded to pathos.

There is the story, for instance, of how little Eliza Donner cried herself to sleep that next night because Miller had promised her a piece of loaf sugar if she would walk a certain distance, and then had harshly told her that there was no sugar. And then how, the morning after, he would have beaten her because she would not walk, if Foster and Eddy had not peremptorily stopped him. But after all, this is only the pathos of childhood, not the tragedy of strong men in the struggle with death. And before we judge Miller too harshly, we must recall his heroism when on the night of the storm he labored with McCutchen to keep the fire going. The man had been in the snow for nearly three weeks, and had been to the lake twice; if his nerves were frayed out, we may forgive him.

And the sufferings of this party were as nothing compared with those of the previous ones. At noon of only the second day after crossing the pass they came up with the almost helpless Breen family. Starks had been having a hard time, but had stuck to his task nobly. His immense strength seemed to bear up all the nine refugees who were with him. He packed the provisions and most of the blankets. Then in addition he sometimes carried one child and sometimes two. He could carry them all, he would say with a laugh, if he only had room on his back; they were so light with starving that one more or less didn't make any difference. Sometimes he would carry one or two children ahead, leave them, and go back for others. In this way he had got on a few miles in the three and a half days that it had taken the others to go to the lake and return.

At just about the same time that the men returning from the lake overtook Starks, they also met a new relief party which had pushed in from Bear Valley to meet them. As it turned out, Glover, Moultry and Coffeemeyer had come back into the mountains and met Woodworth at Mule Springs. There they had shamed him into entering the snow again to make contact with the others. The place of the meeting was somewhere along Yuba Bottoms, not much over a day's journey from Bear Valley. Since the weather still held fair, this sudden accession of food and man-power freed every one from fear of another disaster.

The only question was whether the fresh men might not go ahead and attempt to bring out some of the five who still remained at the mountain camps. But in reply to this suggestion Woodworth said that he could not remain any longer, but would return to Mule Springs and get the horses ready to take everyone out. This lack of official support discouraged the others, and so the whole party turned back.

A week later the refugees were safe at Sutter's where poppies were beginning to bloom and wheat was springing and cattle grazed in knee-deep grass.

But Glover told at Sutter's in no mincing terms of the way Woodworth had flinched at pushing a last relief party ahead, and bluff Sheriff McKinstry wrote a letter. Now McKinstry had a way of putting matters neatly with his pen, and Woodworth probably writhed. In any case he got some men together for another try. They were good men, too—John Rhoads, "Dan" Tucker, Sels, and Coffeemeyer, the mighty John Starks, Foster, and young Billy Graves.

Their attempt, however, was a failure. They went only as far as Bear Valley, and then came back saying that the snow had grown slushy and so soft that they could not advance. It sounds like an excuse, for in the Sierra melting snow consolidates so that it offers easy going. The real trouble was that a storm was blowing up and that the incentive for risking one's life had disappeared. Most of these men, a few weeks earlier, had marched gallantly ahead through incomparably worse dangers. But now who was there to be rescued? George Donner would be dead, or too far gone to move. The same went for old Mrs. Murphy and for Sammie Donner. As for Keseberg, none of them would risk much to save him. And Mrs. Donner—well, she had twice refused to come out, and if she died now, she had merely got what she chose for herself.

Then followed an interlude. The refugees were scattered at the various ranches about Sutter's Fort. Everyone was kind to them; they nursed their frost-bitten toes, and fed themselves back into strength. Most of them were of tough farming stock, and did not take long to get back on their feet again. Billy Graves had been out only about two weeks, when he was considered strong enough to go in with the party which turned back at Bear Valley. The only one that failed to recover was the little Graves baby which Eddy had picked up as it lay beside the dead mother in the snow-pit, and which Stone had carried out. It failed to rally or, as Mr. Thornton most elegantly put the matter: "It drooped and withered away like a flower severed from the parent stem. It now blooms in the paradise of God, in a better and happier clime, where the storms and disasters of life will affect it no more."

A month passed, a time of happy reunion for some, and of loneliness for others. The Reeds had miraculously come through without a single loss, and now were all six recuperating at Sinclair's. The children were proudly picking up a few Spanish words, and were fascinated at the way the *vaqueros* lassoed cattle. The Breens were the only other family who had not lost at least one member. They could well be happy. But Eddy was left entirely alone—wife, son, and daughter, all were gone. The Graves children had lost both father and mother. So had the Jacob Donners. The Murphys had lost heavily, and Mrs. Keseberg was childless, but these, like the children of George Donner, were still in suspense as to what news the next party to cross the mountains would bring to them.

No one about the Fort was greatly interested in relief any more, but as the advance of spring melted the snow farther and farther back and made the passage easier, another motive began to be prominent. California was a frontier country rich in nothing except cattle. Every one knew that the wagons of the emigrants, especially those of the Donners, had contained much of value. Stone, Cady, and Clark had already come back with some good pickings. Every one might admit that the goods in the wagons, or cached beneath the cabins, belonged to the emigrants, and public opinion at Sutter's would not have allowed a mere looting expedition. But the point was that, as soon as the snow melted, the camps would probably be flooded and things washed away or ruined; and after that the Indians would come in from the desert to plunder. So unless some one salvaged the goods soon, the refugees would probably lose everything.

So finally an expedition was got together. The men were to receive a daily wage as members of a relief party, and were also to be entitled to half of what they could carry back. The leader was "Mountaineer" Fallon, or O'Fallon, also know as "Big" or "Le Gros." As his name and nicknames indicate, he was an Irishman of enormous bulk, and one of that most dangerous breed of Rocky Mountain trappers. He had turned up in California about 1845 from nowhere in particular, and since that time had ranged about joining in every revolution or war which happened to turn up handy, and making himself very generally feared, if not always respected.

He enlisted six men for his salvage corps. Four of them were the staunch veterans John Rhoads, "Dan" Tucker, Sels, and Coffeemeyer. Another was Foster, who had crossed with the snow-shoers and again with Eddy. The sixth man was a settler from Johnson's named Keyser. By April 10 they were ready to be off.

30. FALLON LE GROS

FALLON and his men rode away from Johnson's on the evening of April 13. Many miles of the emigrant road were now free from snow, and moving rapidly they came two days later to the lower end of Bear Valley. Here they were forced to dismount and send the horses back in charge of extra men brought along for the purpose. The horses were to be returned to the rendezvous at the end of ten days. Fallon and the others took ten days' rations in their packs, and camped that night at the upper end of the valley.

By this season the snow had packed until a man could walk across it almost as rapidly as over bare ground. Starting the next morning the party made a distance which they estimated at twenty-three miles, and camped well up beyond Yuba Bottoms. Next day when the morning was not far advanced they topped the pass, and looked out upon a view vastly different from that upon which Eddy and Foster had turned their backs a month before. On the heights winter was still unbroken, but at lower levels and in the valley by the lake the snow had the sodden look which comes with spring and on exposed slopes patches of bare ground were showing.

A little after midday they came to the cabins. They found no one alive. Around them lay a scene of filth and mutilated corpses, even worse than that which earlier relief parties had been forced to witness. The seven men stood speechless and awe-struck, and as the intense silence of the forest seemed to sweep in upon them, even Fallon, the mountain-man, felt the creeping horror.

But a sudden shout broke the momentary stillness, and dashing in its direction with aroused hope the men saw three cowardly Diggers running in such panic that they had even left behind their bows and arrows. These had raised the shout probably as a warning to others of their tribe who were prowling around. In any case the presence of Indians in the camp gave little hope that Keseberg or Mrs. Donner or any one else remained alive. The party spent two hours searching about the lake cabins, and then started for the Donner tents where they would find the most valuable goods to be salvaged.

On their way they came upon a fresh trail in the snow, obviously not an Indian's. In their state of mind at the moment they were more fearful lest some one should forestall them at salvaging, than hopeful that they might find anyone alive, and so, as Fallon put it, the trail in the snow "excited our suspicion." Since it ran in the direction that they were going, they followed it along until finally it led them to the Jacob Donners' tent. The man who had made the tracks was not there, but from trail-sign a skilled mountain-man like Fallon had no difficulty in determining that the mysterious maker of the footprints had left the Donner tents only that same morning, and was heading back toward the lake. They must have accidentally missed him in some way, or else he had seen and avoided them.

Around the tents the salvagers found plenty of work to do. The rich property of the Donners lay scattered about everywhere. The melting of the snow and the spring freshets had flooded most of the camp, and sodden in the water lay books, bolts of cloth, tea and coffee, shoes, percussion caps, kitchen ware, and goods of all conceivable kinds which the Donners had hoped to use for themselves or to sell to advantage in California. A survey of the camp revealed worse things. At the entrance to the tent they found a large iron kettle containing human flesh, cut up. Nearby stood a chair, and on it three legs of an ox, which had been buried under the snow all winter and only revealed with the coming of spring. The men examined the beef, and found it well preserved by having been continuously frozen. A small piece had been cut from the shoulder, but otherwise there was no evidence that anyone had used the meat for food. The melting of the snow had also revealed a dead horse.

Further search disclosed the body of George Donner carefully wrapped in a sheet, the last tender attention of his wife. But this care had not prevented the mutilation of the body. The head had been split open and the brains removed; flesh had also been taken for the kettle. He had not been dead long, so the men judged, not more than four days probably. They found no trace of Tamsen Donner.

By this time it was too late in the day for much work of salvage. They gathered up some of the goods, and camped for the night. The next day they spent in collecting and drying the articles which they considered most valuable and most suitable to be carried in their packs across the snow. While they labored they had two good topics for conversation and argument. Who was it had made those tracks in the snow? Where was all the Donners' money? As they went through the jumble of goods, and ransacked every nook of the camp, the latter question became more irksome. There had certainly been plenty of money, both in gold and in silver. Hadn't Halloran, as every one knew, when he died by the Great Salt Lake, left George Donner fifteen hundred dollars in cash? And hadn't Mrs. Donner offered that same sum in silver to Eddy for taking the children? Perhaps she had cached it, or perhaps the man who had left the tracks could tell something. The next day they would try to solve the two mysteries.

On the following morning three men remained with Fallon at the camp. They were to continue the search for the money, and also as a protection against the weather and against Indians or other marauders to cache all the goods except the comparatively small amount which they could carry away on their own backs. Then later in the year when the pass was open to pack-trains other salvaging parties could come across, or perhaps some of the emigrants themselves might return with ox-teams and finally take their wagons through to California.

The other three men, Foster, Rhoads, and Sels, set out to follow the tracks across the snow. But the trail was now old, and the snow had been melting rapidly. They soon found themselves at a loss, and so struck out directly for the lake cabins. When they arrived, they found the answer.

In one of the cabins, amidst the human bones, lay Keseberg. Beside him was a large pan full of liver and lights freshly taken from a human body. To the question as to what had become of Mrs. Donner and the others—they were, he said, all dead. The puzzle of the footprints now became clear. Keseberg, going from the lake to the Donner tents, had made the tracks in the snow. Upon his return he had lost the trail, and thus had not met Fallon and his party. After falling into a stream and wandering about more or less lost, he had sighted the Graves's cabin at dusk, and finally after dark, exhausted, with his clothing frozen about him, he had dragged into his own cabin. He was too much done-up to eat or build a fire, but had merely rolled himself in blankets, and after shivering most of the night had finally fallen into a deep sleep. On awakening he had immediately seen in the light of day that someone had visited the cabin, broken into his goods, and thrown them into confusion.

Keseberg was the only one left to tell the story of the last weeks at the mountain camps. After the departure of Eddy and Foster, so his version ran, old Mrs. Murphy lingered on about a week, and died. Then for about another week, but he was naturally a little vague about the time, Keseberg lived on in the cabin, gathering fuel as well as he could in his weakness, eating what was at hand, existing in solitude except for the wolves who came scratching about the cabin in the darkness. Then about the middle of a bitter night Tamsen Donner came. Her husband was dead. He had died just at nightfall, and after she had laid his body out decently, her dominating will, so long under so great strain kept firm upon her duty to her husband, had suddenly in all its power sprung back and fixed upon her children. She seemed to Keseberg a little crazed. She kept crying out that she must see her children, that she must go to them at once. Even though it was midnight, she wanted to start over the pass, and was with difficulty persuaded otherwise. She was exhausted, chilled and half-frozen. Her clothing was wet, as if she had fallen into a stream. He put her to bed rolled in blankets. But in the morning she was dead.

As to what happened afterwards, we have only the word of the three men as to what Keseberg told them: "He eat her body and found her flesh the best he had ever tasted! He further stated, that he obtained from her body at least four pounds of fat!" This was the end of life allotted to valiant Tamsen Donner.

To Foster, Rhoads, and Sels the story of the manner of her death failed to ring true. Foster himself, a month before, had seen Mrs. Donner and she had then been in surprisingly good physical condition. It did not seem quite right that she who had clung to life so tenaciously through the whole of that terrible winter should suddenly be snuffed out in a single night. Moreover in looking over the cabin they now came upon two kettles containing what seemed to be human blood. Rhoads asked Keseberg where this came from, and his reply, as they reported it, was: "There is blood in dead bodies." Believing that blood could be obtained only from the living, or dying, the three men began to have an ugly suspicion that Keseberg might actually have murdered Mrs. Donner. They plied him with questions which in their opinion seemed to embarrass him and cause him to equivocate. Finally they asked him where Mrs. Donner's money was, and this again caused him some confusion. He knew nothing about it, he said; she must have cached it before she died.

"I haven't it," they reported his words to have been, "nor the money, nor the property of any person, living or dead!" But on searching a bundle which he had, they found silks and jewelry taken from the camp of the Donners and amounting in value to two hundred dollars, and they also found upon him two pistols which they recognized as George Donner's. As they were prudently removing these from him, they felt something in his waistcoat. It proved to be two hundred twenty-five dollars in gold. Now Mrs. Keseberg, before the salvage party had left the settlements, had said that her husband had little money with him, so that the three men were more than ever convinced, in spite of his protests to the contrary, that Keseberg had forestalled them in their search for the gold. Besides what he had on his person, it was likely, they decided, that he had found much more and hidden it. They resorted to threats, telling him that some of the men now at the Donner camp would be ready, if he continued refusing to talk, to string him up to the nearest tree. Rhoads then took him aside, and in as kindly fashion as he could, tried to persuade him to tell the story; he promised in that case the best of treatment, but otherwise offered no prospect but a quick and brutal death at the hands of such a desperado as Fallon was known to be. But Keseberg merely protested his innocence. Finally, secure in their knowledge that he could not escape, they left their packs with him at the cabin, told him that he had better make up his mind during the night, and took the trail to the Donner camp.

Next morning early, each of the seven shouldered a back-breaking pack of a hundred pounds, and they all set out for the lake. What happend after their arrival is best told in the terse language of Fallon's journal, which the editor of the *California Star* declared he printed word for word:

Came within a few hundred yards of the cabin which Kiesburg occupied and halted to prepare breakfast, after which we proceeded to the cabin. I now asked Kiesburg if he was willing to disclose to me where he had concealed that money; he turned somewhat pale and again protested his ignorance: I said to him, "Kiesburg, you know well where Donner's money is, and d—n you, you shall tell me! I am not going to multiply words with you, nor say but little about it—bring me that rope!" He then arose from his pot of soup and human flesh and begged me not to harm him—he had not the money nor the goods; the silk clothing and money which were found upon him the previous day, and which he then declared belonging to his wife, he now said was

the property of others in California. I then told him I did not
wish to hear more from him, unless he at once informed us
where he had concealed the money of those orphan children, then
producing the rope I approached him; he became frightened, but
I bent the rope about his neck, and threw him, after a struggle,
upon the ground, and as I tightened the cord, and choked him
he cried out that he would confess all upon release; I then
permitted him to arise. He still seemed inclined to be obstinate,
and made much delay in talking, finally, but with evident reluc-
tance, he led the way back to Donner's camp about 10 miles
distant, accompanied by Rhodes and Tucker. While they were
absent, we moved all our packs over to the lower end of the
lake, and made all ready for a start when they should return.
Mr. Foster went down to the cabin of Mrs. Murphy, his mother-
in-law, to see if any property remained there worth collecting and
securing; he found the body of young Murphy, who had been
dead about three months, with the breast and skull cut open,
and the brains, liver and lights taken out; and this accounted for
the contents of the pan which stood beside Kiesburg when he
was found. It appears that he had left at the other camp the
dead bullock and horse, and on visiting this camp and finding
the body thawed out, took therefrom the brains, liver and lights.

Tucker and Rhodes came back the next morning, bringing
$273, that had been cached by Kiesburg, who after disclosing
to them the spot, returned to the cabin. The money had been
hidden directly underneath the projecting limb of a large tree,
the end of which seemed to point precisely to the treasure buried
in the earth.—On their return, and passing the cabin, they saw
the unfortunate man within, devouring the remaining brains and
liver, left from his morning repast! They hurried him away, but
before leaving, he gathered together the bones and heaped them
all in a box he used for the purpose, blessed them and the cabin,
and said, "I hope God will forgive me what I have done, I
couldn't help it! and I hope I may get to heaven yet!" We asked
Kiesburg why he did not use the meat of the bullock and horse
instead of human flesh, he replied he had not seen them. We
then told him we knew better, and asked him why the meat in
the chair had not been consumed, he said, "Oh! it's too dry
eating!" the liver and lights were a great deal better, and the
brains made good soup! We then moved on, and camped on the
lake for the night.

The end of Fallon's account was brief:

April 21st. Started for Bear River valley this morning, found the snow from six to eight feet deep, camped on Juba River for the night.—On the 22d., traveled down Juba about 18 miles, and camped at the head of Bear River valley.—On the 25th., moved down to the lower end of the valley, met our horses, and came in.

With them came Keseberg. The crossing of the Donner Party was accomplished. The last man was in.

PART III

THEY REST

Hi motus animorum atque haec certamina tanta
Pulveris exigui iactu compressa quiescunt.

Georgicon IV

FOREWORD

THE year of the Donner Party is within the memory of
many living persons. While these lines were being first written, a last survivor still lingered. At the lake, tall stumps cut
by starving men who stood on top of deep snow have not
yet decayed and fallen. And yet that era in the West seems
almost as distant as the times of Neolithic man, and this particular story, for all it is so well attested, appears so startling,
isolated, and incredible, that it might well be taken for fiction.

Probably the best way to feel the actuality of the story is
to travel through its setting. For the country is tangible and
solid, now as then. And for this reason, I have in the telling
often stressed the scene until the reader has, I hope, come to
feel the land itself as one of the chief characters of the tale.

And the land, in spite of certain scratchings of man, remains essentially wilderness, and presents much the same appearance as it did during the nine months of the story. In
the course of time the route which the Donner Party attempted to follow across the Sierra has become the main gate-
way to central California from the east; and since it leads to
the harbor of San Francisco and the commerce of the Orient,
the route is an important link in world traffic. You may
cross here by paved highway, by double-tracked railroad,
or by aeroplane; or you may still follow mountain trails horseback or afoot. But no matter how you travel, you will see
the places through which the men and women and children
of the Donner Party struggled and in which they died.

The human characters have passed. Whether their bones
lie buried in the plain or are scattered upon the mountains

seems now to make curiously little difference. But the land remains. Still the long ridges descend toward the valley, and the peaks lift their crags above the pass; still the Yuba and the Bear and the American carve at their channels.

31. CAUSES

With the escape of Keseberg the actual story comes to an end. Of the eighty-seven emigrants who had pierced the Wahsatch and camped in the valley of the Great Salt Lake, five had died before reaching the mountain camps, thirty-four either at the camps or upon the mountains while attempting to cross, and one just after reaching the valley. To the number of dead may also be added Sutter's two Indian *vaqueros*, Luis and Salvador. The totals are therefore: dead, forty-two; survived, forty-seven.

In addition, many emigrants and men of the relief parties had lost toes from frost-bite and were otherwise injured. The oxen and dogs had all perished, and the horses and mules, too, with the possible exception of three which Stanton, McCutchen, and Reed may have taken through to Sutter's. Most of the emigrants' property had been left scattered along the way, or had been ruined by exposure. In short, the disaster was the most spectacular in the record of western migration.

The very fact that it may be called spectacular should warn us, however, against the fallacy of considering it typical. It is no more typical of the wagon-journey to California than the last voyages of the *Titanic* and the *Lusitania* are typical of the trans-Atlantic passage. Emigrants ordinarily suffered hardships along the Humboldt, and had a difficult struggle in getting over the Sierra, but they also had some good times upon the road, and often got through to California in good enough health and spirits.

One turns naturally to the question of what caused the disaster of the Donner Party. It was of course the direct result of their taking the so-called cut-off advocated by Hastings. But who was responsible? I have found widely spread a tendency to blame the emigrants themselves, to consider that they, or at least their leaders, were a pig-headed, ignorant lot who thought they knew more about matters than other people did and who by blundering ahead brought upon themselves pretty much what they deserved. As I have tried to show in the first chapters of this book, such an attitude is not well based. The Donner Party took the cut-off upon the advice of Hastings, a man who had crossed the mountains three times and had written a book on the subject. They had also the justification of the large party of emigrants who accompanied Hastings. They had finally the assurances of Vasquez and Bridger. You could hardly ask for more than this.

What made Hastings so blind to the difficulties? One is not altogether without a clue to his motives, and very curious ones they seem to have been. He probably, to be sure, got his guide's fee of ten dollars for each wagon in his company, but this hardly explains all his actions. According to the story told by a confidant, Hastings was playing a deeper game. Before the eye of his imagination hovered the brilliant figure of General Sam Houston, who had carved out from Mexico a republic of his own, and become its president. Hastings wanted to play Houston for California, and to gain a following he had conceived the idea of appearing to the emigrants as a heaven-sent guide and of binding them to himself by fast ties of loyalty and friendship as he led them to the promised land.

He forgot that to be a Sam Houston a man must be wise in council and bold in action, and in attempting to establish his cut-off Hastings was not bold but insanely rash, and not wise but idiotically foolish. In fact the more I look at it, the more strongly I believe that Hastings must have been essentially a salesman, one of California's first go-getters. He "sold" his route and himself to the emigrants, like many a later salesman not stopping to consider whether his wares could live up to his claims for them. But Hastings unfortunately for himself could not merely leave with his commission, and soon he was in a position where salesmanship did little good. The mountains and the desert are indifferent to even the cleverest talker; they possess what might be called a notably high sales-resistance.

But Hastings's own party got through without disaster. Can the troubles of the Donner Party then be ascribed to their own mistakes *after* entering the cut-off? Some have thought so, but the practice of suavely pointing out after the event that a certain person should have acted differently at a particular point has always seemed to me cheap and shoddy, and without a sound, logical basis.

Many after-the-event critics have, for instance, severely blamed the men of the Donner Party for taking the route across the Wahsatch instead of following down Weber Canyon. Actually, how did the emigrants arrive at this decision? They gathered first all information available about the two possible routes; then on the basis of this information they acted. No man can do more upon a similar occasion. Even to declare blandly that by taking the canyon route they would have avoided the final disaster, is totally unwarranted. They might in trying the canyon have smashed wheels upon rocks, lost wagons and oxen over the precipices, and met even worse disaster. The same uncertainty is involved in the other cases in which the men of the Donner Party have been considered foolish, for instance, in their delay at Truckee Meadows to recruit the cattle, and in their failure to realize just when the proper time had come for them to abandon their wagons and goods and push on afoot for their lives.

A more definite charge has, however, been brought against the Donner Party. In an article appearing in the *California Star* soon after the arrival of the snow-shoers at Johnson's the accusation was made that:

the whole party might have reached the California valley before the first fall of snow if the men had exerted themselves as they should have done. Nothing but a contrary and contentious disposition on the part of some of the men belonging to the party prevented them from getting in as soon as any of the first companies.

This article is unsigned, but the writer was probably McKinstry, who had been a member of Hastings's party; his source of information, moreover, can be gathered from other parts of the article, and seems to have been Reed. In spite of obvious exaggeration, therefore, this statement cannot be lightly disregarded. Moreover in his article written in 1871 Reed expressed similar ideas:

The work on the road [in the Wahsatch] slackened and the farther we advanced the slower the work progressed. I here state that the number of days we were detained in road-making was not the cause by any means, of the company remaining in the mountains during the following winter.

This was Reed's version, and there must be something in it, but we must remember that Reed himself was held largely responsible for the company's taking the route across the mountains, that he had been severely criticized as a result, and that his article of 1871 was largely a defense of himself in this and other matters. There must always be differences in point of view, and I make these statements not to insinuate against Reed's honesty, but as a possible expression of the point of view of others in the company. The work on the road naturally would slow down; the men were not used to labor with axes and after a few days many of them would be suffering from blistered hands and sore muscles. Nevertheless in sixteen days they cleared and made passable about thirty miles of road across difficult mountain country and largely through heavy brush. As I calculate it, each man had to make about one hundred fifty yards of road every day besides doing his share of making camp, watching cattle, and bringing the wagons through, often hard and tedious work, after the road was completed. This seems to me no light day's stint. So I reserve my right to believe at least the possibility that what appeared to the impetuous Reed as laziness, or malingering, or contentious shirking was actually genuine fatigue or was perhaps the effect of the free workman's prerogative of estimating for himself when he had done a day's work and not letting any one else make him do more.

I do not maintain that the men, or even the women, of the Donner Party were faultless, that they always made the right decisions, or that they were immune from the ordinary human shortcomings, including that of common stupidity. I do not believe, however, that they had more than their share of such weaknesses. And I object strongly to the smug conviction that because they starved to death we of a later day knowing only very different conditions can conclude that it was all their own fault.

32. AFTERWARDS

As Keseberg and the men of Fallon's party were descending toward the Sacramento Valley, they met a company of horsemen advancing up the emigrant road. Their leader was Elder Sam Brannan of the Church of Latter-Day Saints, and he was on his way to meet the great Mormon emigration with the intention of persuading their leader, President Brigham Young, to continue on to California instead of stopping to colonize in the valley by the Great Salt Lake. Elder Brannan was unsuccessful in this attempt, but incidentally he was the first to carry eastward the news of the catastrophe which had befallen the Donner Party.

The next company to cross was that of General Kearny proceeding eastward fresh from his conquest of California. With him was Fallon, "Le Gros," acting as guide. This party discovered near the road what was left of Stanton's body. Wild animals had almost devoured it, but some of the men identified the clothing and the pistols. On June 21 they found snow near the summit to be still fifteen or twenty feet deep. On the next day they came to the lake cabins, where the ground was then clear of snow. The General ordered a halt for the purpose of burying the few still intact bodies and the great number of mutilated fragments which lay about everywhere. The corpses wasted by famine and shrunken by exposure looked like mummies; summer had not made the butchered remnants any less repulsive.

A more revolting and appalling spectacle [wrote one member of the party] I never witnessed. The remains were, by an order of Gen. Kearny, collected and buried under the superintendence of Major Swords. They were interred in a pit which had been dug in the centre of one of the cabins for a *cache*. These melancholy duties to the dead being performed, the cabins, by order of Major Swords, were fired, and with every thing surrounding them connected with this horrid and melancholy tragedy, were consumed. The body of George Donner was found at his camp, about eight or ten miles distant, wrapped in a sheet. He was buried by a party of men detailed for that purpose.

But it was far from writing *finis* to the melancholy story of the lake cabins. Apparently Major Swords or his detail shirked the labor, so that many bones and fragments remained to the horror of later passers-by. They did not, moreover, burn all the cabins. The diaries of several forty-niners who passed the spot two full years later both note the gruesome sights to be seen and mention at least one cabin as still standing. It was the double one in which the Reeds and the Graveses had passed the winter. Even as late as the sixties the keeper of a public-house a mile or so from the lake on the stage-road exhibited a bag of bones, and a skull said, erroneously no doubt, to be George Donner's.

News of the disaster did not reach New York City by sea until July; those who carried the word overland did not meet the advancing emigrant trains of 1847 until the latter were too far west to consider turning back. Fear inspired by the story of what had happened in 1846 cannot, therefore, have prevented any one from starting for California the next spring, although that statement has sometimes been made. Emigrants, however, frightened by the news learned from Brannan and Kearny, may have abandoned their intention of going to California and turned aside for Oregon.

In other minor ways the catastrophe influenced the history of the West. It gave to the Hastings Cut-off across the Salt Lake Desert such unpleasant notoriety that the route was seldom attempted again. It also led emigrants, somewhat illogically, to view the Truckee route with suspicion, and so to open up the more northerly Lawson route in 1847. Memory of the disaster, moreover, caused the original name of Truckee or Truckee's Lake to become eventually Donner Lake. The names Donner Creek, Donner Pass, Donner Summit, and Donner Peak have also established themselves.

By a strange quirk the road which the men of the Donner Party cut through the Wahsatch turned out to be of more historical significance than anything else which they did. For this rough track hewn out with such travail made possible the quick and easy settlement of the Mormons in the valley of the Great Salt Lake. And the hosts of Zion, as they poured through this passage, made ready and waiting, rendered scant acknowledgment or thanks; they even named the road "Pratt's Cut-off" after one of their own leaders.

The Mormons made only one relocation of any importance. Remember that the men of the Donner Party, wearied with cutting their way, came down at last into a canyon blocked at its outlet with brush. Then they double-teamed, and rather than do any more ax-work hauled their wagons up the steep north side of the canyon. When the Mormon vanguard arrived at this point, they marveled at such a procedure, and going ahead soon cut a road out at the mouth of the canyon. The incident shows how utterly weary the men of the Donner Party must have been of road-making at that moment.

Although the adventure of the Donner Party is thus, historically considered, a minor incident, its spectacular qualities have caused it to become one of the most widely known of western stories, and have led also to the preservation of an unusual amount of reliable testimony concerning it. A curious confirmation of one of the less plausible incidents was furnished in 1891 when a certain Edward Reynolds discovered a considerable sum of money in old coins which had been concealed about four hundred feet from the margin of the central part of Donner Lake, undoubtedly the hoard which Mrs. Graves in her anxiety had hidden on the morning of March 4, 1847.

The amazing preservation of detailed records has not, however, prevented the growth of some legends, for this is the stuff of which folk-tales grow. One of these tells that the old trapper George Yount, living in Napa Valley, dreamed vividly for three successive nights during the winter of 1846. He saw clear as day a lake hemmed in with mountains and a band of emigrants caught in the snow, cold and starving, in their extremity devouring the bodies of the dead. He himself had never seen the place, but so clearly could he describe it from the dreams that others, who knew the mountains better, recognized it. As a result, so the legend runs, Yount organized a party, and guided by those who recognized the description pierced the mountains and achieved the rescue of the Donner Party. The last part is of course pure fiction, and correspondingly throws doubt upon the whole story, which has little enough authority at best. Yount was a man who believed in dreams, and frequently indulged in them. Nevertheless for many years the tale was current, and was even propagated by a bishop.

An even more startling legend has been recorded in Utah, where the people around Grantsville, which the emigrants called Twenty Wells, had their own version of the story. There a general belief among the Mormons was that judgment fell upon the Donner Party as persecutors of the Saints. An angry God, they averred, smote men, women, and children, so that they died of thirst in the desert, all except six who managed, crawling upon hands and knees, to reach water and tell the story. It is a curiously perverted idea of vengeance, for actually the fate which befell the Donner Party was much more terrible than a quick death on the salt plain.

33. THE CHARACTERS

THE men, women, and children of the Donner Party were rapidly absorbed into the population of California, for it was a frontier community where anyone able to use his hands was sure to find plenty of work to do. As always in the early West, women were scarce, and almost before the frost-bite was out of their toes, the girls were receiving advances and accepting suitors. Mary Graves, who had come through the terrible ordeal of the snow-shoers, was married in May, and Elitha Donner in June. The latter was only fourteen, and it was at the time of her marriage only three months since her escape from the snow. Her husband, as it happened, was that Perry McCoon whose little schooner had turned up in the river just in time to ferry Reed and his relief party across the flooded Sacramento. Before the year was out, the widowed Harriet Pike had married again. And Eliza Williams, the hired girl, who had served the Reeds for many years, and was thought to be a hopeless old maid, even she found a husband. Virginia Reed wrote back to her cousin in Springfield with childish glee at the gossip:

Tell the girls that this is the greatest place for marrying they ever saw, and that they must come to California if they want to marry. Tell —— that [Eliza] is engaged to be married. You all think this is a joke, but I tell you 'tis the truth.

The later history of the members of the Party and of their rescuers was on the whole uneventful, and seems even to result artistically in anticlimax. Take gigantic John Starks, for instance, the one who heroically toiled through the snow carrying so many children. To live on for thirty years and then one day to die, like any farmer, of heart failure while at the prosaic enterprise of pitching hay!

No individual connected with the story of the Donner Party rose to very great eminence. Several of the families have, however, been of much local importance. The Breens around San Juan Bautista, the Reeds and the Donners at San José, and the Murphys at Marysville counted for much in the development of their communities, and figure in the regional history.

One of the members for whom I have come to have much admiration is William Eddy. No one excelled him in heroic endeavor, and yet his own story, as recorded through Thornton, is remarkably free from egotism. His fate was tragic, for he lost everything—oxen, wagon, goods, wife, son, and daughter. It is pleasant to be able to record that Eddy restored his fortunes in California, married again, and became the father of another family. He died, however, in 1859, still a young man.

One of the most colorful members of the Party was big McCutchen with his picturesque vocabulary. He lived to a white-bearded and vigorous old age at San José, where he did not lose touch with his comrade of the mountains, James Reed. In 1871 an article appeared in the *Pacific Rural Press* based upon reminiscences of a Mrs. Curtis, none other than the woman whom with her husband the two fathers had found cooking the dog in the snow-buried camp at Bear Valley. Mrs. Curtis attacked both McCutchen and Reed, and as a result we find the two old comrades again off on a rescue party, this time to rescue their own reputations. They decidedly put Mrs. Curtis in her place, but it is a pity that we have only what McCutchen wrote upon this occasion; what he said was probably more vivid.

Reed himself lived and prospered. When banished from the company on the Humboldt, he had managed to carry with him a considerable sum of money, and with this he bought a large tract of land close to the village of San José. Upon the discovery of gold he went to the mines, returned well laden, and again invested in lands. The increase in the value of his property, keeping pace with the rapid growth of the town, made him wealthy. He became one of California's first subdividers, and in 1850 his advertisements of lots for sale were appearing on the front pages of the San Francisco newspapers. He was active in public affairs, and was said to have spent twenty thousand dollars in the effort to have San José made the capital of the state. Later on, he suffered the usual vicissitudes of fortune which hardly any one in the California of those days was able to escape, but he managed in the end to sustain himself. Mrs. Reed, she who had so audaciously dared the snowy summits with Virginia and faithful Milt, lived until 1861. Reed died in 1874. The children—Virginia, Patty, Jim, and little Tommy—all grew to maturity. Virginia, according to her promise in the time of storms, became a Catholic.

It is pleasant to know also that Reed adopted into his family the little Mary Donner whom he had tried to rescue and who had suffered so terribly from frost-bite during the great storm. In 1859 she married S. O. Houghton, a rising young lawyer of San José, but tragedy which had been foiled in the snow still awaited her, and in less than a year she lay dead in childbirth.

The three little daughters of George and Tamsen Donner —Frances, Georgia, and Eliza—got along better than one might have expected. Hiram Miller, who had carried Eliza across the snow, was made their guardian, but they did not see much of him. A kind-hearted Swiss pair named Brunner, who lived near Sutter's, took pity upon the children and gave them a home. The little ones soon were happy again, and called Mrs. Brunner "grandma." They were not entirely destitute, for some of their property had been salvaged and a little money recovered. Afterwards Frances went to live with the Reeds in San José, but the two younger ones continued with the Brunners until they were old enough to go to boarding school. They, and their two elder half-sisters also, were of hardy stock, and seem to have suffered no bad effects from the experiences of the winter. All five of them married, raised families, and lived to a good age, Leanna almost attaining her century. Eliza became the second wife of that same S. O. Houghton who had previously been the husband of her cousin Mary Donner. In 1911 when close to seventy Mrs. Houghton published *The Expedition of the Donner Party,* an account based largely upon printed records, but preserving also some of her own and of her sisters' recollections.

Of the men of the rescue parties little need be told. They got their pay at least. Of so much we can be certain, for after various adventures Captain Kern's papers have finally come to light again, and among them certain sheets filled with lists of names and scratchings of arithmetic, and constituting what may be called the pay-roll of the Donner relief. The men received a dollar and a half a day for general aid, carrying forward supplies, and so forth, but the men of Glover's party got three dollars from the time of their leaving Sutter's. Whether they got the extra two dollars a day which had been promised them in the snow at Bear Valley is not stated on the pay-roll; they most likely received it on a separate account from Sutter and Sinclair. Sometimes amusing and sometimes poignant are the individual items of the pay-rolls. Fifty dollars is listed for William Thompson for carrying out "F. Donough," and the same to John Starks for bringing out "John Graves." One item reads: "Mr. Tucker one Coverlid left with Mr. Denton @ $20 dollars." Redoubtable Ned Coffeemeyer claimed compensation for one flannel shirt, one pair of stockings, and one pair of drawers. Jotham Curtis, whose wagon in Bear Valley had served as a source of supplies, put in a statement of damages which curiously illustrates current values: one buffalo rug, $4.00; three tin buckets, $9.00; two tin cans, $1.50. Some of these claims seem high; I doubt whether Glover's coverlid was actually worth twenty dollars, but for leaving it under the circumstances one would gladly count him entitled to double the amount. Sept Moultry is said at some later date to have pressed a claim upon Congress for twenty thousand dollars in compensation of his heroism in rescuing the emigrants. No one doubted his heroism, but he was never granted the money.

As for Hastings himself, the arch-mover, he lived a life which was marked, it would seem, by tragic frustration. His dream of rivaling Sam Houston vanished with the annexation of California, and with the dreadful aftermath of his own attempt to become the emigrants' guide and savior. Instead of a host of friends and retainers, he found that his summer's endeavor had won him bitter enemies. Some even made threats to kill him. Nevertheless he set up a practice of law in San Francisco, and in 1849 was a member of the State Convention at Monterey. But after that he began to drift about, still full of plans too ambitious for his capabilities. He espoused the Confederate cause, and in 1863 went to Richmond with a scheme for raising forces among sympathizers in California, seizing control of Arizona, and making the Bonnie Blue Flag fly triumphant all the way across the continent. But nothing came of it. After the war he went to South America, and finally in 1870, the old dream of empire still in mind, he died while trying to establish a colony of ex-Confederates in Brazil.

Of all the leaders in the relief of the Donner Party, Selim Woodworth, that son of the writer of the "Old Oaken Bucket," came off with the worst reputation. His own reports leave us with the impression of too great egotism. He certainly seems to be giving the impression that he had actually crossed the mountains, and been in person the leader of the relief parties. Actually he was never even as far as Summit Valley, and the treatment which he receives at the hands of the others connected with the expedition is harsh. They imply that he was a martinet, not always sober, and they even impugn his courage. Yet curiously (or is it only that this is the kind of man who naturally prospers in civilization?) Selim Woodworth was in after life the most successful of all of them. He rapidly went to the front in business in San Francisco. In 1851 he was president of the great Vigilance Committee, an office which in spite of its dubious character was considered both responsible and honorable, and which certainly required courage. In 1854 the *Annals of San Francisco* included his portrait and biographical sketch along with those of about a dozen other outstanding citizens; but its account of his activities in the rescue of the Donner Party sounds suspiciously as if written by himself. ("As bad as Munchausen's or Gulliver's big stories," Billy Graves called it, but he was only a blacksmith at Calistoga, and his word wouldn't count for much in San Francisco.) When the war came, Woodworth rejoined the navy and rose to the rank of Commodore. He died in 1870, still a prominent citizen.

We may spare a word also for Fallon, "Le Gros," who bent the rope around Keseberg's neck. After guiding Kearny eastward, he undertook to return to California the next year. He set out from Fort Hall alone, and, as it went with so many of the mountain-men, simply "got rubbed out." Was it a wide-ranging war-party of Blackfeet, or did his scalp dry in the wickiups of the Shoshones? At least he died in character. From '45 to '48 he marched across the pages of history, and then as he had appeared, he went, mysteriously, and if we may guess it, not peacefully.

Of all those who struggled and endured through that winter of horror, not one remains. Naomi Pike, who had become the wife of John L. Schenck, made a valiant attempt to be the last survivor, but after I had written a first draft of this very passage, news came that she had died, at the age of ninety, in the spring of 1934. Her death left finally Mrs. MacMahon of San Francisco, who had been the infant Isabella Breen. The relief party led by Eddy and Foster had found her close to death in that pit of horrors where the fire burned, hemmed in by high walls of snow. Stalwart John Starks helped rescue her along with the rest of the family, until they met at Yuba Bottoms the valiant men of the first relief advancing again into the snow. She died on March 25, 1935.

34. "KESEBERG VS. COFFYMERE"

THE deeds and character of Keseberg have caused more controversy than any other subject connected with the Donner Party. It is a controversy which I would gladly avoid; but it is, I fear, essential to the completion of the story. It involves, moreover, much besides the character of Keseberg, for if he was blameless, then Eddy, Foster, Tucker, Fallon, Coffeemeyer, and a good many others can be considered nothing better than persecutors and liars.

After Keseberg's arrival at Sutter's Fort some of the men of Fallon's party talked freely about him, with the result that he brought action in the court of Alcalde Sinclair. Little is known of the details, but in the Bancroft Library is still preserved a writ from Sinclair to Sheriff McKinstry with

instructions to summon Mrs. Wolfinger. On the back of the
document is the memorandum: "Mrs. Wolfinger. Witness
for the Plaintiff. Keseberg vs. Coffymere. Action for Def-
amation of Character. Damages $1,000." The date of the
trial was set for May 5, 1847.

The cause of the action was presumably that Coffeemeyer
had declared Keseberg guilty of murdering Tamsen Donner.
The court awarded the plaintiff one dollar of damages, but
apparently forced him to pay costs. This seems in itself a
rather ambiguous verdict, and certainly the trial, like most
of its sort, settled absolutely nothing, except perhaps that no
legal proof of the murder existed. People kept on thinking
and talking. Some said that Keseberg had a hold over Sutter,
something of scandalous nature, so that the latter's pre-
ponderant influence had been brought to bear on the case.
Even after the verdict the *California Star* did not refrain
from publishing Fallon's journal, and although in it no positive statements were made about the murder, still the implica-
tions were strong.

At this time Sutter gave Keseberg command of the
schooner *Sacramento,* which was employed in taking wheat
down to San Francisco. It was a place from which Keseberg
might well have stayed away, for on the word of his land-
ing, Eddy armed himself and set out to fulfill his vow of
killing Keseberg. Luckily for every one, Eddy happened to
meet James Reed and Edwin Bryant, and these two persuaded
him to give up his idea.

In 1848 Keseberg, like almost every one else in California,
went to the mines. Then he came back to the new city of
Sacramento, and with a certain lack of good taste, one might
think, opened up a restaurant. In the boom of the gold rush
he made money rapidly, and bought a hotel. In 1851 bluff
George McKinstry, now no longer sheriff, wrote to Captain
Kern bringing him up to date on what had happened to
some of their old acquaintances; one sentence ran:

Old Keseberg, the Man-eater, has made a fortune, and is now
keeping a Restaurant in K St., Sac. City. I would like to board
there, I wouldn't!

In those early days, we have it on good authority, Keseberg
sometimes actually flaunted his prowess as a cannibal; he was

heard boasting publicly in a bar-room that human liver was the best meat he ever ate. Now the amazing fifties of California had a strong stomach and a prodigious appetite for the horrible and bizarre. Was not Joaquin Murrieta's head put on exhibition? In those times Keseberg's cannibalism might have gained him only a great and not unpleasant notoriety. But with the sixties the times of the frontier and the gold-rush had passed, and solid citizens began to look askance at the big German with the blond beard. He began to feel the chill and to suffer petty persecutions. Urchins jeered at him, and threw stones. He had lost his money, too, and it was not so easy to be nonchalant now that he was poor and growing old. Thus he sank out of sight in the new civilization which was growing up around him; obscurity was perhaps the best thing that he could hope for.

But in 1879 he reappeared from oblivion. In this spring Mr. C. F. McGlashan was working upon his history of the Donner Party. He visited Eliza Donner Houghton, and was surprised to find that she rejected the story that Keseberg had murdered her mother. Thereupon he went on to say that he had enough evidence in a single note-book to convict Keseberg of murder or at the least so to arouse public sentiment against him that he would have to leave the state. At last, however, Mr. McGlashan decided that he would find Keseberg before loosing the hounds of public fury against him. A detective agency quickly located the intended victim near Sacramento, very poor, unwilling to meet any one in a public place, or even to walk the main streets for fear of being recognized. His wife was dead, and he lived in squalor with two imbecile daughters who suffered from violent seizures during which they screamed and fell into fits.

Upon two occasions McGlashan interviewed Keseberg, and finally became convinced of his innocence as regarded the death of Tamsen Donner and of his comparative blamelessness in many other matters. A month later Mrs. Houghton talked with Keseberg, and was reaffirmed in her belief that her mother had not died a violent death. Keseberg could evoke no evidence except his own statement, but his manner was reassuring. "In conversing," wrote McGlashan, "he looks one squarely and steadily in the eye, and appears like an honest, intelligent German." He defended himself against the old charges of malingering by saying that he had injured his foot by stepping upon a sharp stub, part of which had remained deep in the flesh. This made him unable to walk during a large part of the winter, and even after the splinter had worked out and the wound healed, he had again disabled himself by cutting his heel with an ax while chopping wood. These injuries, he said, had prevented his going out with the earlier rescue parties. In corroboration he showed a scar on his heel.

With reference to the death of Tamsen Donner he denied the story of the kettles full of blood, pointing out that the blood would have coagulated. He also declared that he had no reason to have killed her for her money, since she was only too anxious to try crossing the mountains alone and in that attempt would almost certainly have died. He said as a final argument that he had no need of her body as food, for many other corpses remained.

But in this interview, too, his manner more than his argument seems to have convinced his interviewers. He called upon God to be his witness; tears stood in his eyes; he sank upon his knees before Mrs. Houghton. The pity of his situation also moved his hearers. He felt himself to be among the persecuted, declaring on one occasion:

> Only a man conscious of his innocence, and clear in the sight of God, would not have succumbed to the terrible things which have been said of me—would not have committed suicide! Mortification, disgrace, disaster, and unheard-of misfortune have followed and overwhelmed me. I often think that the Almighty has singled me out, among all the men on the face of the earth, in order to see how much hardship, suffering, and misery a human being can bear!

After this time he lived on to the age of eighty-one, and died peacefully in the Sacramento County Hospital in 1895. He made no death-bed confession, and left no message.

By his conversations with McGlashan and Mrs. Houghton Keseberg added little to our general knowledge of the Donner Party, but he succeeded in influencing both his interviewers in his own favor. The manner of his death seems also to have even further established his innocence in the mind of Mrs. Houghton. In their books they therefore considered him largely as a martyr, and some later writing has even attempted to whitewash him entirely. Charitable at this seems from one point of view, it results, as I have already pointed out, in vilifying Eddy and many others concomitantly with clearing Keseberg. It is best to be neutral in such a case, and let all parties be heard. So far as I know, no one has ever attempted to state both sides, and having given Keseberg's defense, I should like to outline what Coffeemeyer, veteran of Glover's as well as of Fallon's party, might state on his account, if he were here to argue his own side of the case.

As for the blood, he might point out that nothing in Fallon's journal indicates that the blood in the kettles was not coagulated. Every fool who has done so much as to cut a finger knows this property of blood, and perhaps to these men accustomed to hunting and to butchering of cattle it seemed incredible that anyone could assume them to mean liquid blood. There is no reason, I think, why one may not speak of a kettle of blood even though it is coagulated. As to the second reason, that Mrs. Donner was about to start over the pass alone, for this there is only Keseberg's own statement; and besides, if she had made the attempt, both her money and her body would probably have been lost. As for the third reason, that many other bodies were available so that he had no need to commit a murder to obtain food, this is by no means certain, for many bodies had probably been laid away in the snow in locations which Keseberg did not know. Moreover, Keseberg made use of Mrs. Donner's body while others were still available, and this in itself gives the suggestion of a motive. Keseberg was certainly in an almost demented state at the time. Even so, he may not have preferred carrion when better fare was available. It is an ugly suggestion, but Coffeemeyer should be allowed the benefit of the argument.

Entirely aside from questions involving the death of Tamsen Donner, doubt may be thrown upon the complete veracity of Keseberg's statement. By a comparison of chronology and in other ways several inaccuracies may be brought out. Most of these may be attributed to mere forgetfulness, but one seems deliberately misleading:

Mrs. Murphy lived about a week after we were left alone. When my provisions gave out, I remained four days before I could taste human flesh.

On its face this seems certainly intended to arouse a belief that Keseberg did not practice cannibalism until the death of Mrs. Murphy about March 20; actually one can scarcely doubt the evidence that he had begun more than three weeks before that date.

The upshot is that lacking further evidence there can be no final decision upon the question of Mrs. Donner's death, and the argument can easily be (perhaps already has been) spun out *ad nauseam*. Altogether I find Keseberg arraigned upon twelve counts, not to mention one or two which seem to be straw-men set up by his defenders in order to be triumphantly knocked down.

On five of the twelve the evidence seems to be from neutral, reliable sources, and I have accordingly stated these as facts in my account. They are, that Keseberg robbed an Indian grave, that he mistreated his wife, that from motives of revenge he was unduly anxious to lynch Reed, that he abandoned Hardkoop heartlessly, and that he boasted of his own cannibalism. It seems probable also on the face of the evidence that he was attempting to make off with some of the Donners' property. Three points seem by their very nature not to be proved one way or the other: that he malingered, and that he killed Tamsen Donner and George Foster. Two charges seem unlikely: that he killed Mrs. Murphy and Samuel Donner. One, never stated by a good first-hand authority, seems entirely unfounded: that he was involved in the death of Wolfinger.

In the face of the almost universal testimony of those who in '46 and '47 came into contact with him, it seems difficult to clear Keseberg entirely or to place implicit reliance upon his own statements. McGlashan in summing up his account of Keseberg states that, although he may be guilty of certain misdeeds, the most careful searcher for evidence cannot find the slightest proof that Keseberg committed any of them. This seems convincing, but it is really only a half-statement. For also, the most careful searcher cannot find the slightest proof that Keseberg did not commit them. In other words, even in McGlashan's time, thirty-two years after the event, it was not a question of proofs, but of human testimony, always liable to err and become confused, but seldom likely to be completely fabricated.

35. TABOO

In considering the case of Keseberg I have given little regard to the question of cannibalism. For there can be no doubt of the fact itself; besides, he did in this matter only what others of the party did; and finally under the circumstances neither he nor the others can be held culpable. One may think him blameworthy for his boasting, his flaunting of the deed, but certainly not for the cannibalism itself. That was the result of necessity, and of a necessity recognized by even such a great authority upon the conduct of life as the Catholic Church.

The Breens, for instance, were Catholics, and seem beyond doubt to have resorted to cannibalism after Reed had left them behind at the camp in the snow. Yet if Patrick Breen later told all this in confession, a priest would have instructed the penitent that he had comitted no sin, and would have prescribed no penance. And he might even have added that in overcoming natural scruples in order to preserve his life a Catholic is thought as much to practice virtue as to commit a sin.

A reasonable man of whatever religion or of no religion at all would hardly, one would think, depart very far from this attitude, and yet the matter of cannibalism seems really to be a kind of taboo in which reason fails to function. Certainly most people regard it with an irrational repulsion entirely out of proportion to any experience which they themselves can have had with it. It is regarded as one of the unclean things, like certain practices of sex, not to be discussed or even thought of. Some, I am sure, will look upon this book as a piece of obscenity, and will be angry with me for touching the subject at all. Nevertheless, the cannibalism, although it might almost be called a minor episode, has become in the popular mind the chief fact to be remembered about the Donner Party. For a taboo always allures with as great strength as it repels.

Such was its power that some of the survivors were led to deceits and falsifications and even inadvertently confessed themselves guilty of worse uglinesses rather than admit this one fact. And why should this have been so? Surely the necessity, starvation itself, had forced them to all that they did, and surely no just man would ever have pointed at them in scorn, or assumed his own superiority. "There but for the grace of God, go I!"—such an attitude is the only one which a decent man can assume in the case.

Even the seemingly ghoulish actions involved in the story may be rationally explained. To open the bodies first for the heart and liver, and to saw apart the skulls for the brain were not acts of perversion. We must remember that these people had been living for months upon the hides and lean meat of half-starved work-oxen; their diet was lacking not only in mere quantity, but also in all sorts of necessary vitamins and mineral constituents, even in common salt. Almost uncontrollable cravings must have assailed them, cravings which represented a real deficiency in diet to be supplied in some degree at least by the organs mentioned. If Keseberg said that human liver was better than lean beef, most likely a starved body more than a perverted mind was speaking.

I myself am a man somewhat squeamish in dietary habits; I am not comfortable in the presence of tripe, and pass with a certain feeling those little shops in the back-streets of French towns where one sees displayed the freshly flayed side of a horse. And yet this horror of cannibalism seems to me disproportionate. Humanity may fall into many worse degradations. Personally I should rather admit to cannibalism under necessity than to some of the actions to which members of the Donner Party admitted in order to escape suspicion of that particular act.

The case of Jean Baptiste is an example. The reader may have noticed that throughout the book I have been at diffi-culty in restraining a dislike for this character; I introduced him under the term "mongrel," and by so doing I intended not only to refer to his mixed blood, but also to indicate that he possessed the qualities conventionally ascribed to dogs of that sort. More than once, it appears, he wished or even at-tempted to escape on his own account and leave the Donners in the lurch, and finally he succeeded in doing so. But this is not the worst. For after getting out of the mountains, Jean Baptiste went to San Francisco where, that same summer, he happened to meet Lieutenant Wise of the United States Navy. To him Jean Baptiste expatiated largely upon the experiences of the Donner Party. He was the hero of his own tale, and his heroism consisted not only in mighty deeds of endurance but also in hair-raising feats of cannibalism. He had eaten Jacob Donner; he had even, but this was perhaps a lie, eaten a baby. Moreover, with a perverted pride, he called attention to himself by wallowing loathsomely in the details; as Wise reported his words: "eat baby raw, stewed some of Jake, and roasted his head, not good meat, taste like sheep with the rot." This was the way in which he pictured himself and his deeds in 1847.

But in 1884 Jean Baptiste came to talk with Eliza Donner Houghton. In spite of his bad qualities the little Mexican had apparently been fond of the children, and they in their turn had liked him. He was much affected as he talked with Mrs. Houghton, and while his voice trembled and the tears coursed down his cheeks he denied flatly that any cannibalism at all had occurred at the Donner camp. The hair and bones found, he said, were those of cattle; the bodies of the dead were never disturbed, and as the snow deepened even the location of the graves was lost.

Now even if a little boastful, what Jean Baptiste told to Lieutenant Wise was much nearer the truth than what he told later to Mrs. Houghton. Certainly one tale or the other must be a downright lie. And as for the accompaniments of coursing tears and a trembling voice—when I consider such hypocrisy I feel a longing for the society of an honest cannibal!

But to end on this note of disgust would be false, and would place too much emphasis upon the merely anthropophagic phase of the story. The emigrant train formed, as I have already suggested in the first chapter, a microcosm or little world in itself, and to judge it properly, as with the greater world, we must, in Matthew Arnold's well-worn phrase, see it steadily and see it whole. Hypocrisy there is in the story, and weakness, false pride and vaunting, deceit, poltroonery, ugly perversions, and baleful frenzies. But there is more also. Through the story runs the scarlet thread of courage and the golden thread of heroism. There is even humor, as when bluff Sheriff McKinstry writing to Kern and Woodworth warns them to "look out for those man eating

women," and adds a ribald comment as to the size of the
pieces in which those women are said to prefer their meat.
But along with ribaldry, constancy is there too, and strength
of body and mind, love and self-sacrifice, ingenuity of thought
and long-suffering endurance. They were strong timber, those
who lived through that winter, and like all strong timber
they had their scarcely suspected roots gripping hard to life
and reaching deep into the ugliness of clay and worms.

The story of their ordeal is not pleasant. Few, I fear, will
find it always easy reading. But after all, the merely pleasant
is thin and bloodless; a picnic in the park scarcely gives humanity a chance to show of what it is capable. Not of that
sort, all will agree, is this adventure in the snow. Here, if
anywhere, we see men and women and children put to the
final strain of body and spirit. Yet suicide finds no place in
the story. And since these too in great part endured, others
in evil circumstance may be encouraged to fight boldly. By
this, their story may even be said to meet the demands of
some that literature should serve an extraneous social purpose. For though despair is often close at hand, it never tri-
umphs, and through all the story runs, a sustaining bond, the
primal force which humanity shares with all earthly creatures,
the sheer will to live.

SUPPLEMENT–1960

FOREWORD

SINCE I first worked on this book, a quarter-century ago, a great deal has happened. I now read the first sentence of the Foreword to Part I with a sense of shock. When written, the idea there expressed seemed mere fantasy, though useful as a literary device—that a man might hover in space some hundreds of miles above the surface of the earth, thence to survey the landscape below. Now, however, we appear to be just upon the edge of doing that very thing, and perhaps within another twenty-five years some observer will take his position there to see whether my description is correct.

But within this time-span, in spite of the invasion of space and other events, people have continued to be interested in the Donner Party. And this interest, more deeply considered, is not surprising. The story is basically one of people under stress. As such, it speaks to us still. The cause of the stress is not important—the smashing of a wagon wheel or of an atom, a fall of snow or of strontium 90. The human element remains the same.

One might even assemble evidence to show that interest in the story has actually intensified. Not only have many books and articles based more or less directly upon the story appeared in print, but also the name Donner Trail appears to be taking over, even on official maps, such older designations as the California Trail and the Truckee Route. It is now in use from Utah westward.

Also to be noted is the establishment and maintenance of Donner Memorial State Park, visited yearly by many thousands. Plans have been initiated for the building of a museum in which memorials of the Donner Party will be displayed.

A much visited feature of the park is the big rock, now bearing a bronze plaque with the names of the members of the party, and securely identifying the location of what has come to be known as the Murphy cabin. A bronze statuary group of heroic size marks, either exactly or approximately (there has been controversy on the question), the site of the so-called Breen cabin.

The use of this name is a further demonstration of the way in which the incidents of the Donner story have tended to displace others. The cabin was actually built by Joseph Foster, Allen Montgomery, and Moses Schallenberger of the Stevens Party, in late November, 1844. The narrative left by Schallenberger is the chief record of the discovery of the pass and of his own solitary wintering in the cabin. In *The Opening of the California Trail* (1953) I have reprinted his narrative, and have attempted to do justice to the pioneers of 1844. None the less, while the name Stevens may be known to one, the name Donner is known to a hundred. . . .

Two collections of material have become available since the original publication of this book. One of these is that presented to the Sutter's Fort Museum by the descendants of James F. Reed. Most of this material has been edited by Carroll D. Hall, and published as *Donner Miscellany* (1947). It consists of some brief letters, some miscellaneous papers, such as receipts, and two diaries. One of these last is published in this volume as the Reed Diary. The other, often mentioned as the Miller-Reed Diary, is also a document of some importance. Although the earlier entries are in two different hands, the handwriting from July 3 onward has been identified as that of James F. Reed. As the composite authorship would indicate, the manuscript is to be considered, not a personal diary, but a kind of log-book for the party as a whole.

The new evidence thus afforded, within the interval covered, confirms the major events of the story, as they are already told in this volume. Questions are raised upon some details which can scarcely be considered important. For instance, was Reed's axle broken on the shore of the lake (p. 32) or in the mountains? Was Halloran buried at Black Rock (p. 32) or a day's journey farther west? Did the Indian named Thursday travel with the company on Friday (p. 49) or on Tuesday? But before getting much concerned about such discrepancies we should note that the log-book confirms previous evidence on the events themselves, that is, that Reed's wagon suffered a broken axle, that Halloran died and was buried, and that an Indian traveled with the emigrants for a day.

The log-book thus differs from previous evidence principally in chronology. Some of its entries, however, were demonstrably not written on the date given but on a later date, and errors of chronology are thus possible.

In preparing my *Itinerary* for the original edition I was chiefly dependent upon Thornton. But his chronology was often impossible. I therefore revised it as well as I could in the light of time and distance and what other testimony was available. The chronology as now supplied by the log-book I consider to be much more reliable than that of Thornton, and better than that of the *Itinerary*. On the other hand, I am not convinced that it is absolutely correct.

The best procedure, doubtless, is merely to record the log-book chronology, and thus to allow anyone who wishes to do so to check it against the *Itinerary* (p. 293). Only seven entries are affected.

August 11–22. Cross Wahsatch Mountains.
August 23–28. Travel from near [Salt Lake City] to springs in [Skull Valley].
August 29. Rest at springs in [Skull Valley].
August 30–September 3. Cross Salt Lake Desert to springs at base of [Pilot Peak, Nevada].
September 4–9. In camp resting.
September 10–26. Travel *via* [Silver Zone Pass etc.], rejoining Fort Hall Road about ten miles southwest of [Elko].
September 27–October 12 [?]. Travel along Humboldt River to its sink.

This chronology makes a difference in time expended in the crossing of the Wahsatch. My summation on page 31 was to the effect that this part of the journey, including the time in camp, consumed twenty-one days. This figure may now have to be revised to seventeen days. Nevertheless, the time thus lost remains critical in causing the final disaster.

After the last log-book entry we become dependent again upon Thornton, supplemented by "dead-reckoning" as to how many days would reasonably be expended by jaded oxen passing over an estimated distance. This part of the itinerary can therefore be left as it appears on pages 293–95, with the advice that the dates before the arrival at the lake be accepted with caution, as is indicated by the note on page 304.

On the whole, as I see it now, the thirteen days that I originally allowed for the journey down the Humboldt would scarcely have been sufficient. The extra days allowed by the log-book chronology could have been expended upon this leg of the journey, so that the arrival at the sink may still be put at October 12, if not, indeed, even a day or two later. If we accept this latter possibility, the halt at Truckee Meadows (pages 64–66) would have been shorter, and this would be reasonable, since the length of the rest there has never seemed to me quite explicable in the circumstances, though seemingly necessitated by the record.

And—to digress for a moment—I may state that some further knowledge of the tribes of the region has cleared up for me a point about the relations with the Indians. As long as the wagon-train was in Shoshone country, there was no trouble. The depredations commenced as soon as the emigrants came into contact with the Piutes.

The log-book also presents some possible evidence as to one small section of the route. On pages 42–43 and on the map (p. 30) I indicated that the Donner Party departed from Hastings's route at one point. The entries in the log-book, however, can be taken to indicate that the Donner Party followed Hastings over the longer route, *via* the point which the Jefferson map indicates as Chiles Cache.

I am, however, for various reasons, inclined to think the log-book in error. First, Thornton is here rather circumstantial. Second, the account in the *California Star* of February 13, 1847, states that Stanton and McCutchen left when the party was recruiting after "the second long drive of 35 miles"; this would mean that the two left on September 18 and took with them the memory that there was a second long drive, of about the same length as that mentioned by Thornton. Finally, the distance between the last camp in the lake bed and "Basin Camp" was thirty-six miles, according to the log-book; forty, according to the estimate in Thornton. But the distance by way of Chiles Cache, according to Jefferson, was fifty miles. Thus even the log-book, in its estimate of only thirty-six miles, speaks for the shorter route, though in other ways it indicates the longer one.

As for details or "color" the log-book may be described as a log-book, and nothing more. It is little concerned with personal matters, and from internal evidence anyone would even have difficulty in judging it to be Reed's work. It chiefly records the miles traversed and the conditions of travel. The ordinary entry runs to only a few words.

Typical entries are: "Made this day nearly due north in Sinking Creek Valley about ten miles owing to water," or "Left camp about ten o'clock and made this day 12 miles down the river." The record for days when no traveling was done is likely to be even shorter—"Rested in camp," or "Still in camp." Upon almost the only occasion when an interesting incident seems to be in the background, the record is tantalizingly brief. This is the entry for September 14: "left the Basin Camp or Mad Woman Camp, as all the women in camp were mad with anger." As to what had aroused the distaff side, we are thus left entirely and eternally in ignorance. . . .

Differing vastly from the thin log-book, the McGlashan papers, as yet uncatalogued in the Bancroft Library, are voluminous. In 1878 Charles Fayette McGlashan was thirty-one years old, editor of the *Truckee Republican*. One day a gentleman entered the office and proved to be Judge James F. Breen, that son of Patrick Breen who had been about four years old in 1846. There ensued a conversation in the course of which Breen promised, in McGlashan's words, "he would help me write the history of the Donner Party."

Judge Breen was not in a good position to help anyone very much in writing such a history. He did not even possess an accurate copy of his father's famous diary, but he kept his word by supplying some information. He really accomplished his purpose, however, by igniting McGlashan's tremendous and long-continuing energy.

McGlashan, we must remember, was editor of a small-town newspaper, not a trained historian. His idea of how to collect information was to interview the survivors, either by letter or directly. He made little allowance for what might have happened to people's memories in thirty years, and he was not trained in appraising documentary evidence.

Breen had visited McGlashan late in 1878; after only a few months, early in 1879, articles on the story appeared in a special number of the *Republican*. A small book, *History of the Donner Party, A Tragedy of the Sierra,* appeared late in 1879, was published in a revised edition in 1880, and since that time has been often reprinted.

The acceptance and the success of this hastily compiled volume was amazing. Hubert H. Bancroft, in the fifth volume of his massive *History of California,* appearing in 1886, commented, "C. F. McGlashan published a volume on the subject in 1879, treating it in a manner that has left little or nothing to be desired." Perhaps because of this eulogy, the work has received high praise from later historians.

As the record would indicate, I do not agree with this opinion. If I had agreed, I should obviously not have tried to write my own history. McGlashan's work seems to me hazy in chronology and topography, overloaded with miscellaneous notes about the survivors, and composed in a bad style of nineteenth-century sentimental oratory. It sometimes misquotes its originals; it indulges in almost ludicrous eulogy of individuals. It is far from complete—in particular, omitting most of the references to cannibalism.

Its author was, however, an assiduous collector. Through interviews and correspondence, by copying diaries and journals, he amassed a large collection.

McGlashan died in 1931. When I was working on the story, I tried to gain access to his materials, but was unable to do so, except for a volume of letters by Virginia Reed (listed in the bibliography as ReVL). Only a few years ago was the whole collection made available to me through the kindness of the late Dr. Douglas M. Kelley, McGlashan's grandson.

The papers fill two large cardboard cartons, one of these containing the Donnerana. I approached this collection with hope that much new light might be shed upon the story and in some trepidation that my own work might be thus overthrown. Both hope and trepidation were unwarranted.

There were many copies of documents, but all of the important ones had been already available to me. There were numerous photographs, but these were chiefly of individuals as they looked in the eighteen-seventies. There were many newspaper clippings, but these contained nothing of importance. There were, finally, a large number of letters from the survivors. The expression "large number" must be taken

seriously; McGlashan once stated that he had received a
thousand such letters, and this would seem to me a fair estimate for those included in the papers.

But the letters too were disappointing. The great majority
of them had nothing about the Donner story at all. Mc-
Glashan, in fact, had almost become the captive of his own
project. By being the historian, he had become a kind of
official friend and counselor of the survivors. With some of
them he carried on a correspondence for upwards of forty
years. Everything that they remembered about 1846–47 they
naturally exhausted in two or three letters. All the rest dealt
with anniversaries, births, and deaths, or was merely chit-chat
between friends.

Even in the earlier letters there is less than one would have
hoped to find. We must remember that during thirty years
these people had been trying to forget the starvation, squalor,
and death. They had been forced to think of themselves, not
as heroic pioneers, but as people who had loathsomely indulged in cannibalism, or were suspected of having done so.
At first, almost without exception, each person kept his guard
up. Later on, some of them let go, and even became loqua-
cious. But they had difficulty, even so, in pulling back from
thirty years the memories of what they had been trying to
forget.

Here and there we pick up details, which are, if of no
great significance, of some interest. Thus we learn, what
might have been deduced from the evidence already available,
that both Baylis Williams and his sister Eliza were somewhat
abnormal. Baylis, perhaps a partial albino, could not see well
by day, but could see at night. Eliza was extremely deaf.

Other passages, of considerable interest, were not used by
McGlashan, perhaps because of their too gruesome quality, or
perhaps merely because his book was already becoming as
long as he wished it to be.

Patty Reed, though only eight at the time, seems to have
had some vivid memories. As she wrote in touching sim-
plicity:

My memory tells me, Spitzer died in Mr. Breen's cabin, to the
right hand of the fireplace, feet near the door, and imploring
Mrs. Breen to just put a little meat in his mouth so he could
just know it was there and he could die easy and in peace. I

do not think the meat was given him, but he gave up the ghost, and was no more.

Seared into her memory was the plight of the McCutchen baby, after its mother had departed with the snowshoers: "When the lice (pardon me, sir) were literally eating it up alive. It had scratched, broken the skin over its little bones." The adults in the cabin, apparently recognizing the child's fate, but with euthanasia not part of their philosophy, tied its hands down so that it could no longer scratch, and let it cry until the crying ceased. As Patty added: "God's kind ministering angels surely were not in that mountain prison!" In the tradition of the story, Tamsen Donner has become the outstanding heroine. Curiously, however, she scarcely survived in the memories of the children who later wrote these letters. But they remembered Aunt Betsy, Mrs. Jacob Donner, who had the true motherly touch for any child. Thus Patty wrote on May 7, 1879 and we may here attempt to reproduce her own unusual and almost hysterical style of writing:

Has any one, been kind, & thoughtfull, in giving you, a *word* of praise, *due* the memory, of Mrs. Jacob Donner, one of the most thoughtful, & generous, & hospitable, "Mothers" "of the Donner Party," I, never saw, her good face, at the camp, at the *Lake, no,* they were so far behind us, we never, *met* any of them, until relief came to us. But, we heard *once* through poor Milton, but my memory, prompts me, to say, She was a Mother, *devoted, meek, retired,* & one of the most *industrious,* in all the *Party,* She was allways ready, to assist, & offer her, sympathy (& that was *much* in this party) to any one, in distress! sorrow! or grief! She, had a heart, willing to provide the *last crumb,* I shall all-ways remember a little kindness to *us,* when we came up, to *their* wagons in the *desert,* found them all asleep. We laid down, upon the *salt* to rest (& came very near, yes! *near* freezing, to *death, only!* the dogs! saved us, *then!* from cold death, & a *poor little dog,* saved us, from, *death of hunger,* at the Breen cabin, *dog!* is *good!* any *way!* or *where!* you may *try* don't! *doubt,* me, Mr. McGlashan, this is true;) as soon as day light, appeared, we sent to their wagon, Papa wishing to assertain, if any, *word,* had reached *them,* from, those who had gone on, with the cattle, to the springs, we had crackers, & some loaf Sugar (the Sugar, was to quench thirst) with us, to eat, as, we moved on, this salt desert, but! Mrs Donner said, "no, Mr Reed, let

Mrs Reed & the children, stay, with us, & ride in our wagon, to the spring, Papa *thankfully*, excepted, of Mrs. D. generous request, as his little ones were, very tired. . . . . *poor! Parents! were! so!* anxious! but we, little ones, were *glad!* with the thought, of rideing with, Aunt Betsy, she made fire, fried bacon, & made *white*, or milk gravey, poured over it, & had some nice, salt, rising, bread, & *poor Ma* said, a *good cup of tea*, the breakfast tasted so *nice*, to us little ones after, walking *10 miles* (so said) leaving our wagons, at *sunsett*. we *were*, tired, & hungry, We have never, forgotten that meal, brother Tom, seldom eats cream gravey, at our table, that he don't say, "Sister, *do you*, yet,— remember, Mrs. Donners nice gravey," & we have not, forgotten that *kind* heart! or that friendly! look, of Mrs. Donner,. Also when *"one"* of our party would whip, or beat his Wife, Mrs. Donners tears, were the first, to start with sympathy, & mingle in friendship, with that poor afflicted one.

The letters supply copious information as to the survivors themselves in later life. Some seem to have passed through their troubles without damage, and a few could even see some humor. Such a one was Billy Graves, who wrote on February 28, 1879:

After they got through to where S. E. Woodworth was, Mrs. Breen remarked how they had suffered in the mountains. Then Woodworth said to her, "You may thank me, Mrs. Breen, for your safe delivery."

"Thank you, I thank nobody but God and Stark and the Virgin Mary," she said, putting Stark second best, and I think he deserved it.

A survivor who lived through into a calm and secure maturity was Georgia Donner, a four-year-old in 1846–47, who became Mrs. W. A. Babcock. Among McGlashan's correspondents she seems most at peace with the world, ready to admit her own cannibalism as a child of four, careful in her judgment of others, seeming to realize—as no one else in the party seemed able to do—that hard circumstance, and not perversity of character, was to blame. Thus she wrote on April 19, 1879:

A strange feeling comes over me while I look at Keseberg's picture. How I wish he could tell the truth, and that we the sur-

vivors might know if we blame him more than we should.—
While we (Donner children) were at his cabin he seemed to be
the strongest of the number there. Kept the children in their
beds. He said that we were in the way. When Mrs. Murphy
expected him to be absent a little while she would allow us to
get up and move about to rest us. When she did not hear him
in time to warn us that we might get to bed before he came in,
he was angry but did not strike us. Mrs. Murphy was so kind
to the little children that we remember her affectionately. It
was always my impression that the last relief party took from
the cabin Frances, Georgia and Eliza Donner, and Simon Murphy.
As we were ready to start, Mrs. Murphy walked to her bed, laid
down turned her face toward the wall. One of the men gave her
a handful of dried meat.—She seemed to realize that we were
leaving her, that her work was finished.

Mrs. Babcock alone seems to have felt a kind of responsibility to history in making the facts known. "Duty," she
wrote in that same letter, "calls from us the dreadful truth."
Then she continued:

And we who are willing the veil should be removed from the
past to reveal knowledge kept from each other many years, feel
that we are speaking to a world in which we have found many
friends. And while their thoughts are lead by our sad story,
may they learn from what we say that our friends did cast their
bread upon the waters to return after many days. We show our
appreciation by giving them the truest history the world will ever
have of what took place at Donner Lake.

In that same spirit of looking history squarely in the face,
of trying to preserve the true record, she seems to have
written on June 15, 1879, though her opening sentence reads
almost as an apology for her realism:

I do not know why but I feel I ought to write the following
lines.
The dead child that Keseberg hung on the wall was not eaten
by him alone. A part was given to my sisters and myself, and
Simon Murphy whom I remember so kindly cut a piece, laid it
on the coals, cooked and ate it. I do not remember to whom
Mrs. Murphy was speaking when she accused Keseberg of kill-

ing it (I said persons; it might have been children.) I was more interested in what she was saying, than in those to whom she was speaking. . . .

When I spoke of human flesh being used at both tents, I said it was prepared for the *little ones in* both tents. I did not mean to include the larger (my half sisters) children or the grown people, because I am not positive that they tasted of it. Father was crying and did not look at us during the time, and we little ones felt that we could not help it. There was nothing else. Jacob Donners wife came down the steps one day saying to mother "What do you think I cooked this morning?" Then answered the question herself, "Shoemaker's arm."

Later in this same letter, Mrs. Babcock came the closest to pronouncing the benediction:

My heart has always ached when I thought of Mr. and Mrs. Foster, and felt a kind interest in all of the survivors, and since we have been hearing from each other it seems like a family had met after a separation of 33 years and a feeling of sadness steals over me when I think the time will soon be at hand for us to say goodbye again.

In contrast to Mrs. Babcock some of those who had been children during that winter seem never to have attained a normal maturity. Most striking is the case of one of them who refused to correspond with McGlashan. Nancy Graves had been nine years old at the time of the disaster. We learn of her later troubles in a letter written by Eliza Donner Houghton. One should note also the oversentimental style of the letter itself. Though this may be called characteristic of the period, it is so pronounced in these letters of the survivors that one wonders whether it may not be a kind of protective mechanism. At least, she wrote on August 8, 1879:

But I cannot speak to you within doors—take this armchair on the porch and the gentle breeze through the leaves of the elms, acacia, & locust will whisper peace to my saddening heart, as I repeat the story of a sorrowing little girl. It was here I sat one lovely evening, a number of weeks ago, watching the beauties which surrounded me—a friend joined me—and as the shadows disappeared, our voices grew merry,—then low and sad, for we were talking of "by gone" days;—we reviewed her happy childhood days, as with jingling bells, then we paused; for she mentioned one name familiar to me through suffering, and she said, "I never recall my first schooldays in San Jose, without thinking of poor little Nancy G—— who used to cry so much in school. Why that poor child used to break right out during schooltime, and it often seemed to me her heart would break." "Did you ever know why she was so unhappy?" "No." "Did you not ask her?" "Yes, one day my sister and two or three others, gathered around her; we cried with her; and begged her to tell us what troubled her so much; and between sobs and sighs she told us of her being at 'Starved Camp'—how her mother died, how part of the flesh was prepared for food without her knowledge— and how she was told of it after she had partaken of it, and how perfectly heartbroken she had been ever since. We tried to soothe and comfort her but it seemed no use; for she would cry *'How can I* forget it; or *forgive* myself?' "

On the whole, the McGlashan papers require no changes to be made in the structure of the story, though they present a certain number of interesting, isolated details as here quoted, not previously available. . . .

A few articles in scholarly journals deserve mention. . . . In the *Masterkey*, May, 1944, Frances E. Watkins published "News from a Far Country: An Unpublished Letter of Virginia Reed." The letter was written before July 20, the opening date of *Ordeal by Hunger,* but along with the editor's comments it is of interest.

To the *California Historical Society Quarterly,* March, 1945, P. M. Weddell contributed "Location of the Donner Family Camp," a review of the author's investigations on the ground, over a period of years. The results are confirmatory of his earlier conclusions, as already checked and accepted in this book (p. 304).

In 1951, Volume XIX of the *Utah Historical Quarterly* was given over to the posthumously published *West From Fort Bridger,* collected and annotated by J. Roderic Korns. The major documents here presented had already appeared in print, and some of them had long been well known to historians of the West. I thus have difficulty in understanding how Mr. Korns could have written, "All the books about the Hastings Cutoff and the Donner party must be rewritten under the impact of these new-found records." Perhaps the

records were "new-found" as far as Mr. Korns was concerned. The documents by Clyman, Bryant, and Jefferson
will be found listed in the *Bibliography* (pp. 297–98). The log-
book had appeared in print four years before Mr. Korns's
version reproduced the already printed text. In addition, all
these documents touch only the prologue of the story. I
therefore see no reason why any book on the Donner Party
needs to be rewritten because of this reprinting of already
known sources. Mr. Korns's notes are of value, particularly in
connection with the route as far as central Nevada.

In February, 1958, Professor David E. Miller published
"The Donner Road through the Great Salt Lake Desert," in
the *Pacific Historical Review*. This article sums up the result
of the author's investigations by jeep and plane in 1956. It is
confirmatory of previous studies, and presents a more detailed
map than has hitherto been available. One should note here
the use of the term Donner Road, though the route actually
examined, as the author indicates, must be that of the large
number of wagons that crossed in 1850. Presumably these
wagons followed the general line of the Donner track, but I
do not see how we can be sure that they everywhere followed
it exactly. The designation Donner Road is thus used, even
though Hastings's wagons were the trail-breakers, and many
others came later. This is thus another instance of the way
in which the name associated with this famous story has taken
over—just as with Donner Pass, which was discovered by the
Stevens Party in 1844 and which with all justice to Elisha
Stevens should have been called by his name. . . .

During the course of the years various readers have pointed
out errors, though some of these I decided, upon investiga-
tion, were really not errors. Some mistakes and possible
mistakes as regards chronology and route I have already discussed. Others, when winnowed down, prove to be, in my
opinion, both gratifyingly few and definitely peripheral:

p. 12   Reedowsky should be Reednowsky.

p. 29   The big mountain was not a divide between two
branches of the Bossman, but that between the drainages of
Weber and Jordan rivers.

p. 29   "North wall" should be "south wall," and the emigrants at this point came out into open country.

p. 50   It is questionable whether the Donner Party can

be said to have gained on Hastings, especially since both parties had split into sections.

p. 55   Sallee was not a member of the Hastings Party, but had gone by Fort Hall.

p. 220   There was some heavy travel on the Hastings cut-off in 1850.

p. 220   The Lawson (better spelled, Lassen) route was first traveled in 1848.

I may also, with pleasure, record that the newly discovered materials have in some instances confirmed conclusions which I had hitherto based largely upon inference. Thus the log-book, if we accept its chronology, would go far toward establishing my date of September 18 for the departure of Stanton and McCutchen, since it specifies a halt for the party on that day. So also a statement by George Tucker in the McGlashan papers does something to confirm the southerly route of the snow-shoers, and the manner in which Eddy killed the deer (p. 112). . . .

Two matters which were not settled by the original edition of this book may be further considered here. They are of some interest in themselves, and are of even more interest as illustrating the way in which the human mind is likely to work in connection with famous stories.

As the opening words of his Chapter IV in the revised edition, McGlashan wrote, "Gravelly Ford, on the Humboldt River, witnessed a tragedy." He is here referring to the killing of Snyder by Reed. This ford is not mentioned in records of 1846, so far as I have discovered, and is apparently a name given at some later date.

When working on the story, I soon came to the conclusion that McGlashan was wrong in thus locating the incident. I could establish that on October 5 the wagon-train was already several days' journey west of Gravelly Ford. I later had the experience (rather unusual in research) of discovering what seemed to be the exact source of McGlashan's error.

In that chapter he acknowledged much indebtedness to a narrative by William C. Graves, published in 1877 (see p. 298, GWC). In particular, this narrative contains the only mention of Gravelly Ford that I have discovered among documents dealing with the story. What Graves actually wrote was:

Then we had no more trouble till we got to Gravelly Ford, on the Humboldt, where the Indians stole two of father's oxen, and in two days after they stole a horse: but we pushed on.

He then, in the next paragraph, tells of the killing of Snyder. This is a clear statement that the killing occurred, not at the ford, but at some point reached more than two days later. But McGlashan, apparently reading in haste, assumed that the "trouble" was the killing, and not the depredations of the Indians. In my own account, therefore, I did not locate the incident at Gravelly Ford, and on p. 303 I inserted a brief note, pointing out McGlashan's error and its apparent cause. This, it seemed to me, should settle the matter.

In thus thinking, I showed myself better as a reader of documents than as a judge of human nature. Contrary to the poet's statement of the case, error did not writhe and die, but continued to flourish. More recent books—for example, the WPA guide to Nevada—have continued to state that Snyder died at Gravelly Ford. His grave is even exhibited to tourists who make the pilgrimage to Beowawe.

The situation is rendered more striking by the discovery of the log-book, which has the party near the ford on September 29, a week before Snyder's death!

I question whether anything can be done about the matter now. Doubtless it is, in any case, of no great consequence. But the working of the folk-mind still interests me.

In spite of all evidence, does poor Snyder continue to die at Gravelly Ford, because the ordinary person finds it imaginatively more satisfactory that a particular incident should happen at a definitely named place, and not merely somewhere along the road? Or, as one interested in place names, should I conclude that the name itself supplies the key? Robert Louis Stevenson once wrote of some places demanding particular kinds of events: "Certain dank gardens cry aloud for a murder." Perhaps it is the same with names. Gravelly Ford may seem to people to be especially fitting as a scene of violence and death. . . .

Also tending to become legendary is the matter of the alleged mistake about the road. As I have heard this account told, the Donner Party arrived at the lake after the ground was covered with snow; they therefore lost "the road," which is conceived as going by way of Cold Stream, the next canyon to the south; instead, they went along the north side of the lake and tried to go directly over the pass; this proved to be impossible, and they were thus trapped, whereas they would have been able to cross if they had followed "the road." Something of this version is preserved in the statement on a bronze plaque, placed near one of the highways, that "the road" went by way of Cold Stream Canyon.

In statements by the survivors I was able to find no mention of any such mistake, and only one late mention of the Cold Stream route. This latter is in McGlashan's Chapter V:

W. C. Graves says the old emigrant road followed up Cold Stream, and so crossed the dividing ridge. Some wagons were drawn up this old road, almost to the top of the pass, others were taken along the north side of Donner Lake, and far up toward the summit. Some of these wagons never were returned to the lake, but were left imbedded in the snow.

Since these details are not included in Graves's narrative, McGlashan probably got them by conversation, as the word "says" would indicate. Graves was here drawing on his thirty-year-old memories, and the whole passage can be considered to have little authority, in view of the general unreliability of Graves's reminiscences.

There were, however, two roads. The original one followed along the north shore of the lake and crossed the pass about where the railroad now crosses. Its existence is made clear by the testimony of Schallenberger (for 1844), Simeon Ide (for 1845), and Bryant (for early 1846). From the evidence I could find when I was working in the early nineteen-thirties, I was unable to determine surely when the second road was opened, and I stated my doubts in a note (p. xiii). I later came to the tentative conclusion from further study of Jefferson's map that the new road was opened in late 1846. Settlement of the problem has come with the researches of Irene G. Paden (*Pacific Historical Review*, February, 1949), who has shown on the evidence of emigrants' diaries that a road up Cold Stream Canyon was first used in late September, 1846— and therefore in time for the Donner Party.

The reason behind the emigrants' going to the work of opening up a new road may be a simple one. The year 1846 saw a much heavier traffic in wagons than the route had ever had to handle before. Getting wagons over the pass was slow work. There may therefore have been what amounted to a traffic jam. Learning that they would have to wait several days, some of the emigrants probably explored around, and developed a new road. The establishment of an alternate route would not mean that the original one was abandoned, or even that it immediately became secondary.

When the Donner Party arrived, they could not have been ignorant of the second route, since Stanton would have informed them. He had recently traveled both ways across the mountains, would have seen the new road and have heard about it, and might even have traveled it. Some of the emigrants may therefore have tried it, as Graves stated.

If they so attempted, they probably found that route harder than the one along the lake. It has easier grades, but is correspondingly longer. It ascends to high altitude and remains there over a much longer distance than does the road by the lake, and it crosses the divide by a pass several hundred feet higher. It would therefore have had deeper snow over a longer distance, and under the conditions faced by the Donner Party might have been quite out of the question.

We can only regret that "the road" has been given authority by being recorded on long-enduring bronze. There is only dubiously late testimony that it was ever involved with the Donner story at all. This road later came to be the dominant one, as is indicated by the Perkins diary (p. xiii) and other evidence, but it was certainly not the first or only one. . . .

At this point I again take leave of my story, though now— perhaps grown wiser after twenty-five years—with less hope that the complexities of historical evidence will prevail against the charming simplicities of legend.

Taking advantage of this new edition, I here offer three original documents which present the story with a moving immediacy.

DIARY OF PATRICK BREEN

NOVEMBER, 1846–MARCH, 1847

THE MANUSCRIPT of Breen's diary, in the Bancroft Library of the University of California, consists of eight sheets of note-paper, crudely trimmed and folded, apparently by the author himself, to make a booklet of thirty-two pages. This booklet has been rebound in half-calf and marbled paper, but some old needle-holes indicate an original sewing. Each page measures about 3¾ by 6¼ inches. The diarist used the first twenty-nine pages. The paper is yellowed; the ink is faded; several pages are badly blotted.

The history of the manuscript is simple. Breen took it with him when he left the camp. On his arrival at Sutter's Fort he gave it to Sheriff McKinstry, who wanted it in order to use the material for making out his report to Captain Hull. Years later, probably in 1871, McKinstry passed it on to H. H. Bancroft, who was then collecting materials on which to base his history of California. Bancroft had the diary rebound, and it remained in his private library until that collection came into the possession of the University of California in 1905.

The great interest of the diary was immediately recognized in 1847. McKinstry supplied the *California Star* with what he declared to be a verbatim copy. Actually, when this version was published on May 22, 1847, there were large omissions; blanks were substituted for some names; explanatory notes, not distinguished from the text, were added; spelling and punctuation were radically revised.

This quite inadequate text was widely reprinted, and remained the basis of all other texts until 1910. Frederick J. Teggart then edited it in Volume I of the *Publications of the Academy of Pacific Coast History*. This version is an excellent one, though in the transfer of such a document from script to print there is always room for some differences of personal opinion.

When working on *Ordeal by Hunger*, I used the original manuscript, occasionally departing from Teggart's text when

I thought myself justified. In 1946 I edited the diary for an edition of 300 copies issued by the Book Club of California. In this volume the text was presented in facsimile, and a fuller history was offered than is given here. The present text is essentially the same as that of 1946.

The very nature of a manuscript such as this one renders any printed version something of a falsification. Doubtful abbreviations, superscripts, and various conventional symbols cannot be properly reproduced. Even the most careful editor cannot always be sure whether the diarist intended *today* and *o'clock* to be one or two words. In particular, Breen made use of what seems to be a conventional symbol resembling *d* to indicate the *-ed* ending of verbs.

Still, in spite of these difficulties, the script is remarkably legible. Not more than two or three words can be considered really doubtful.

In general, then, the manuscript has been reproduced as closely as print will allow, except for a few obvious alterations in the interest of more ready reading. To this end, spaces have been inserted in lieu of punctuation. A few letters and names have been supplied in brackets.

Fortunately Breen's Irishisms survive in print. We may note his *shanty* where an American would probably have put *cabin,* and his *dale* for *deal.* Patty he once rendered as Pat, and again as Paddy. The German name Donner he wrote as the Irish name Donough.

Factually, the diary nearly always proves to be correct, when it can be checked. (For a defense of the chronology, see pp. 307–08.) A few possible minor errors may be noted.

Breen's statement that he "gave" a yoke of oxen to Foster is rendered doubtful by Thornton's assertion that Breen took from Foster a gold watch and other property in security.

The mention of Lewis Suitor with reference to the Keseberg baby may be a mere error; Breen's eye could have caught the name Suitor (his spelling of Sutter) from higher up on the page. Or possibly a baby born on the plains had been given a middle name in honor of the goal of the journey. On the other hand William R. Grimshaw ("Narrative of Events, 1848–50," MS, Bancroft Library) states that Keseberg had had some previous connection with Sutter, and the name may be a reflection of this fact.

According to Virginia Reed's letters, she and her mother

buried Milt Elliott; Breen states that it was his sons John and Edward. Quite possibly they all worked together.

Breen states that twenty-four left on February 22; the correct number, as gathered from other sources, was twenty-three. But Breen's figure is certainly very close.

Since a good deal has already been presented about diarist and diary (see especially Chapters 2, 12, and 18), no further analysis need be given here.

THE DIARY

FRIDAY Nov. 20th 1846   came to this place on the 31st of last month that it snowed   we went on to the pass   the snow so deep we were unable to find the road, when within 3 miles of the summit   then turned back to this shanty on the Lake, Stanton came one day after we arriveed here   we again took our team & waggons & made another unsuccessful attempt to cross in company with Stanton   we returned to the shanty it continueing to snow all the time we were here   we now have killed most part of our cattle having to stay here untill next spring & live on poor beef without bread or salt   it snowed during the space of eight days with little intermission, after our arrival here, the remainder of time up to this day was clear & pleasant frezeing at night the snow nearly gone from the valleys.

sat. 21st   fine morning   wind N:W   22 of our company are about starting across the mountain this mor[n]ing including Stanton & his indians,   some clouds flying   thawed to day   wnd E

Sunday 22nd   froze hard last night   this a fine clear morning,   wind E.S.E   no account from those on the mountains

monday 23rd   Same weather wind W   the Expedition across the mountains returned after an unsuccsful attempt

tuesday 24th   fine in the morning   towards eve[ni]ng Cloudy & windy   wind W   looks like snow   freezeing hard

wendsday 25th   wind about WNW   Cloudy   looks like the eve of a snow storm   our mountainers intend trying to cross the Mountain tomorrow if fair   froze hard last night

Thurssday the 26th   began to snow yesterday in the evening now rains or sleet the mountaniers dont start to day the wind about W. wet & muddy

Friday 27 Continues to snow, the ground not covered, wind W dull prospect for crossing the mountains

Saturday 28th Snowing fast now about 10 o clock snow 8 or 10 inches deep soft wet snow, weather not cold wind W

Sunday 29th still snowing now about 3 feet deep, wind W killed my last oxen today will skin them tomorrow gave another yoke to Fosters hard to get wood

Monday 30th Snowing fast wind W about 4 or 5 feet deep, no drifts looks as likely to continue as when it commenced no liveing thing without wings can get about

December 1st Tuesday Still snowing wind W snow about 5½ feet or 6 deep difficult to get wood no going from the house completely housed up looks as likely for snow as when it commenced, our cattle all killed But three or four [of] them, the horses & Stantons mules gone & cattle suppose lost in the Snow no hopes of finding them alive

wedns. 2nd. Continues to snow wind W sun shineing hazily thro the clouds dont snow quite as fast as it has done snow must be over six feet deep bad fire this morning

Thursd. 3rd Snowed a little last night bright and cloudy at intervals all night, to day cloudy snows none wind S. W. warm but not enough so to thaw snow lying deep allround Expec[t]ing it to thaw a little to day the forgoing written in the morning it immediately turned in to snow & continued to snow all day & likely to do so all night

Friday 4th Cloudy that is flying clouds neither snow or rain this day it is a relief to have one fine day. wind E by N no sign of thaw freezeing pretty hard snow deep

Saturday 5th fine clear day beautiful sunshine thawing a little looks delightful after the long snow storm

Sund. 6th The morning fine & Clear now some Cloudy wind S-E not [melting] much in the sunshine, Stanton & Graves manufactureing snow shoes for another mountain scrabble no account of mules

Mond. 7th beautiful clear day wind E by S looks as if we might [have] some fair weather no thaw

Tues 8th fine weather Clear & pleasant froze hard last night wind S.E deep snow the people not stiring round much hard work to [get] wood sufficient to keep us warm & cook our beef

Wedns. 9th Commenced snowing about 11 Oclock wind N:W snows fast took in Spitzer yesterday so weak that he cannot rise without help caused by starveation all in good health some having scant supply of beef Stanton trying to make a raise of some for his Indians & self not likely to get much

Thursd. 10th Snowed fast all night with heavy squalls of wind Continues still to snow the sun peeping through the clouds once in about three hours very difficult to get wood to day now about 2 Oclock looks likely to continue snowing don't know the debth of the snow may be 7 feet

Friday 11th snowing a little wind W sun vissible at times not freezeing

Satd. 12th Continues to snow wind W weather mild freezeind little

Sunday 13th Snows faster than any previous day wind N:W Stanton & Graves with several others makeing preperations to cross the Mountains on snow shoes, snow 8 feet deep on the level dull

monday 14 fine morning sunshine cleared off last night about 12 o clock wind E:S:E dont thaw much but fair for a continueance of fair weather

Tuesday 15th Still continues fine wind W: S: W

Wed'd 16th fair & pleasant froeze hard last night & the Company started on snow shoes to cross the mountains wind S.E looks pleasant

Thursd. 17th Pleasant sunshine today wind about S.E bill Murp[hy] returned from the mountain party last evening Bealis [Williams] died night before last Milt. [Elliott] & Noah [James] went to Donnos 8 days since not returned yet, thinks they got lost in the snow. J Denton here to day

Frid'd. 18 beautiful day sky clear it would be delightful were it not for the snow lying so deep thaws but little on the south side of shanty saw no strangers today from any of the shantys

Satd. 19 Snowed last night commenced about 11 Oclock. squalls of wind with snow at intervals this morning thawing wind. N by W a little Singular for a thaw may continue, it continues to Snow Sun Shining cleared off towards evening

Sund. 20 night clear froze a little now clear & pleasant wind N W thawing a little Mrs Reid here. no account of Milt. yet Dutch Charley [Burger] started for Donnghs turned back not able to proceed tough times, but not discouraged our hopes are in God. Amen

Mond. 21 Milt. got back last night from Donos camp sad news. Jake Donno[,] Sam Shoemaker[,] Rinehart, & Smith are dead the rest of them in a low situation snowed all night with a strong S-W wind to day Cloudy wind continues but not snowing, thawing sun shineing dimly in hopes it will clear off

Tuesd. 22nd Snowed all last night Continued to snow all day with some few intermissions had a severe fit of the gravel yesterday I am well to day, Praise *be to the God of Heaven*

Wend. 23rd Snowed a little last night clear to day & thawing a little. Milt took some of his meat to day all well at their camp began this day to read the Thirty days prayer, may Almighty God grant the request of an unworthy sinner that I am. *Amen*

Thursd. 24th rained all night & still continues to rain poor prospect for any kind of Comfort Spiritual or temporal, wind S: may God help us to spend the Christmass as we ought considering circumstances

Friday 25th began to snow yesterday about 12 o clock snowed all night & snows yet rapidly wind about E by N Great difficulty in getting wood John & Edwd. has to get [it] I am not able offered our prayers to God this Cherimass morning the prospect is apalling but hope in God *Amen*

Satd. 26th Cleared off in the night to day clear & pleasant Snowed about 20 inches or two feet deep yesterday. the old snow was nearly run soft before it began to snow now it is all soft the top dry & the under wet wind S.E

Sun 27 Continues clear froze hard last night Snow very deep say 9 feet thawing a little in the sun scarce of wood to day chopt a tree dow[n] it sinks in the snow & is hard to be got

Monday 28th Snowed last night Cleared off this morning snowed a little now Clear & pleasant

Tuesday 29th fine clear day froze hard last night. Charley sick. Keysburg has Wolfing[er]s Rifle gun

Wedsd. 30th fine clear morning froze hard last night Charley died last night about 10 Oclock had with him in money $1.50 two good loking silver watches one razor 3 boxes caps Keysburg tok them into his possession Spitzer took his coat & waistcoat Keysburg all his other little effects gold pin one shirt and tools for shaveing.

Thursday 31st last of the year, may we with Gods help spend the comeing year better than the past which we purpose to do if Almighty God will deliver us from our present dredful situation which is our prayer if the will of God sees it fiting for us Amen—morning fair now Cloudy wind E by S for three days past freezeing hard every night looks like another snow storm Snow Storms are dredful to us snow very deep crust on the snow

Jany. 1st 1847 we pray the God of mercy to deliver us from our present Calamity if it be his Holy will Amen. Commenced snowing last night does not snow fast wind S.E sun peeps out at times provisions geting scant dug up a hide from under the snow yesterday for Milt. did not take it yet

Sat. 2nd fair & thawey snow got soft wind S-E looks thawey froze pretty hard last night

Sund. 3rd continues fair in day time freezeing at night wind about E Mrs. Reid talks of crossing the mountains with her children provisions scarce

Mond. 4th fine morning looks like spring thawing now about 12 o clock wind S:E Mrs. Reid[,] Milt.[,] Virginia & Eliza started about ½ hour ago with prospect of crossing the mountain may God of Mercy help them left ther children here Tom with us Pat with Keysburg & Jas with Graveses folks, it was difficult for Mrs. Reid to get away from the children

Tuesd. 5th Beautiful day thawing some in the sun Wind S-E snow not settleing much we are in hopes of the rainy time ending

Weds. 6th fine day clear not a cloud froze very hard last night wind S:E Eliza came back from the mountain yesterday evening not able to proceed, to day went to Graves, the others kept ahead

Thursd. 7th continues fine freezeing hard at night very cold this morning wind S.S.E. dont think we will have much more snow snow not thawing much not much dimeinished in debph

Friday 8th fine morning wind E froze hard last night very cold this morning Mrs. Reid & company came back this mor[n]ing could not find their way on the other side of the Mountain they have nothing but hides to live on Martha is to stay here Milt. & Eliza going to Donos Mrs. Reid & the 2 boys going to their own shanty & Virginia prospects Dull may God relieve us all from this difficulty if it is his Holy will *Amen*

Satd 9th Continues fine freezeing hard at night this a beatiful morning wind about S.S.E Mrs. Reid here virginias toes frozen a little snow settleing none to be perceived.

Sund. 10 began to snow last night still continues wind W N W.

Mond. 11th still continues to snow fast, looks gloomy Mrs Reid at Keysburgs virg. with us wood scarce difficult to get any more wind W

Tuesd 12th snows fast yet new snow about 3 feet deep wind S:W no sign of clearing off

Wends. 13th snowing fast wind N.W snow higher than the shanty must be 13 feet deep dont know how to get wood this morning it is dredful to look at

Thursd. 14th new moon Cleared off yesterday evening snowed a little during first part of night Calm but a little air from the North very pleasant to day sun shineing brilliantly renovates our spirits prais be to God, *Amen*

Frid. 15th fine clear day wind N W Mrs. Murphy blind Lanth[ron Murphy] not able to get wood has but one axe betwixt him & Keysburg, he moved to Murphys yesterday looks like another storm expecting some account from Suiters soon

Satd. 16th wind blew hard all night from the W. abated a little did not freeze much this is clear & pleasant wind a little S of W no telling what the weather will do

Sund. 17th fine morning sun shineing clear wind S.S.E Eliza came here this morning, sent her back again to Graves Lanthrom crazy last night so bill says, Keyburg sent bill to get hides off his shanty & carry thim home this morning, provisions scarce hides are the only article we depend on, we have a little meat yet, may God send us help

Mond. 18th fine day clear & pleasant wind W, thawing in the sun Mrs. Murphy here to day very hard to get wood

Tuesd. 19th Clear & pleasant thawing a little in the sun wind S.W Peggy & Edward sick last night by eating some meat that Dolan threw his tobacco on, pretty well to day (praise God for his blessings,) Lanthrom very low in danger if relief dont soon come hides are all the go, not much of any other in camp

Wed. 20th fine morning wind N froze hard last night. Expecting some person across the Mountain this week

Thursd. 21 fine morning wind W did not freeze quite so hard last night as it has done, John Battice & Denton came this morning with Eliza she wont eat hides Mrs Reid sent her back to live or die on them. Milt. got his toes froze the donoghs are all well

Frid. 22nd began to snow a little after sunrise likely to snow a good dale wind W came up very suddenly, now 10 Oclock

Satd. 23rd Blew hard & snowed all night the most severe storm we experienced this winter wind W sun now 12 oclock peeps out

Sund. 24th Some cloudy this morning ceased snowing yesterday about 2 Oclock. Wind about S.E all in good health thanks be to God for his mercies endureth for ever. heard nothing from Murphys camp since the storm expe[c]t to hear they suffered some

Mod 25th began to snow yesterday evening & still continues wind W

Tuesd 26 Cleared up yesterday to day fine & pleasant, wind S. in hopes we are done with snow storms. those that went to Suitors not yet returned provisions geting very scant people geting weak liveing on short allowance of hides

Weds 27th began to snow yesterday & still continues to sleet thawing a little wind W Mrs. Keyber[g] here this morning Lewis Suitor she says died three days ago Keysburg sick & Lanthrom lying in bed the whole of his time dont have fire enough to Cook their hides. Bill & Sim. Murphy sick

Thursd. 28th full moon cleared off last night & froze some to day fine & warm wind S.E looks some like spring weather birds chirping qute lively full moon today

Frid 29th fine morning began to thaw in the sun early. wind S.W froze hard last night there will be a crust soon God send *Amen*

Satd. 30th fine pleasant morning wind W beginning to thaw in the sun John & Edwd. went to Graves this morning the Graves seized on Mrs Reids goods untill they would be paid also took the hides that she & family had to live on. she got two peices of hides from there & the ballance they have taken you may know from these proceedings what our fare is in camp there is nothing to be got by hunting yet perhaps there soon will. God send it *Amen*

Sund. 31st The sun dont shine out brilliant this morning froze prtty hard last night wind N.W. Lantron Murphy died last night about 1 Oclock, Mrs. Reid & John went to Graves this morning to look after her goods

Mond. February the 1st froze very hard last night cold to day & Cloudy wind N W. sun shines dimly the snow has not settled much John is unwell to day with the help of God & [deleted] he will be well by night amen

Tuesday 2nd began to snow this morning & Continued to snow untill night now clear wind during the storm S-W

Wend. 3rd Cloudy looks like more snow not cold, froze a little last night wind S.S.W. it was clear all last night sun shines out at times

Thurd. 4th Snowed hard all night & still continues with a strong S:W. wind untill now [not?] abated looks as if it would snow all day snowed about 2 feet deep, now

Frid. 5th snowed hard all [yesterday] until 12 O'clock at night wind still continud to blow hard from the S.W: to day pretty clear a few clouds only Peggy very uneasy for fear we shall all perrish with hunger we have but a little meat left & only part of 3 hides has to support Mrs. Reid she has nothing left but one hide & it is on Graves shanty Milt is livi[n]g there & likely will keep that hide Eddys child died last night

Satd 6th it snowed faster last night & to day than it has done this winter & still Continues without an intermission wind S.W Murphys folks or Keysburgs say they cant eat hides I wish we had enough of them Mrs Eddy very weak

Sund. 7th Ceased to snow last [night] after one of the most Severe Storms we experienced this winter the snow fell about 4 feet deep I had to shovel the snow off our shanty this morning it thawed so fast & thawed during the whole storm. to day it is quite pleasant wind S.W. Milt here to day says Mrs. Reid has to get a hide from Mrs. Murphy & McCutchins child died 2nd of this month

Mond 8th fine clear morning wind S.W. froze hard last [night] Spitzer died last night about 3 o clock to [day?] we will bury him in the snow Mrs. Eddy died on the night of the 7th

Tuesd. 9th Mrs. Murphy here this morning pikes child all but dead Milt at Murphys not able to get out of bed Keyburg never gets up says he is not able. John went down to day to bury Mrs Eddy & child heard nothing from Graves for 2 or 3 days Mrs Murphy just now going to Graves fine mor[n]ing wind S.E. froze hard last night begins to thaw in the Sun.

Wedndd. 10th beautiful morning Wind W: froze hard last night. to day thawing in the Sun Milt Elliot died las[t] night at Murphys Shanty about 9 Oclock P:M: Mrs. Reid went there this morning to see after his effects. J Denton trying to borrow meat for Graves had none to give they have nothing but hides all are entirely out of meat but a little we have our hides are nearly all eat up but with Gods help spring will soon smile upon us

Thursd 11th fine morning wind W. froze hard last night some clouds lying in the E: looks like thaw John Denton here last night very delicate. John & Mrs Reid went to Graves this morning

Frid. 12th A warm thawey morning wind S.E. we hope with the assistance of Almighty God to be able to live to see the bare surface of the earth once more. O God of Mercy grant it if it be thy holy will *Amen*

Sat. 13th fine morning clouded up yesterday evening snowed a little & continued cloudy all night. cleared off about daylight. wind about S:W Mrs. Reid had headacke the rest in health

Sund 14th fine morning but cold before the sun got up. now thawing in the sun wind S E Ellen Graves here this morning John Denton not well froze hard last night John & Edwd. burried Milt. this morning in the snow

Mond. 15 mor[n]ing Cloudy untill 9 Oclock then Cleared off warm & sunshine wind W. Mrs. Graves refused to give Mrs. Reid any hides put Suitors pack hides on

her shanty would not let her have them   says if I say it will
thaw it then will not, she is a case

Tuesd. 16th Commenced to rain yesterday Evening
turned to Snow during the night & continud untill after daylight this morning it is now sunshine & light showers of
hail at times   wind N.W by W. we all feel very weakly to
day snow not geting much less in quantity

Wedsd 17th froze hard last night with heavy clouds run-
ing from the N.W. & light showers of hail at times to day
same kind of Weather wind N.W. very cold & Cloudy
no sign of much thaw

Thrsd 18th Froze hard last night to day clear & warm
in the sun cold in the shanty or in the shade   wind S.E
all in good health Thanks be to Almighty God *Amen*

Frid. 19th froze hard last night 7 men arrived from Colifornia yesterday evening with som provisions but left the
greater part on the way to day clear & warm for this region some of the men are gone to day to Donnos Camp
will start back on Monday

Saturd. 20th   pleasant weather

Sund 21st thawey warm day

Mond 22nd the Californians started this morning 24 in
number some in a very weak state fine morning wind S.W.
for the 3 last days Mrs Keyburg started & left Keysburg
here unable to go I burried pikes child this mor[n]ing in the
snow it died 2 days ago, Paddy Reid & Thos. came back
with Messrs Grover & Mutry

Tuesd. 23 froze hard last night to day fine & thawey
has the appearance of spring all but the deep snow wind
S:S.E. shot Towser to day & dressed his flesh Mrs Graves
came here this morning to borrow meat dog or ox they
think I have meat to spare but I know to the Contrary they
have plenty hides I live principally on the same

Wend. 24th froze hard last night to day Cloudy looks
like a storm wind blows hard from the W. Commenced
thawing there has not any more returned from those who
started to cross the Mts.

Thursd. 25th froze hard last night fine & sunshiny to
day wind W. Mrs Murphy says the wolves are about to
dig up the dead bodies at her shanty, the nights are too cold
to watch them, we hear them howl

Frid 26th froze hard last night today clear & warm

Wind S: E: blowing briskly Marthas jaw swelled with the toothache: hungry times in camp, plenty hides but the folks will not eat them we eat them with a tolerable good apetite. Thanks be to Almighty God. *Amen* Mrs Murphy said here yesterday that [she] thought she would Commence on Milt. & eat him. I dont [think] that she has done so yet, it is distressing The Donnos told the California folks that they [would] commence to eat the dead people 4 days ago, if they did not succeed that day or next in finding their cattle then under ten or twelve feet of snow & did not know the spot or near it, I suppose they have done so ere this time

Satd 27th beautiful morning sun shineing brillantly, wind about S. W. the snow has fell in debth about 5 feet but no thaw but [in] the sun in day time it freezeing hard every night heard some geese fly over last night saw none

Sund. 28th froze hard last night to day fair & sunshine wind S.E. 1 solitary Indian passed by yesterday come from the lake had a heavy pack on his back gave me 5 or 6 roots resembleing Onions in shape taste some like a sweet potatoe, all full of little tough fibres

Mond. March the 1st to [day] fine & pleasant froze hard last night there has 10 men arrived this morning from bear valley with provisions we are to start in two or three days & Cash our goods here there is amongst them some old [mountaineers] they say the snow will be here untill June

DIARY OF JAMES F. REED

FEBRUARY–MARCH, 1847

AMONG the holdings of the Sutter's Fort State Historical Monument is a notebook of twenty-four unlined pages, 6½ inches by 7½ inches, with gray paper covers. It has been folded once, longitudinally, so as to be carried in a pocket. Though the paper is a little yellowed, the notebook is in remarkably good condition—considering the rains, floods, and snowstorms through which its contents indicate that it has passed. Most of the pages are covered with badly written lines in pencil, in many places so blurred as to be scarcely legible. From the information that it provides and also from the mere appearance of its smudged pages, the notebook can be made to reveal an interesting story.

On February 7, 1847, James F. Reed left Yerba Buena. The citizens had just contributed $1300 to help save the emigrants, and Reed was carrying with him a considerable amount of this cash. He was also carrying the notebook.

The money and the notebook were intimately connected. Reed would have to render an account of the funds expended, and the blank pages supplied his means of keeping the record straight. In fact, on leaving the town, he set down notations of expenditures made at the *embarcadero*. He entered other expenditures on later days.

The notebook was Reed's record not only of funds, but also of the lives for which he became responsible. Before leaving the lake camp for the return, he carefully listed the seventeen whom he was taking with him, and on one of the inside covers he made what seems to be a preliminary notation, indicating how many children would have to be carried, and how many were "able." No wonder it is, then, that he preserved the notebook carefully.

Only as something of an afterthought, apparently, did he begin a diary. Obviously, a man having to justify his actions in spending money or otherwise will do well to keep a daily record. So, leaving room for the primary matter of listing

268

expenditures, Reed began writing on page 11. Apparently he made this first entry when at Sonoma on February 9, but he then made an entry also for the departure from Yerba Buena.

Quite possibly, indeed, Reed had still another motive for maintaining a current record, and keeping it always with him. He already knew the perils of the snow. He must soberly have faced the possibility that he would die upon the storm-swept mountains. If his body should then be found later, the notebook would survive as a record and memorial.

Reed continued his practice of bringing the account up-to-date every few days. Thus, strictly speaking, the record is not a diary, though during about three weeks it is so close to being one that we need not quibble about the term.

Exactly when Reed made the last of these "current" entries cannot be surely determined. Perhaps it was on the evening of March 2, but possibly the later entries as far as the first part of that for March 5 were written at the time indicated. But after that morning of March 5 Reed became involved in strenuous events that would probably have prevented Samuel Pepys himself from a daily stint. At the bottom of the page below the entry for March 5, in smaller handwriting, Reed crowded some additional information, including some that he could not have learned until several days later. The rest of the later part of the narrative also contains scattered bits of similar information. Nevertheless, much of this part is expressed in the present tense, as if the writer were experiencing the events as he was writing. This effect could also have been produced if an original diary had been copied and expanded, but everything about the scrawled and smudged pencil-written pages suggests that no copying was done.

What seems likely, then, is this. . . . Shortly after the events Reed decided to finish the record by setting down his experiences at "Starved Camp." He used the present tense, perhaps because the happenings were still so vivid in his mind, more likely because he believed that the diary style should be continued for what we might call artistic purposes. He could hardly have written with any serious intent to deceive, for his insertions of later-learned details are undisguised.

After Reed's return from the mountains the diary was preserved among his papers. McGlashan, when preparing his *History of the Donner Party* in 1879, had access either to the diary or some copy of it. He reprinted large sections, but in a form which has been so highly edited as to be really re-written. When I was working in the nineteen-thirties this was the only version of the diary that was available to me, and the quotations in the text therefore differ from the diary as here reproduced.

Eventually, by gift of Reed's descendants, the diary be-came the property of the Sutter's Fort Museum. It was published by Carroll D. Hall in *Donner Miscellany* (1947). This version has been of much help to me, and I gratefully acknowledge its assistance, though I differ from Mr. Hall's interpretation in some details. The present text is primarily based upon first-hand examination of the manuscript.

The entries preceding that of February 21/22 are here omitted. They are brief notes of no great interest, and the events are sufficiently well summarized in Chapter 23. Anyone wishing to examine the whole diary may consult *Donner Miscellany*.

The attempt is here made to present the diary, just as it was written, though the neatly marshaled lines of print can never hope to reproduce the emotional effect of the blurred, pencil-written scrawl. Many misspellings, which stand out so blatantly in print, are really to be considered lapses of pencil (e.g., *mak* for *make*) or the mere illegibility resulting from a dull pencil-point. Especially at the end of a line Reed let the word disappear into a scrawl, so that *yesterday* appears as *yesty;* in many such instances I have given him the benefit of the doubt. In other places his apparent misspellings are really his use of colloquial forms and pronunciations, as with *give* (for *gave*), *come* (for *came*), and *ware* (for *were*).

To make the task of reading easier, I have inserted a few letters and words in brackets. The notation [?] indicates that the single preceding word must be considered doubtful. In the original the dates are written in the margin, along with a figure indicating the estimated number of miles traveled. Frequently there is difficulty in determining whether these dates refer to the day of the events described or to the day on which the writing was done. I have therefore deleted these marginal dates, and inserted my own in brackets. My dates refer, as well as can be ascertained, to the days on which the described events actually occurred. I have made no note of Reed's own deletions (which are not important) except when some of the words must be supplied to make the sense clear, and in one instance when the deletion itself was of interest.

In so far as it can be checked, the diary appears to be highly accurate. In stating that his camp in Summit Valley was 8300 feet above sea-level, Reed was merely calculating from an accepted figure of the time. Although the exact site of the camp still awaits discovery, its altitude must have been about 6800.

Reed is naturally the central figure of his own narrative, but he is not boastful. He records his incapacity during the emergency of the storm, and the heroic labors of McCutchen. Apparently to spare the feelings of the other refugees he deleted the words indicating that of them all his wife alone did not cry out for food.

Reed's use of the present tense is, consciously or not, deceptive. In writing Chapter 25, I was dependent upon McGlashan's rendering of the text, since the original was not then available, and I therefore wrote as if Reed were putting the words down while he huddled at the fire in the snow-pit. Such a belief is no longer possible.

Nevertheless, Reed wrote very soon after the events, when the experience was vivid in his memory. His words remain as the stark record of a man close to the last extremity in a Sierra snowstorm—starving, his sight failing, almost freezing, weighed down with the care of seventeen refugees, many of them helpless children, his own little son and daughter among them.

THE DIARY

[February 21/22] this morning the men arrived with out any accident excepting one horse that run back I got him from Mr Combs at Mr Gordons. I kept fire under the Beef all night which I had on the scafold and next morning by sun rise I had about 200 lbs dryed and bag[g]led we packed our horses and started with the [several words deleted] our supplies 700 lbs flour including what Greenwood had dried Sunday 4½ Beeves [several words deleted] and Mr Greenwood had 3 men including himself traveled this days about 10 miles.

[February 23] left camp early this morning and packed today and encamped early on acct grass tomorrow we will reach the snow

[February 24] encamped at the Mule Spring this evening made preparations to take the snow in the morning here we left at camp our saddles Bridles etc

[February 25] started with 11 horses & mules lightly packed average pack about 80 *lbs.* traveled about 2 miles and left one mule, and pack, made this day with hard labour for the horses, in the snow about 6 miles Our start was late.

[February 26/27] left our encampment early thinking the snow would bare the horses. proceeded 200 yard with dificulty when we were compelled to unpack the horses and take the provision on our backs · here for a few minutes there was silence with the men when the packs ware ready to sling on the back the hilarity commenced as usual made the head of Bear Valley a distance of 15 miles we met in the valley about 3 miles below the camp Messrs Glover & Road belonging to the party that went to the lake for people who informed me they had started with 21 persons 2 of whom had died John Denton of Springfield Also & a child of Keesberger Mr. Glover sent 2 men back to the party with fresh provisions they men were in a starving condition and all nearly perished [?] I here lightened our packs with a suficiency of provisions to do the people when they should arrive and [several words deleted] I sent back to our camp of the 26 2 men to bring provision they will return tomorrow and left one man to prepare for the people which were expected today and I left camp early on a fine hard snow and proceeded about 4 miles when we met the poor unfortunate starved people, as I met them scattered allong the snow trail I distributed Sweet bread that I had backed the 2 nights previous I give in small quantities, here I met Mrs. Reed and and two children two still in the mountains I cannot describe the death like look they all had Bread Bread Bread Bread was the beging of every Child and grown person [the words *except my wife* deleted] I give to all what I dared and left for the sene of desolation and now am camped within 25 miles which I hope to mak this night and tomorrow we had to camp soon on account of the softness of the snow, the men falling in to their middles. Two of the party one man and one child died since the party left   One of the party that passed us today a little boy Mrs. Murphy's son was nearly blind, when we met them.   they ware over-joyed when we told them there was plenty of provision at camp   I made a cach 12 miles and encamped 3 m eastward on Juba, snow about 15 feet.

[February 28/March 1] left camp about 12 o'clock at night and was comp[elled] to camp about 2 o'cl the snow still being soft.   left again about 4 all hands and made this day 14 miles   in camp early   snow soft. Snow her[e] 30 feet   3 of my men Cady, Clark & Stone [Interlined: *I told if they wished the(y) might*] kept on during the night [Interlined: *which they intended but halted*] within 2 miles of the cabins and remained without fire during the night on acct of 10 Indians which they saw [Interlined: *the boys not having arms*] and supposed they had taken the cabins and destroyed the people   in the morning they started and arrived   all alive in the houses   give provision to Keesberger, Brinn, Graves and two then left for Donners a distance of ten miles which they made by the middle of the day   I come up with the main body of my party   Informed [?] the people that all who ware able should have to start day after tomorrow   made soup for the infirm   washed and clothed afresh Mrs Eddy & Fosters children and rendered every assistance in our power   I left with Keesbergs people Mr Stone to cook and watch the eating of Mrs Murphy Keesberger & 3 children

[March 2] left early this morning with 3 of the men and went to Donners where Cady & Clark had arrivd yesty   found all alive   cheered [?] them [?] and sent Cady back for more provisions [two words illegible] of any   found here but 3 child of J Donner that could com with us   at George Donner tent there was 3 Stout harty children   his wife was able to travel but preferred to stay with her husband until provision should arrive, which was confidently expected by Comd [?] Woodworth, who was at Cap Suters the day before I left Mr. Johnsons,   here I left two of my men Cady & Clark one with each tent to cook and as fast as possible resusitate the enfeebled so that they might in a few days start,   took 3 children of J Donner and the men I took in and returned the same day making this 20 miles carrying 2 of the child   got back to the other cabins about 8 o'ck,

much worn down,   as I passed Mrs Graves told them I would
be of[f] in the morning,   the men that remained with her
today cached the principal of her effects and got for her out
of one of the waggons about 800 in gold & silver which was
concealed in a slat [word illegible] or bracket that was nailed
in the middle of the bed the money being placed in grooves
[word illegible] made for the purpose.

[March 3] after leaving with Keesberger camp 7 day[s]
prov[isions] and Mr. Stone to get wood cook and take care
of the helpless I left with the following persons   P Brin
Mrs Brin, John Brin, young man and 4 other smaller children
2 of which had to be carried   in all of Brins 7—Mrs Graves
—& 4 children 2 of which had to be caried   in all of her
family 5   Solomon Hook young man and Ma[r]y & Isaac
Donner in all 3—with two children of my own   one a girl
of 9 Years the other a little boy 4   in all 2—making in all
17 souls—proceeded about 2 miles and incamped on the edge
of the lak[e] on a bare spot of ground

[March 4] left camp early   traveled on the lake 2 miles
an[d] encamped under the mountain   made this day about
4 miles,   nothing of interest occ[urre]d.

[March 5] this morning [Interlined, apparently inserted
later: *after Breakfast I had 2 scanty meals left for all hands
which would do to the night following*] I sent ahead 3 men
J Jondrou M Dofar & Turner who ware of my best men for
the occasion, to push to our first cach and if not disturbed
to bring it up while the other two proceed on and bring up
our second [Crowded in at bottom of page in smaller handwriting, inserted later, since it contains information not
known on this date: *and if they should meet our supplies
which we all expected clace [close] at hand to hurry them
on, but to our misfortune there was none nigher than 65
miles and at this Juncture no prospect of starting which I
learned afterwards, to be the fact from Comd [?] Woodworth
himself.*]

[On the following page occur some financial notes; on the
second following page the "diary" resumes, but seems to
have been written after the return and not on the dates given.
See pp. 269–70.]

I moaved camp and after a fatiguing day arrivd at the
praire now Starved Camp at the head of Juba   it was made
by the other Compy. who had passed in but a few days

previous. here the men began to fail being for several days on half allowance, or 1½ pints of gruel or sizing per day. the sky look like snow and everything indicates a storm god forbid wood being got for the night & Bows for the beds of all, and night closing fast, the clouds still thicking terror terror I feel a terrible foreboding but dare not communicate my mind to any, death to all if our provisions do not come, in a day or two and a storm should fall on us, very cold, a great lamentation about the cold.

[March 6/7] Still in camp the last of our provisions gone looking anxiously for our supplies none. My dreaded Storm is now on us comme[nce]d Snowing in the first part of the night and with the snow comme[nce]d a perfect Hurricane in the night. A great crying with the children and with the parents praying crying and lamentations on acct of the cold and the dread of death from the Howling Storm the men up nearly all night making fires, some of the men began to pray several became blind I could not see even the light of the fire when it was blazing before me I continued so to the next day then my sight returned *Young Brine* [Breen] fell of[f] his feet into the pit the heat of the fire had made in the snow to the depth of 15 feet. it has snowed already 12 inches, still the storm continues the light of Heaven, is as it ware shut in from us the snow blows so thick that we cannot see 20 feet looking against the wind I dread the Coming night 3 of my men only able to get wood the rest give out for the present. After some time wood being secured we had a great dificulty in fixing a foundation for our fire the snow having melted to a great depth I think now 15 feet—and no earth in sight it must be from 6 to 10 feet [more?] snow before the earth is seen in the fire pit, the manner of making our fires on the snow are as follows, we lay 2 ps [pieces] of timber or saplin about 10 feet apart—then Roll close together large green logs on the two pcs in a transverse position these form a bed for the dry logs to lie on so as to prevent the coals of the dry wood which we lay on from falling through into this deep pit which has melted below Still storming verry cold so much so that the few men employed in cutting the dry trees down have to come and warm about every 10 minutes. Hunger hunger is the cry with the children and nothing to give them freesing was the cry of the mothers with [word illegible] to their starving freezing children night Closing fast and with it the Hurricane Increases—not quite so much snow falling as before night.

[March 8] thank God day has once more appeared although darkened by the storm snowing as fast as ever and the Hurricane has never ceased for ten minutes at a time during one of the most dismal nights I ever witnessed and I hope I never shall witness such in a similar situatate of all the praying and crying I ever heard nothing ever equaled it several times I expected to see the people perish by the extreme cold at one time our fire was nearly gone and had it not been for Mr McCutchen's exertions it would have entirely disapeared had the fire been lost Two thirds of the camp would have been out of their misery before morning but as God would have it we soon got it blazing in comfortable order and the sufferings of the people became less—At this time hope began to animate the bosoms of many young and old when the cheering blaze Rose through the dry Pine logs we had piled together, one would say thank god for this fire another how good it is the little half starved half frozen poor children would say I'm glad I'm Glad we have got some fire Oh how good it feels, it is good our fire didn't go out At daylight I discovered the storm to slack by hushing as it were entirely for a few minutes and then it would burst forth with such fury that I felt often alarmed for the safety of the people on acct of the tall timber that surrounded us—the storm continues to lull Snow now nearly Ceased, the location of our camp a bleak point under the summit of the great California Range about 1000 feet consequently our altitude about 8300 above the *Sea* with a small Prarie on our south and west about 3 miles in length & one in breadth here the snow and wind had full sweep this camp was used by the other party that had passed out of the mountain the under or bed logs for the fire having remained it saved the men from considerable labor in cutting and rolling green logs together I estimate the snow in this valley about 20 feet deep and at the cabins on the east side of the mountain about 10 feet on the average the storm did not rage with such fury on the east side of the great Chain as with us as I learned by two of my party that left the cabins the day after the storm was over.

LETTER OF VIRGINIA REED

MAY 16, 1847

ONE DAY about three months after her rescue from the snow-covered cabin, Virginia Reed sat down to write a letter to her cousin Mary C. Keyes, back home, in Springfield, Illinois. At this time Virginia was staying, with her mother and the other children, at Yount's Ranch in the Napa Valley.

She had the requisites for writing a good letter—pen and ink, note-paper of a size a little smaller than a present-day typewriter-sheet, and (most important of all) plenty to write about. Obviously the twelve-year-old was delighted at the opportunity to amaze her stay-at-home cousin with the tale that Othello himself might have told to awe-struck Desdemona. It was full of "most disastrous chances," and of "hairbreadth scapes" among "hills whose heads touch heaven." If there were no "men whose heads do grow beneath their shoulders," there certainly were "anthropophagi." Virginia undoubtedly saw herself becoming a veritable story-book character among "all the girls i know" back in Springfield. Besides, she seems to have been very fond of Mary Keyes.

Seldom, indeed, has such a youthful writer been granted such subject-matter. In almost epic style she announced as her theme: "our trubels geting to Callifornia."

With the whole story of the Donner Party—which she knew and of much of which she was a part—thus present in her immediate memory, the words flowed out, uninhibited by spelling or grammar. Page after page she finished, until in mere length the letter became remarkable for a writer of that age. But besides wordage she was also producing a complete child's version of one of the world's great stories.

Having finished with the "trubels," Virginia apparently broke off writing. Beginning again, perhaps the next day, she wrote a new salutation, "My Dear Cousin," and proceeded to tell a little of what California was like and to add a few touches of personal news. Also, apparently on a separate page, perhaps for the enlightenment or amusement of "Dochter

Maniel," she told about certain customs of folk-medicine in this new country. Of this last page we are not certain, but such a supposition seems best to account for a passage in one of the printed versions and to explain why a description of the letter written in 1879 notes eight pages, whereas now only seven are known.

The history of the letter after its writing is almost as interesting as the letter itself. In ending, Virginia wrote, "pa is yerbayan"—a cryptic statement, which is probably to be taken as, "Pa is at Yerba Buena." In later years, however, Virginia was quoted as having said that her father kept looking over her shoulder as she wrote, and that he later corrected "a few misspelled words." Let the timing be what it may, throughout the letter, in her father's much heavier handwriting, are many deletions, corrections, and even some rewritings of short passages. Many spellings are corrected, though for Reed to be revising anyone's spelling was certainly, as his own diary would indicate, a bizarre idea. (At least, he spelled a little better than Virginia did.)

Reed's changes were sometimes for greater specificity. He inserted the names of the oxen lost at Big Sandy as "Bulley and George." He added the names of the dogs: "Tyler, Barney, Trailer, Tracker, and little Cash." In place of Virginia's curiously derogatory "that man," he wrote, "Mr. Stanton." Others of his alterations were in the interests of accuracy. Once he changed "March" to "February." His daughter's, "the couldes night you most ever saw," he qualified, "for the season." She wrote that the "Bears" had robbed the caches: he changed this to "Cacadues or Fishers"—the first of these being his rendering of the French-Canadian carcajou, or wolverine. For greater accuracy, also justifying his own failure to get through, he altered the passage where Virginia had written briefly of his first attempt: "Pa sta[r]ted out to us with provision and then came a storm and he could not go." This he made:

Pa sta[r]ted out to us with provisions on the first of November and came into the Great California Mountain, about 80 miles and in one of the severest storms known for years past, raining in the valley and a Hurricane of snow in the mountains. It came so deep the horses and mules swamped so they could not go on any more.

Because of the alterations the letter became of more historical value, though it lost something of the artistic unity with which the twelve-year-old had unconsciously endowed it.

Once the letter was finished, the problem of how it was to be forwarded must have become important. Lacking a regular mail, letters were generally sent back across the plains by the courtesy of someone who was returning on horseback. One may hazard an informed guess that the carrier of Virginia's letter was her father's friend Edwin Bryant, who set out in June, 1847.

The next we know for certain is that on December 16, 1847, the *Illinois Journal* of Springfield published Virginia's work under the well-justified title, "Deeply Interesting Letter." We may take it as certain that Congressman Abraham Lincoln read this item in his home-town paper; he would have a special interest since he and Reed had served in the same company during the Black Hawk War.

As was customary at the time and as writers expected, the letter had been heavily edited before publication. Though crediting the work to "a little girl, aged about twelve years, step-daughter of Mr. James F. Reed," the editor had naturally accepted Reed's emendations as authoritative, though he had sometimes been unable to make the handwriting out, so that "Bulley" became "Riley." Both fishers and cacadues were apparently unknown creatures to the people of Springfield, and the editor put "Martens" instead. (This version of the letter was reprinted in *Westways,* December, 1934.)

He also printed the passage about doctoring, which is of sufficient interest to be quoted, even though it does not concern the Donner Party:

Tell Doctor——that they doctor the funniest in this country that he ever saw. They grease the sick all over with mantaja and kill a bienna and cut it in four pieces, and put a great piece of fat carrina on the wrist, and kill a sheep and wrap the sick up in the skin.

Obviously Virginia was trying to show off her newly acquired Spanish, and making a hash of the spelling. We may take *mantaja* as *manteca,* butter or lard; *carrina* is probably for *carne,* meat. As for *bienna,* my guess is that is is for *gallina,* hen; when we consider what Virginia could do with

English spelling, we should not underestimate what she might do with Spanish.

Fortunately, even after the printed version had appeared in 1847, the original of the letter was preserved. At some later time it was returned to Virginia. But the hypothetical extra sheet, about the doctoring, disappears from history.

When McGlashan was collecting Donner materials, in 1878 and the years following, he maintained a voluminous correspondence with Virginia, who had then become Mrs. John M. Murphy. (Her husband was not of the Murphys of the Donner Party, but had crossed with the Stevens Party of 1844.)

In the McGlashan papers are several of Mrs. Murphy's letters which make reference to this one of 1847, and there are two versions of the letter itself. One of these is considerably rewritten, probably by its author, with an eye toward magazine publication. The other, though giving the date as May 10, is a very accurate rendering, accepting Reed's emendations.

At some still later period the letter was defaced, and one short passage was thoroughly inked out. Probably no one but Mrs. Murphy herself would have taken such a liberty. We can only guess that she became embarrassed at her realism in writing about little Cash: "we ate his entrails and feet & hide & evry thing about him." Fortunately the words are preserved in the *Illinois Journal,* and the "May 10 version" gives even the spelling.

Some years after 1900 George Wharton James was working on his book *Heroes of California,* in which is included a chapter on Virginia. At this time, probably, a photographic copy of the letter was made for him. After his death, this copy went to the Southwest Museum, where it remains. Toward the end of her life Mrs. Murphy showed the original letter to a young friend, Lucia Shepardson De Wolf, and had her make two copies of it. Mrs. Murphy died in 1921 at the age of eighty-six—seventy-four years after writing the letter! After her death, according to Mrs. De Wolf, the letter was "searched for in vain."

In 1935 Mrs. De Wolf printed her version under the title *A Happy Issue.* This version, as compared with the photographic copy and the other texts, makes many and sometimes puzzling omissions, presents different readings in some places, and only half-preserves the spelling.

We have, then, the interesting situation of a letter existing in five different versions, all apparently based upon the original but no one of them being the original or exactly representing it. The photographic copy comes close to doing so, but has been rendered illegible in some places and presents also the necessity of distinguishing between the original text and Reed's emendations.

I have here used primarily the photographic copy, have called upon the "May 10 version" to supply the text about "little Cash," and have used the *Illinois Journal* for confirmation and for the "doctoring" passage, as quoted above. In a few places Reed's deletions were so heavy that Virginia's original words cannot be made out; I have then used his words, marking each with an asterisk.

As with the other original texts, I have used spaces for punctuation at the end of sentences, and have inserted a few words and letters in brackets for the aid of the reader. I have omitted the original page numbers and pagination. I have kept the spelling. Now and then Virginia's orthography yields startling results, as in the statement, "they raped the children up." Doubtless she meant "wrapped," and I have ventured that emendation. Startling also are Virginia's assertions that everyone had gained weight so that her mother weighed 10040 pounds and Eliza 10072 pounds. On second thought we see that these were only Virginia's devices for writing 140 and 172. Similarly, "that was the hades thing" is not to be taken as mild profanity, but by comparison with spellings elsewhere is seen to be, "that was the hardest thing."

A photographic copy is seldom wholly satisfactory, and this one may have been made after the original had already lost some of its legibility. Nevertheless, though the writing demands minute study, it can be made out. There may be a few differences of personal opinion about some letters, but I have only once thought it necessary to insert a question mark after a word. The existence of so many versions, some of them made when the manuscript was new, helps considerably with the decipherment.

Since Virginia figures largely in the pages of the book itself, no introduction of her is here necessary. Neither have I thought it required to correct her errors, as her father did.

That she makes some factual mistakes is to be expected. Anyone caring to make the comparison will see that the text of the book does not always agree with her statements. The letter is here reproduced, not as a summary of the story, but as a record of the impression that the experience made upon a twelve-year-old girl.

There is little need, also, to point out what that impression was. The letter speaks for itself. One can note, perhaps, the stark realism and the accompanying restraint of language which this document shares, along with most of the others dealing immediately with the Donner experience. These people had passed through so much, had looked death in the face so often and for so long, that they apparently had no need to build up their ordeal with high-flown words. One can note also the sense of family love and pride, and also a sense of pride in herself, though this never stands out to become offensive. In spite of its childish misspellings, the letter displays a remarkable maturity.

The chief omission, readily understandable, is that there is no reference at all to Reed's killing of Snyder. The statement is merely, "pa had to go on to Callifornia for provisions."

Her sentence, "they are all in from the mountains now but four," has led some to think that the letter may have been written some time before May 16. More likely, however, news of Fallon's expedition, which returned to Sutter's Fort in the last week of April, had not yet reached an isolated ranch in Napa Valley. . . .

Along with the Breen and Reed diaries, Virginia's letter may be termed, I think, a "natural" of literature.

THE LETTER

Napa Vallie
California
May 16th 1847

My Dear Cousin   May the 16   1847

I take this oppertunity to write to you to let you now that we are all Well at present and hope this letter may find you all well to My Dear Cousin I am going to write to you about our trubels geting to Callifornia. We had good luck til we come to big Sandy thare we lost our best yoak of oxens we come to Brigers Fort & we lost another ox we sold some of our provisions & baut a yoak of Cows & oxen and thay pursuaded us to take Hastings cutof over the salt plain thay said it saved 3 Hundred miles. we went that road & we had to go through a long drive of 40 miles With out water Hastings said it was 40 but i think 80 miles We traveld a day and night & a nother day and at noon pa went on to see if he coud find Water. he had not bin gone long till some of the oxen give out and we had to leve the wagons and take the oxen on to water one of the men staid with us and the others went on with the cattel to water pa was a coming back to us with water and met the men & thay was about 10 miles from water pa said thay [would] get to water that nite and the next day to bring the cattel back for the wagons and bring some water pa got to us about noon the man that was with us took the horse and went on to water We wated thare [thinking] he [would] come we wated till night and We thought we [would] start and walk to Mr Donners* wagons that night we took what little water we had and some [?] bread and started pa caried Thomos and all the rest of us walk we got to Donner and thay were all a sleep so we laid down on the ground we spred one shawl down we laid down on it and spred another over us and then put the dogs on top it was the couldes night you most ever saw the wind blew and if it haden bin for the dogs we would have Frosen as soon as it was day we went to Mrs Donners she said we could not walk to the Water and if we staid we could ride in thare wagons to the spring so pa went on to the water to see why thay did not bring the cattel when he got thare thare was but one ox and cow thare none of the rest had got to water Mr. Donner come out that night with his cattel and brought his wagons and all of us in we staid thare a week and Hunted for our cattel and could not find them so some of the compania took thare oxens and went out and brout in one wagon and cashed the other tow and a grate many* things all but What we could put in one wagon we Had to devied our provisions out to them to get them to carie it* We got three yoak with our ox & cow so we went on that way a while and we got out of provisions and pa had to go on to Callifornia for provisions we could not get along that way. in 2 or 3 days

after pa left we had to cash our wagon and take Mr graves
wagon and cash some more of our things. well we went
on that way a while and then we had to get Mr eddies
wagon we went on that way a while and then we had to
cash all our close except a change or 2 and put them in Mr
Bri[ns] Wagon and Thomos & James rode the other 2 horses
and the rest of us had to walk. we went on that way a
While and we come to a nother long drive of 40 miles and
then we went with Mr Donner We had to walk all the
time we was a travling up the truckee river we met a man
and to Indians that we had sent on for provisions to Suter
Fort thay had met pa not fur from Suters Fort he looked
very bad he had not ate but 3 times in 7 days and the
three* last* days without any thing his horse was not abel
to carrie him thay give him a horse and he went on so
we cashed some more of our things all but what we could
pack on one mule and we started Martha and James road
behind the two Indians it was a rain[in]g then in the Vallies
and snowing on the montains so we went on that way 3
or 4 days till we come to the big mountain or the Callifornia
Mountain the snow then was about 3 feet deep thare was
some wagons thare thay said thay had atempted to croos
and could not. well we thought we would try it so we
started and thay started again with those wagons the snow
was then up to the mules side the farther we went up the
deeper the snow got so the wagons could not go so thay
pack thare oxens and started with us carring a child a piece
and driving the oxens in snow up to thare wast the mule
Martha and the Indian was on was the best one so thay
went and broak the road and that indian was the Pilet so
we wint on that way 2 miles and the mules kept faling down
in the snow head formost and the Indian said he could not
find the road we stoped and let the indian and man go
on to hunt the road thay went on and found the road to
the top of the mountain and come back and said thay thought
we could git over if it did not snow any more well the
Weman were all so tirder caring there Children that thay
could not go over that night so we made a fire and got
something to eat & ma spred down a bufalo robe & we all
laid down on it & spred somthing over us & ma sit up by
the fire & it snowed one foot on top of the bed so we got
up in the morning & the snow was so deep we could not go

over & we had to go back to the cabin & build more cabins & stay thar all winter without Pa we had not the first thing to eat Ma maid arrangements for some cattel giving 2 for 1 in callifornia we seldom thot of bread for we had not any since I [remember] & the cattel was so poor thay could not git up when thay laid down we stoped thare the 4th of November & staid till March and what we had to eat i cant hardley tell you & we had that man & Indians to feed to well thay started over a foot and had to come back so thay made snowshoes and started again & it come on a storm & thay had to come back it would snow 10 days before it would stop thay wated till it stoped & started again I was a going with them & I took sick & could not go. thare was 15* started & thare was 7 got throw 5 weman & 2 men it come a storme and thay lost the road & got out of provisions & had to eat them that Died not long after thay started we got out of provisions & had to put matha at one cabin James at another Thomas at another & Ma and Elizia & Milt Eliot & I dried up what little meat we had and started to see if we could get across & had to leve the childrin o Mary you may think that hard to leve theme with strangers & did not now wether we would see them again or not we couldnt hardle get a way from them but we told theme we would bring them Bread & then thay was willing to stay we went & was out 5 days in the mountains Eliza giv out & had to go back we went on a day longer we had to lay by a day & make snowshows & we went on a while and coud not find the road so we had to turn back I could go on verry well while i thout we were giting along but as soone as we had to turn back i coud hadley get along but we got to the cabins that night & I froze one of my feet verry bad that same night thare was the worst storme we had that winter & if we had not come back that night we would never got back we had nothing to eat but ox hides o Mary I would cry and wish I had what you all wasted Eliza had to go to Mr. Graves cabin & we staid at Mr Breen thay had meat all the time. & we had to kill littel cash the dog & eat him we ate his entrails and feet & hide & evry thing about him o my Dear Cousin you dont now what trubel is yet. Many a time we had on the last thing a cooking and did not now wher the next would come from but there was awl weis some way provided there was 15 in the cabon we was in and half of us had to lay a bed all the time thare was 10 starved to death then we was hadly abel to walk we lived on little cash a week and after Mr. Breen would cook his meat we would take the bones and boil them 3 or 4 days at a time ma went down to the other cabin and got half a hide carried it in snow up to her wast it snowed and would cover the cabin all over so we could not git out for 2 or 3 days we would have to cut pieces of the logs in sied to make the fire with I coud hardly eat the hides and had not eat anything 3 days Pa sta[r]ted out to us with provisions and then come a storm and he could not go he cash his provision and went back on the other side of the bay to get a compana of men and the San Wakien [Joaquin] got so hye he could not cross well thay Made up a Compana at Suters Fort and sent out we had not ate any thing for 3 days & we had onely half a hide and we was out on top of the cabin and we seen them a coming

O my Dear Cousin you dont now how glad i was we run and met them one of them we knew we had traveled with him on the road thay staid thare 3 days to recruit us a little so we could go thare was 21 started all of us started and went a piece and Martha and Thomas give out and the men had to take them back Ma and Eliza & James and I come on and o Mary that was the hades thing yet to come on and leiv them thar did not now but what thay would starve to Death Martha said well Ma if you never see me again do the best you can the men said they could hadly stand it it maid them all cry but they said it was better for all of us to go on for if we was to go back we would eat that much more from them thay give them a little meat and flore and took them back and we come on we went over great hye mountain as strait as stair steps in snow up to our knees litle James walk the hole way over all the mountain in snow up to his waist. he said every step he took he was a gitting nigher Pa and somthing to eat the Bears took the provision the men had cashed and we had but very little to eat when we had traveld 5 days travel we me[t] Pa with 13 men going to the cabins o Mary you do not now how glad we was to see him we had not seen him for 6 months we thought we woul never see him again he heard we was coming and he made some s[w]eet cakes to give us he said he would see Martha and Thomas the naxt day he went in tow days what took us 5 days some of the compana was eating them that Died but Thomas & Martha had not ate any Pa and the men started with 17 peaple Hiram G. Miller carried Thomas and Pa caried Martha and thay wer caught in [storms] and thay had to stop two* days it stormed so they could not go and the Bears took their provisions and thay were 4 days without any thing Pa their provisions and thay were 4 days without any thing and Hiram and all the men started one Donner boy [sentence unfinished] Pa a carring Martha Hiram caring Thomas and the snow was up to thare wast and it a snowing so thay could hadly see the way. thay [w]rap[p]ed the children up and never took them out for 4 days thay had nothing to eat in all that time Thomas asked for somthing to eat once them that thay brought from the cabins some of them was not able to come and som would not come that was 3 died and the rest eat them thay was 11 days without any thing to eat but the Dead Pa braught Tom and pady on to where we was none of the men was abel to go there feet was froze very bad so thay was a nother Compana went and brought then all in thay are all in from the mauntains now but four thay was men went out after them and was caught in a storm and had to come back thare was* a nother compana gone thare was half got through that was stoped thare thare was but [2] familes that all of them got [through] we was one O Mary I have not rote you half of the truble we have had but I have rote you anuf to let you now that you dont now what truble is but thank god we have all got throw and the onely family that did not eat human flesh we have left everything but i dont cair for that we have got throw with our lives but Dont let this letter dish[e]a[r]ten anybody never take no cutofs and hury along as fast as you can.

My Dear Cousin
We are all very well pleased with Callifornia particulary with the climate let it be ever so hot a day thare is allwais cool nights it is a beautiful Country it is mostley in vallies it aut to be a beautiful Country to pay us for our trubel giting there it is the greatest place for cattel and horses you ever saw it would Just suit Charley for he could ride down 3 or 4 horses a day and he could lern to be

Bocarro [vaquero] that one who lases [lassos] cattel the spanards and Indians are the best riders i ever saw they have a spanish sadel and woden sturups and great big spurs the wheels of them is 5 inches in diameter and they could not manage the Callifornia horses without the spurs. thay wont go atol if thay cant hear the spurs rattle that have littel bells to them to make them rattle thay blindfold the horses and then sadel them and git on them and then take the blindfole of and let [them] run and if thay cant sit on thay tie themselves on and let them run as fast as they can and go out to a band of bullluck and throw the reatter [riata] on a wild bullluck and put it around the horn of his sadel and he can hold it as long as he wants another Indian throwes his reatter on its feet and throw them and when thay take the reatter of of them thay are very dangerous thay will run after them hook there horses and run after any person thay see thay ride from 80 to 100 miles a day some of the spanard have from 6 to 7000 head of horses and from 15 to 16000 head cattel we are all verry fleshey Ma waies 10040 pon and still a gain[in]g I weight 81 tell Henriet if she wants to get Married to come to Callifornia she can get a spanyard any time. that Eliza is a going to mariye a spanyard by the name of Armeho [Armijo] and Eliza weigh 10072 We have not saw uncle Cadon yet but we have had 2 letters from him he is well and is a coming here as soon as he can Mary take this letter to uncle Gursham and to all that i know to all of our neighbors [Interlined: *and tell Dochter Maniel*] and every girl i know and let them read it Mary kiss little Sue and Maryan for me and give my best love to all i know to uncle James aunt Lida and all the rest of the famila and to uncle Gursham and aunt Percilla and all the Children and to all of our neighbors and to all the girls i know Ma sends her very best love to uncle James aunt Lida and all the rest of the famila and to uncle Gursham and Aunt Persilla all of the Children and to all of our neighbors and to all she knows. pa is [at] yerbayan [Yerba Buena] so no more at present

My Dear casons
VIRGINIA ELIZABETH B REED

ROSTER OF THE DONNER PARTY

CONDENSED ITINERARY OF
THE DONNER PARTY

BIBLIOGRAPHY

NOTES AND REFERENCES

INDEX

ROSTER OF THE DONNER PARTY

THE figures after the names indicate the age as accurately as can be determined. Spellings of names have been normalized; in the original sources spellings frequently differ. For the arrangements of families by wagons, see note to Chapter 1.

Antonio (Antoine), 23, from New Mexico, probably employed to herd the loose cattle.

Breen family. Patrick, ca. 40, from Iowa, born in Ireland; Margaret (Peggy), ca. 40, his wife; their children, John, 14; Edward J., 13 (?); Patrick, Jr., 11 (?); Simon P., 9 (?); Peter, 7 (?); James, 4; Isabella, 1.

Burger, Karl ("Dutch Charley"), ca. 30, from Germany, probably a teamster for Keseberg.

Denton, John, 28, from Sheffield, England, traveling with the George Donner family.

Dolan, Patrick, ca. 40, from Iowa, born in Dublin, Ireland.

Donner family (George). George, 62, from Springfield, Illinois; Tamsen, 45, his wife; their children, Frances E., 6; Georgia, 4; Eliza P., 3. George Donner's children by a former wife: Elitha Cumi Donner, 14; Leanna C. Donner, 12.

Donner family (Jacob). Jacob, 65, from Springfield, Illinois, brother of George; Elizabeth, ca. 45, his wife; their children, George, 9; Mary M., 7; Isaac, 5; Samuel, 4 (?); Lewis, 3 (?). Elizabeth Donner's children by a former husband: Solomon E. Hook, 14; William Hook, 12.

Eddy family. William H., ca. 28, from Illinois; Eleanor, ca. 25, his wife; their children, James P., 3; Margaret, 1.

Elliott, Milford (Milton, or Milt), ca. 28; from Springfield, Illinois, teamster for Reed.

Fosdick, see under Graves family.

Foster, see under Murphy family.

Graves family. Franklin Ward ("Uncle Billy"), 57, from Illinois; Elizabeth, 47, his wife. Their unmarried children, Mary Ann, 20; William C., 18; Eleanor, 15; Lavina, 13; Nancy, 9; Jonathan B., 7; Franklin Ward, Jr., 5; Elizabeth, Jr., 1. A son-in-law, Jay Fosdick, 23, and his wife, Sarah Graves Fosdick, 22.

Halloran, Luke, ca. 25, from Missouri, an invalid traveling with the George Donners.

Hardkoop, ——, ca. 60, from Cincinnati, Ohio, born in Belgium, traveling with the Kesebergs.

Herron, Walter, ca. 25, a teamster for Reed.

Hook, see under Donner family (Jacob).

James, Noah, ca. 20, a teamster for one of the Donners.

Jean Baptiste, see Trubode.

Keseberg family. Lewis, 32, from Germany; Phillipine, ca. 32, his wife; their children, Ada, 3; Lewis, Jr., 1.

McCutchen family. William ("Mac"), ca. 30, from Missouri; Amanda, ca. 24, his wife; their child, Harriet, 1.

Murphy family. Lavina, 50, a widow, from Tennessee, but lately resident in Missouri; her unmarried children, John Landrum, 15; Mary M., 13 (?); Lemuel B., 12; William G., 11; Simon P., 10. Two sons-in-law with their wives and families: Foster, William M., ca. 28; Sarah Murphy Foster, 23, his wife; their child, George, ca. 4. Pike, William M., ca. 25; Harriet Murphy Pike, ca. 21, his wife; their children, Naomi L., 3; Catherine, 1.

Pike, see under Murphy family.

Reed family. James Frazier, 46, from Springfield, Illinois; Margaret W., 32, his wife; their children, Martha J. (Patty), 8; James Frazier, Jr., 5; Thomas K., 3. Mrs. Reed's daughter by her first husband: Virginia E. Backenstoe, 12, generally known as Virginia Reed.

Reinhardt, Joseph, ca. 30, from Germany, said to have been a partner of Spitzer.

Shoemaker, Samuel, ca. 25, a teamster for one of the Donners.

Smith, James, ca. 25, a teamster for Reed.

Snyder, John, ca. 25, a teamster for Graves.

Spitzer, Augustus, ca. 30; from Germany, said to have been a partner of Reinhardt.

Stanton, Charles Tyler, 35, from Chicago, traveling unattached.

Trubode, Jean Baptiste, ca. 23, from New Mexico, teamster for George Donner.

Williams, Baylis, ca. 24, a hired man for Reed.

Williams, Eliza, ca. 25, a hired girl for Reed, sister of Baylis Williams.

Wolfinger family. Wolfinger's first name and age are not known; his wife, name and age not known.

CONDENSED ITINERARY
OF THE DONNER PARTY

DATES as applied to camps indicate the night following the date mentioned, e.g., July 19 for the night of July 19–20. Place-names not used at the time of the Donner Party are bracketed.

July 19, 1846. Camp at Little Sandy Creek [Wyoming].
July 20-28. Travel from Little Sandy Creek to Fort Bridger.
July 28-30. At Fort Bridger.
July 31-August 6. Follow Hastings's trail from Fort Bridger *via* Bear River, and Echo Canyon [Utah], to Weber River.
August 6. Find Hastings's note at Weber River crossing.
August 6-11. In camp at the crossing; Reed and others sent ahead.
August 12-27. Cross Wahsatch Mountains *via* [Little East Canyon Creek], Bossman [East Canyon] Creek, [Big Mountain], [Parley's Canyon], and [Emigration Canyon].
August 28-September 1. Travel from near [Salt Lake City] *via* Black Rock and Twenty Wells [Grantsville] to springs in [Skull Valley].
September 2. Rest at springs in [Skull Valley].
September 3-8. Cross Salt Lake Desert to springs at base of [Pilot Peak, Nevada].
September 9-15. In camp resting.
September 16-30. Travel *via* [Silver Zone Pass], [Flowery Lake], [Independence Valley], [Ruby Valley], [Huntington Creek], and [South Fork of Humboldt River], rejoining Fort Hall road about ten miles southwest of [Elko].
September 18 (?). Stanton and McCutchen sent ahead.
October 1-12. Travel along Humboldt River to its sink.
October 5. Snyder killed, near [Stone House].
October 8. Hardkoop left behind, near [Cosgrave].
October 13-14. Cross desert between Humboldt Sink and Truckee River; Wolfinger remains behind.
October 15. In camp on Truckee River near [Wadsworth].
October 16-19. Travel up canyon of Truckee River to Truckee Meadows near [Reno].

October 19. Stanton, with two Indians and pack-train, rejoins.

October 20-25. Resting in Truckee Meadows. (Approximate dates.)

October 20. Pike killed.

October 25(?)-30. Travel in three sections *via* [Dog Valley] to Truckee [Donner] Lake.

October 28-29. First heavy snowfall on mountains.

October 31-November 3. Attempt to cross pass with wagons. Snow and rain during much of this time.

October 31. Reed and McCutchen leave Sutter's attempting to bring back food.

November 4. The Party returns to Donner Lake and establishes camp there.

November 4-11. Storm continues, rain and snow. (This first storm lasted with intermissions from October 28 to November 11.)

November 12. First attempt to escape across pass on foot.

November 20. Breen begins his diary.

November 21-22. Second attempt to escape across pass on foot.

November 25-December 3. Second storm. (These storms might better be called "periods of stormy weather," for they usually included lulls and intervals without precipitation. On the other hand, briefer storms often of several hours' duration sometimes occurred in periods which I have not indicated as stormy.)

December 9-13. Third storm.

December 15. First death (Baylis Williams) at Truckee Lake.

December 16-January 17, 18. Journey of snow-shoers from Truckee Lake to Johnson's Ranch.

December 23-25. Fourth storm. Snow-shoers' fire extinguished.

January 2. Reed at Battle of Santa Clara.

January 4-8. Mrs. Reed, Virginia, and Milt Elliott attempt to cross pass on foot.

January 9-13. Fifth storm.

January 22-27. Sixth storm.

January 31. Glover's relief party leaves Sutter's.

February 2-6. Seventh storm.

February 3. Meeting held at Yerba Buena [San Francisco] for raising of relief funds.

February 4-18. Glover's relief party journeys from Johnson's to the Lake.

February 7. Reed, Greenwood, and Woodworth with supplies and funds for relief leave Yerba Buena.

February 22-27. Glover's relief party with refugees journeys from the Lake to Bear Valley.

February 22-March 1. Reed's relief party journeys from Johnson's to the Lake.

February 27. Reed's relief party meets Glover's relief party with refugees.

March 1. Last entry in Breen's diary.

March 3-5. Reed's relief party with refugees journeys from the Lake to [Summit Valley].

March 6-8. Eighth storm. Reed's relief party with refugees storm-bound.

March 8-10. Reed with some of the refugees continues journey to Bear Valley.

March 7-13. Eddy and Foster journey from Johnson's to the Lake.

March 13-17. Eddy and Foster with refugees journey from the Lake to Bear Valley.

March 19. Mrs. Murphy dies at Lake (approximate date).

March 23-28 (?). Another relief expedition sent out from Johnson's but fails to advance beyond Bear Valley.

March 26. Tamsen Donner comes to the Lake (approximate date).

March 28-April 3. Ninth storm (approximate dates).

April 13-17. Fallon's party journeys from Johnson's to the Lake.

April 21-22. Fallon's party with Keseberg journeys from the Lake to Bear Valley.

BIBLIOGRAPHY

THIS list includes works preserving independently the testimony of members of the Donner Party and of the various relief parties, works which attempt to interpret this material, and works which by indirect means—e.g., by giving information about the road, contemporary conditions, etc.—add to our knowledge of the events. Among these last might be included the maps of the U. S. Topographical Survey, and the *American Almanac* (Boston, James Munroe & Co.) for 1846 and 1847.

The works listed differ greatly in value, and some of them I even consider highly misleading. Nevertheless I have included these latter to show that, if I have not made use of the "information," I have at least weighed and considered it. Definitely fictional interpretations have not been included.

My knowledge of topography is based chiefly upon personal study, largely made on foot, of the country between Donner Lake and Sacramento.

To economize space, works are cited under the abbreviation, and page and chapter references are given only for direct quotations or when the material referred to occurs out of chronological order or for other reasons might be difficult to locate.

I suggest a threefold classification of the sources in decreasing scale of dependability:

(1) Contemporary letters and journals (except for BPD these are all in printed form), and accounts which more or less directly reproduce these. Journals include those of Breen, Eddy, Reed, Ritchie-Tucker-Glover, Fallon (see BPD, ReIJ, McG, Th). These sources are invaluable for establishing dates, places, and names, and the skeleton of events, but are generally brief and lacking in detail.

(2) Works written and published soon after 1847. Th is outstanding in this group. It is based largely upon the material included under (1), and in addition makes use of much oral testimony which the writer collected during his visit

to San Francisco in 1847. Special pleaders have attacked the accuracy of Th, but I have found it extremely trustworthy. It contains some errors, but so do all the others, even Breen's diary.

(3) Works written and published after the revival of interest in the story (ca. 1870). These include retellings of the whole story as in Ba, Ho, McG, controversial and interpretative articles, letters, reminiscences, etc. The last two are in general just the opposite of those listed under (1); they are rich in detail, but sketchy and untrustworthy for dates, places, etc. Theoretically, letters and reminiscences of the survivors should rank as primary authorities; actually, I find that in the interval of thirty years or more the writer has usually reshaped the story to fit his own ideas of what should have happened.

AA	Allen, William Wallace, and Avery, Richard Benjamin: *California Gold Book*. San Francisco and Chicago, 1893.
Alley	Alley, Bowen & Co.: *History of Sonoma County*. San Francisco, 1880.
Al	Alter, J. Cecil: *James Bridger*. Salt Lake City [1925].
Ba	Bancroft, Hubert Howe: *History of California*. San Francisco, 1884-90.
Bid	Bidwell, John: *Echoes of the Past*. Chicago, 1928.
Big	Bigler, H. W.: "Diary of a Mormon in California." MS. in Bancroft Library.
Bo	Boggs, William Montgomery: "Statement of Crossing the Plains, 1846." MS. in Bancroft Library.
BJPM	Breen, John: "Pioneer Memoirs." MS. in Bancroft Library.
BPCP	Citizenship papers of Patrick Breen. MS. in Bancroft Library.
BPD	Breen, Patrick: "Diary." MS. in Bancroft Library. *Diary of Patrick Breen*, Ed. Frederick J. Teggart, Berkeley, Cal., 1910, is excellent, but earlier printed versions are untrustworthy.
Bry	Bryant, Edwin: *What I Saw in California*. New York, 1848.
Bur	Burnett, Peter Hardeman: *Recollections and Opinions of an Old Pioneer*. New York, 1880.
GlG	Clayton, William: *The Latter-Day Saints' Emigrants' Guide*. St. Louis, Mo., 1848.

GlJ   Clayton, William: *William Clayton's Journal*. Salt Lake City, Utah, 1921.

Cly   *James Clyman, American Frontiersman*. Ed. Charles L. Camp. San Francisco, 1928.

Cu   Cutts, James Madison: *The Conquest of California and New Mexico*. Philadelphia, 1847.

Far   Farnham, Eliza W.: *California, In-Doors and Out*. New York, 1854.

FSD   "Fort Sutter Diary." MS. in Bancroft Library.

FSP   *A Transcript of the Fort Sutter Papers*. Published by Edward Eberstadt, n.d.

GWC   Graves, William C.: "Crossing the Plains in '46." *The Russian River Flag* (Healdsburg, Cal.), April 26, May 3, 10, 17, 1877. See also December 30, 1875.

Hall   Hall, Frederick: *History of San José*. San Francisco, 1871.

Har   Harlan, Jacob W., *California, '46 to '88*. San Francisco, 1888.

Has   Hastings, Lansford Warren: *The Emigrants' Guide to Oregon and California . . . with Historical Note and Bibliography by Charles Henry Carey*. Princeton, 1932.

Ide   Ide, Simeon: *Biographical Sketch of the Life of William B. Ide*. Claremont, N. H., 1880.

Ja   James, Geo. W.: *Heroes of California*. Boston, 1910.

Je   Jefferson, T. H.: *Map of the Emigrant Road from Independence, Mo., to St. Francisco, California* (1849).

Ke   Kelly, Charles: *Salt Desert Trails*. Salt Lake City, Utah, 1930.

McC   McCutchen, William: "Statement of Wm. McCutchen." *Pacific Rural Press*, April 1, 1871.

McD   McDougal, Frances H.: "The Donner Tragedy." *Pacific Rural Press*, January 21, 1871. See also April 29, 1871.

McG   McGlashan, C. F.: *History of the Donner Party*. Truckee, Cal., 1879. The First Edition differs considerably from later ones; my quotations are from the Second Edition.

McK   McKinstry, George: "Documents for the History of California, 1846-8." MS. in Bancroft Library.

No   North, Arthur W.: "The Cut-Off." *Sunset Magazine*, December, 1915.

Pa   Parkman, Francis, Jr.: *The California and Oregon Trail*. New York, 1849.

Po   Power, John Carroll: *History of the Early Settlers of Sangamon County, Illinois.* Springfield, Ill., 1876.

Ra   Rabbison, Antonio B.: "Growth of Towns." MS. in Bancroft Library.

Re   Reed, James Frazier: "The Snow-Bound, Starved Emigrants of 1846." *Pacific Rural Press,* March 25, April 1, 1871.

ReIJ   Reed, James Frazier: "Narrative of the Sufferings of a Company of Emigrants in the Mountains of California, in the Winter of '46 and '7." *Illinois Journal* (Springfield), December 9, 1847. See also December 23, 1847.

ReSJ   Reed, James Frazier: "From a California Emigrant." *Sangamo Journal* (Springfield, Ill.), November 5, 1846.

ReVC   Murphy, Virginia Reed: "Across the Plains in the Donner Party (1846)." *Century Magazine,* July, 1891.

ReVIJ   Murphy, Virginia Reed: "Deeply Interesting Letter." *Illinois Journal* (Springfield), December 16, 1847.

ReVL   Murphy, Virginia Reed: Letters to C. F. McGlashan, MSS. in possession of the McGlashan estate.

Rh   Rhoads, Daniel: "Relief of the Donner Party." MS. in Bancroft Library.

Star   *California Star* (Yerba Buena, San Francisco).

Sto   Stokes, Frank, Jr., "The Last Man Out." *Touring Topics,* February, 1929.

SPR   Sutter, John A., "Personal Reminiscences." MS. in Bancroft Library.

Swo   Swords, Thomas: *Report of a Journey from California by the South Pass to Fort Leavenworth in 1847.* (537) Ex. Doc. I of H. R. 30 Cong. 2 Sess. (1848), pp. 226-236.

Th   Thornton, Jessy Quinn: *Oregon and California in 1848.* New York, 1849. (2 vols.) All page references are to Volume II.

ThM   Thornton, Jessy Quinn: "Oregon History." MS. in Bancroft Library.

Ty   Tyler, Daniel: *A Concise History of the Mormon Battalion in the Mexican War.* Salt Lake City, 1881.

Wa   Waggoner, W. W.: "The Donner Party and Relief Hill." *California Historical Society Quarterly,* December, 1931.

Wi   Wise, Henry Augustus: *Los Gringos.* New York, 1849.

Yo   "Biographical Obituary, Samuel C. Young." *Pioneer* (San José, California), November 9, 1878.

ADDENDUM

Ho   Houghton, Eliza P. Donner: *The Expedition of the Donner Party and Its Tragic Fate*. Chicago, 1911.

NOTES AND REFERENCES

PAGE

5. CHAPTER 1. Chief sources: Has, Ho, Th. Also: Bry, ClJ, Cly, Har, ReVC, Star (Feb. 13, 1847).

5. Twenty wagons. Star (Feb. 13, 1847), upon information drawn apparently from Reed, gives the number of wagons in the Donner Party as twenty-three. This apparently refers to the maximum number of wagons, after Graves with his three had joined. From scattered references the wagons may be assigned: George Donner, Jacob Donner, Reed, Breen, three each; Keseberg, two; Eddy, Dolan, Pike, Wolfinger, one each. Of the two remaining, one must be assigned without definite evidence to Foster-Murphy and the other probably to Spitzer-Reinhardt.

6. Copies of Hastings's book. One copy brought across by the Donner Party is now in the Bancroft Library.

10. CHAPTER 2. Sources: Ba (Pioneer Register and Index), BJPM, BPCP, BPD, Bry, Cly, Hall, Has, Ho, McG, McK, Pa, Po, Ra, Re, ReVC, ReVL, Th, ThM. Letters, Mrs. Martha Reed Lewis to Dr. C. W. Chapman, Sept. 25, 1910, and April 14, 1921, in possession of Dr. Chapman.

12. "Even in . . ." Has, p. 83.

12. "a pleasure . . ." Martha Reed Lewis to C. W. Chapman, April 14, 1921.

13. "There is . . ." Cly. Clyman reports Reed as saying "nigher," but that is probably Clyman's own rendering; I have found nothing to indicate that Reed spoke such a dialect.

14. "known as . . ." Bry, p. 250.

18. "Many of . . ." Pa, p. 9.

19. CHAPTER 3. Chief sources: Re, ReIJ, ReSJ, Th. Also Bry, Har, Ho, McK, ReVC, ReVL. On the road, Bry, ClG, ClJ. On Fort Bridger, Bry, Al.

20. "I know . . ." ReVL, p. 139.

20. Arrival at Fort Bridger. The date of departure is set definitely as the thirty-first by ReIJ, with confirmatory evidence from McK, ReSJ, and ReVC. Th gives date of departure as July 28, as does Ho following Th. Thornton probably mistook the date of arrival for that of departure.

21. "two very . . ." ReSJ.

22. "Since I . . ." Bry, p. 145, and Har, pp. 41-42, both tell the story, and give Bill's words in different form; since the authorities differ, I have reshaped the quotation after my own opinion of what Bill would have said. Bry gives the name as "Bill Smith," but the character involved was apparently the well-known Bill Williams.

23. McCutchen. Th gives Pike instead. But Re gives McCutchen, and since Reed himself was a member of the party, he seems a better authority than Th. McG follows Th, and most later writers follow McG.

24. CHAPTER 4. Chief sources: Ho, Re, Th; also Far, ReVL, Sacramento (Cal.) *Daily Union,* Oct. 1, 1866. On the road and country: Bry, ClG, ClJ, Je, No, Yo.

26. "Exceedingly rough . . ." ClJ.

27. Eighty-seven. This is the number as determined by McGlashan, with allowance for his inclusion of Mrs. Keyes, Luis, and Salvador. Other accounts check well enough with this except that ReIJ gives the number before the arrival of the Graveses as eighty-two. Possibly a group turned back at Bear River, for from this point Stanton was able in some way to send a letter to his brother (McK).

32. CHAPTER 5. Chief sources: Ho, Re, ReVIJ, Th; also, ReVL. On the road and country: Bry, Je, Ke.

34. Hastings's note. A. B. Hulbert in his *Forty-Niners* praises Hastings in connection with this note upon the assumption that he or some one sent by him recrossed the desert to leave this warning. The note, however, must have been left before the crossing was attempted, for Hastings's own party took several days to cross, and for him to have sent back *false* information clear across the desert is as unthinkable as it would have been criminal. After all there is no reason against the note's having been left beforehand. On Hastings's own crossing see: Har, Je, Yo.

40. CHAPTER 6. Chief source: Th. Also: GWC, Re, Star (Feb. 13, 1847). On the road and country: Je, Ke.

41. Caching Reed's goods. Ke points out the difficulty of digging a hole in the sink. In 1933 the remains of a cache were discovered, possibly that made by the Donner Party; it had been made in the way which I have indicated (Letter from Charles Kelly, Oct. 28, 1933).

42. Chronology. I follow Th in assuming that the Party left Pilot Peak on September 16. Comparison of Th and Je

indicates that the Donner Party, every night from Flowery Lake to the Humboldt, camped where Hastings had camped. The exact time when McCutchen and Stanton went ahead is doubtful. Star (Feb. 13, 1847) gives the most reliable statement, but this might be taken to indicate a day or even two days earlier than the eighteenth, or might possibly refer to the morning of the nineteenth.

46. "Nothing transpired . . ." Re.

47. CHAPTER 7. Chief source: Th, pp. 110-12, 182-83. Also: BJPM, GWC, Ja, McG, Re, ReVC, ReVL. On the country: Bry.

49. Thursday. October 2, 1846, was actually Friday.

51. Reed-Snyder affair. This is naturally one of the most controversial incidents of the whole story. Three versions exist: (1) pro-Reed, e.g., McG, Ja, ReVC, ReVL; (2) pro-Snyder, e.g., GWC; (3) an intermediate version (Th) based upon information from Eddy. I have followed the last, which by the rules of evidence seems decidedly preferable to either of the others; it is closer to (1) than to (2). McG, apparently from a misreading of GWC, gives the scene of Snyder's death as Gravelly Ford. Actually GWC places the scene several days' journey west of that point, and this checks with the date as given in Th. Later writers have, however, copied McG.

51. "Uncle Patrick . . ." McG, p. 47.

51. "I am . . ." McG, p. 47.

53. CHAPTER 8. Chief source: Th. Also: GWC, Ho, McG, ReIJ. On the country: Bry.

57. Hundred cattle. This is about the total of the figures given in Th; it seems large and may be slightly swelled by exaggeration, but is not impossible. A train as large as the Donner Party's would have required normally well over a hundred team-oxen in addition to the loose herd, so that even after the loss of a hundred they might still have been able to move as many as fifteen lightly loaded wagons. The Indians sometimes shot, sometimes drove off or stampeded the cattle; the sources are often vague. The failure of the men to guard their cattle is one of the worst indictments against them, but may be to some extent excused on the grounds of their inexperience and their exhausted condition.

60. CHAPTER 9. Chief sources: Far, Th. Also: BPD, Bry, GWC, Har, Ho, Je, McG (pp. 53-59; 208-09), Re, REIJ, ReVC, ReVIJ. On the road and country: Bry, Ide.

60.   River of Heaven. J. R. Ridge: "The Humboldt Desert" in *Poetry of the Pacific* (San Francisco, 1867).

61.   Wolfinger affair. My account follows Th. McG follows largely a very garbled account given by GWC, based upon recollections thirty years after the event. GWC does not mention the Hardkoop affair and apparently telescopes it with that of Wolfinger, thus involving Keseberg.

64.   Chronology. The length of the stay in Truckee meadows cannot be determined accurately. The dates for arrival at the lake, etc., in Th are three days off, as checked by BPD, Far, ReVIJ, and Sinclair's letter in Bry. These four authorities settle these dates definitely, and I have followed them in the narrative. The journey from the meadows to the lake may have taken as much as a week, so that the date in Th for the last crossing of the Truckee (October 25) may be correct.

70.   Pine trees. Here and elsewhere I have used this term after common practice to include the various kinds of conifers which form the mixed forests of the Sierra.

76.   CHAPTER 11. Chief sources: Re, ReIJ, Th. Also: Bry, McD.

79.   Jotham Curtis. For the experiences of Reed and Mc-Cutchen with the Curtises I have followed Re, and Th. McD puts a very different face on the matter, but does not seem to me such a credible authority.

79.   "very good . . ." Re.

82.   CHAPTER 12. Chief sources: BPD, Th. Also: Bry, Far, Ho, McG, and a picture drawn from description of Wm. G. Murphy. Letter, Martha Reed Lewis to C. W. Chapman, March 4, 1922.

84.   Donner camp. Mr. P. M. Weddell locates this camp on one of the feeders of Alder Creek approximately one half mile north-west of the point marked Prosser House on the U. S. Topographical Map (Truckee quadrangle, ed. 1895). I have examined the ground in detail, and am convinced that this is the proper location. References to the location in the literature are vague. This spot fits them as well as any; it shows several of the tall stumps characteristic of trees cut in deep snow. On November 12, 1935, I did some excavation at this site, finding at two places layers of charcoal deposits about four inches below the present ground-level.

85.   Fishing. Many cocksure people have belabored the Don-

ner Party for the failure to catch fish. For a more authoritative opinion I wrote to the California Fish and Game Commission, and E. L. Macaulay, Chief of Patrol, writes me under date Feb. 15, 1934: "We doubt whether their efforts would meet with much success as the fish feed very little in the winter and usually inhabit the deepest portions of the lake. In our opinion it would be most difficult to catch them in sufficient quantities for food purposes at that time of the year."

90.   "nothing but . . ." GWC.

91.   CHAPTER 13. Chief sources: BPD, Th (pp. 127-29, 137, 240). Also: Bry, Far, GWC, McG, ReIJ.

96.   CHAPTERS 14, 15, 16. Chief sources: Bry (pp. 251-55), ReIJ, Th (pp. 129-56, 240-46). Also: BPD, Bur, McG.

96.   Chronology of the snow-shoers. Bry (Sinclair's statement), ReIJ, and Th all give many exact dates based upon Eddy's testimony, but they show some discrepancies. Bry and ReIJ agree much more closely than either does with Th, and these two also check much more closely with the geography. I have therefore almost neglected Th as far as chronology is concerned, although for details it is important. Bry and ReIJ can generally be reconciled, so that in the final analysis they are seldom more than a day apart. They keep together for the first four days. Bry gives the date of Stanton's remaining behind at the camp-fire as the 20th; ReIJ as the 21st. By checking with the weather conditions (BPD), I accept in this case the date given by ReIJ, and follow this authority until the 24th. From the 25th to the 29th Bry for various reasons seems the more reliable. From the 30th to the 1st the two authorities agree. The next difficulty can be explained, for ReIJ certainly records as of the Jan. 2, 3, and 4 what should have been the entry for Jan. 2 alone. With the acceptance of this correction the two accounts offer no further discrepancy of moment.

97.   Route of the snow-shoers. Wa advances the (amazing) theory that the snow-shoers, and the relief parties as well, followed a route which ran by Relief Hill, between the Middle and South Forks of the Yuba. The only positive evidence adduced is the statement of some unnamed "old residents" who have since died! The only account of the Donner Party which Mr. Waggoner seems to know is McG.

The more detailed accounts of the experiences of the snow-shoers as given in Bry, ReIJ, and Th make Wag-

PAGE

goner's theory untenable. Under the guidance of Stanton and the Indians the snow-shoers followed the route of the emigrant road about as far as the divide between the Yuba and American basins. Thereafter, losing the way, they wandered probably through Six-Mile Valley, and toward the southwest (ReIJ: "Went down the mountain in a southerly direction"). The scene of their camp in the snowstorm I should place not far from Onion Valley. After the storm they followed Saw-tooth Ridge. From the end of this ridge the Sacramento Valley is easily visible. They crossed the canyon of the North Fork between Humbug and Euchre Bars, and then went near Iowa Hill. They descended into the North Fork canyon again, and crossed the stream probably north of Indian Creek (Th: "They went down to the north branch of the American fork of the Sacramento"). One would grant that the snow-shoers cannot have been sure at the time what stream they were crossing, but after his arrival at Johnson's, Eddy would certainly have had time to talk with men familiar with the country, and so find out where he had wandered. From this point landmarks are less notable, and the record is less exactly preserved. Johnson's Ranch lay approximately west of the point of their second crossing of the North Fork, and no difficult natural barrier lay in their way. This route is not greatly longer than that of the emigrant road, but it traverses much more difficult country; in addition they probably made many minor wanderings which cannot now be determined. I should say that in addition to studying the available records I have taken the trouble to go over the most questionable portions of the route on foot.

99.   "Your own . . ." This and other direct quotations in Chaps. 14, 15, and 16 are from Th (pp. 129-56) except as otherwise noted.

99.   "Yes . . ." McG, p. 73.

111.   The details of the killing of the deer (tears, prayers, etc.) are from Thornton's account. I have suspected a certain elaboration upon his part, for he was both sentimental and religious, whereas Eddy was usually neither. On the other hand the incidents cannot be rejected merely because they are strange and improbable from our cynically modern point of view. We are dealing with a man and woman under the greatest physical and mental stress.

115.   SPR gives a somewhat different version of the killing of

the Indians, stating that they were digging in the snow for acorns when shot. My account follows Th which is based on Eddy. The reader should remember the possibility that in this case Eddy may be whitewashing himself to some extent.

116.   "Here are . . ." McG, p. 109, from statement by Mary Graves.

119.   CHAPTER 17. Chief sources: ReIJ, Star (Feb. 6, 1847), Th. Also: Hall, McK, Rh. On the Santa Clara campaign: Ba.

121.   "sailors, whalers . . ." ReIJ.

124.   "nearly every . . ." Th, p. 159.

124.   "This speaks . . ." Star (Feb. 6, 1847).

126.   "Yours of . . ." McK.

127.   CHAPTER 18. Chief source: BPD. Also: Ho, ReVC, ReVL, ReVIJ.

132.   "Children, eat . . ." McG, p. 98.

133.   CHAPTER 19. Chief source: BPD. Also: Ho, ReVL, ReVIJ, Th.

140.   CHAPTER 20. BPD notes the arrival of Glover's party as of February 18. February 19 is given in Tucker's diary which I believe to be the same as that credited to Glover by McKinstry. This latter is quoted in McG (p. 120) and by McKinstry (see Star, March 13, 1847, and Bry, p. 255), but neither can be relied upon to quote *verbatim*. Th is based on the account given by McK, with additions of details probably from verbal sources.

This raises the question as to whether Breen or Tucker was a day off in the chronology. But Breen notes the arrival of Reed's party as of March 1, and this agrees with the dates given in McG (p. 158, Th quoting Reed's diary), and in Th (p. 196). Since Th is a secondary authority and is inconsistent as well, the conflict is reduced to Breen and Reed against Tucker, and it seems proper to take the double testimony against the single.

The cessation of the storm noted by Breen as of February 7, and by Ritchie (who preceded Tucker in keeping the diary) as of the eighth shows the inconsistency probably existing as far back as this date. On the other hand, Kern's pay-rolls (FSP) check with Th to establish January 31 as the date of leaving Sutter's. The difficulty arose, I have concluded, most likely when Ritchie at the time of leaving

Johnson's thought the day to be the fifth when it was really the fourth. My chronology is worked out upon this belief.

146. Milt's burial. I follow Virginia Reed's version. But see also BPD, entry of Feb. 14.

149. "I will . . ." Star, March 13, 1847.

151. CHAPTER 21. Chief sources: BPD, Bry, McG, Th. Also: GWC, ReVL, Rh.

152. "Are you . . ." Rh.

152. "Relief, thank . . ." ReVL, p. 53.

152. "Have you . . ." Th, p. 169.

157. CHAPTER 22. Chief source: Th. Also: Bry, BPD, FSP, GWC, McG, Re, ReIJ, ReVIJ, ReVL.

157. "Are you . . ." Th, p. 173.

158. "Well, mother . . ." ReVIJ.

162. "Bread! Bread!" McG, p. 154.

162. "Is Mrs. . . ." This and the other direct quotations which follow in the chapter are from ReVL, pp. 73, 74, 77, 126.

165. CHAPTER 23. Chief sources: BPD, McG, Th. Also: Ba (Pioneer Register and Index), Bry, p. 356, GWC, Re, ReIJ.

167. "I had . . ." Bry, p. 356.

169. Ten Indians. These and the one seen by Breen on the same day were probably Piutes who wintered usually on the lower Truckee. Traditions of the Donner Party survived among these Indians (see S. W. Hopkins: *Life among the Piutes*, Boston, 1883, pp. 12-13). They would not normally have entered the higher mountains during the time of heavy snow; perhaps they had learned earlier in the season that the whites were encamped by the lake, and came at this time in hope of plunder or out of mere curiosity.

172. CHAPTER 24. Chief sources: Th, Re, ReIJ. Also: Ho, ReVIJ, Wi. The facts are plainly and circumstantially stated in Th. Re passes over the cannibalism; ReIJ tells it without mentioning names but in such a way as to confirm Th. Jean Baptiste's account as preserved by Lieut. Wise is of some confirmatory value, although it contains also some boastful inaccuracies. Virginia Reed makes the statement: "We are the only family that did not have to eat human flesh" (VRIJ). Mrs. Houghton passes the matter over without specific mention, but tries to confute the fact of any cannibalism at Alder Creek. So great is her desire for this end that, after using Th implicitly as her chief authority for the earlier part of her narrative, she passes over his version

of this incident entirely and even (pp. 342-43) quotes him as if to refute it! McG says nothing about the matter one way or the other.

175.   CHAPTER 25. Chief sources: McG, Re, ReIJ, Th. Also: Far, McC.

180.   "I dread . . ." McG, p. 174.

180.   Second night of the storm. The experiences of this night are, as might be expected under the circumstances, confused in the various accounts. My own account is something of a synthesis put together in the attempt to present clearly what most likely happened.

181.   "I'm glad . . ." McG, p. 175

182.   "was leaning . . ." Th, p. 215.

184.   CHAPTER 26. Chief sources: Ho, McG. Also: Th.

188.   CHAPTER 27. Chief source: Th. Also: Far, GWC, McG, Star (March 13, April 3, 1847), ThM. The happenings in the camp at the head of the Yuba (Starved Camp) form one of the controversial parts of the story. The longest account is in Far, but this is so sentimentalized and so obviously a defense of Mrs. Breen (who supplied the information) that it is not to be trusted.

189.   "I shall . . ." Star, March 13, 1847.

191.   "that they . . ." Th, p. 218.

191.   "had become . . ." Th, p. 218.

196.   CHAPTER 28. Chief source: Th. Also: Ho (pp. 111-14, 120, 124), McG, Star (April 3, 1847). Little accurate detail is preserved upon the section covered by this chapter. Th, based upon Eddy, is best, but has been somewhat confused in transmission. McGlashan used an account as recollected after thirty years by Georgia Donner, who was only five years old in 1847; he also may have had material supplied by William G. Murphy which represented the tradition of the Murphy-Foster families. Mrs. Houghton used Th, her sisters', and possibly her own recollections. Star supplies only a few notes.

Several controversial points are involved. Th states (p. 225) that one of Jacob Donner's children was living at the time of Eddy's arrival at the lake, and Star confirms this. I see no reason to doubt this contemporary testimony. With Samuel Donner still living, Thornton's accusations against Clark are well based, and Tamsen Donner's dilemma becomes more complicated, but not less difficult, than has been ordinarily represented. There is of course something romantically appealing in having her make a clean-cut decision between husband and children; Thornton yielded to the temptation and on pages 227-28 introduces a wholly imaginary conversation between husband and wife. He apparently forgot that the scene of Tamsen's parting with her children was at the lake-camp, while her husband was lying at the other camp. I have tried to represent the situation with the complexity which it actually must have had.

198. "in sight . . ." McG, p. 200.

201. CHAPTER 29. Chief source: Ho (pp. 124-34, 140). Also: McG, ReVIJ, Star (April 3, 1847).

203. "It drooped . . ." Th, p. 221.

204. CHAPTER 30. Chief source: Star (June 5, 1847). Also: Bry, 261-63; Ho, 356-70; McG, 199-224. Fallon's "diary" is almost the only original source; its first published form (Star, *loc. cit.*) does not differ materially from later versions. (All the quotations in the chapter are from Star.) It has been attacked as untrustworthy, but it was not so attacked until long after the event. Such good judges as Bryant and Thornton accepted it at face value. We must remember also that it had the tacit support of such men as Foster and Tucker who, no matter what Fallon may have been, are known as responsible and fair-minded persons. I have given Keseberg's side of the matter in Chapter 34.

213. PART III. Since this part deals chiefly with the interpretation and review of matters already treated, a general chapter-by-chapter statement of sources is unnecessary. For the later lives of the characters the following contain material: Ba, BJPM, FSP, GWC, Hall, Has, McC, McD, McG, McK, Ra, Re, ReSJ, ReVIJ, ReVL. For the aftermath of the Donner Party: Ba, Bid, Big, Bry, Cu, ClJ, McG, SW. On the legends: Alley, Ke. On the Keseberg controversy: Ba, Far, FSP, Ho, McD, McG, McK, Ra, Sto, Wi. On Hastings: Bid, Has (Historical Note).

216. Bridger: Bridger's responsibility in connection with the Donner Party is definitely shown in ReSJ.

217. "the whole . . ." Star, March 13, 1847.

219. "A more . . ." Bry, p. 263.

220. George Donner's skull. Sacramento *Union*, September 27, 1866.

221. Mrs. Graves's money: San Francisco *Call*, May 16, 1891.

222. "Tell the . . ." ReVIJ.

PAGE
226.   "As bad . . ." GWC.
228.   "Old Keseberg . . ." FSP.
229.   "In conversing . . ." This and the next two quotations are
       from McG, pp. 206-22.
235.   "eat baby . . ." Wi, p. 75.
235.   "look out . . ." FSP.

INDEX

The index includes only proper names. A few constantly recurring place-names such as *California* have been omitted. Material in the 1960 Supplement (pp. 237-88) has not been indexed.

Glover, Aquilla, 120, 140-42, 149, 151, 156, 157, 158, 159, 161, 162, 166-67, 177, 178, 192, 197, 202, 225, 231

Gordon's Ranch, 165

Grantsville, 222

Graves, Eleanor, 155
Elizabeth, 27, 61, 141, 150, 155, 170, 175-77, 182, 195, 196, 221
Elizabeth, Jr., 176, 196, 203
F. W., 27, 50, 51, 54-56, 86, 87, 88, 92, 94, 101-03, 190, 195
Jonathan, 196, 225
Lavina, 155
Mary, 27, 86, 94, 97-99, 110-12, 114, 115, 222
Nancy, 196
W. C., 27, 155, 157, 163, 202, 203; quoted, 90, 226

Graves family, 36, 49, 66, 84, 86, 134, 143, 146-47, 152, 175, 188, 189, 192, 194, 203, 207, 220

Greasy Jim. *See* Brueheim.

Grayson, A. J., 76

Great Basin, 2

Great Salt Lake, 2, 5, 6, 23, 25, 28, 30, 206, 215, 219, 220

Great Salt Lake Desert, 35-40

Green River, 19, 21

Green Mountains, 92

Greenwood, Caleb, 125-27, 165, 167
Brit, 126, 167, 175, 180, 192

Greenwood's route, 5, 21

Halloran, Luke, 17, 27, 32, 33, 65, 206

Ham's Fork, 19

Hardkoop, ———, 17, 27, 54, 55, 56, 65, 87, 132, 232

Hardy's Ranch, 126, 166

Hargrave, John, 32-33

Hastings, L. W., 6-7, 11, 12, 21, 23, 24, 25, 26, 30, 31, 32-36, 38, 41, 45, 50, 55, 60, 62, 216-17, 220, 225; quoted, 6, 12

Herron, Walter, 15, 38, 55, 62, 63, 81, 192

Hook, Solomon, 173, 175, 182
William, 163

Houghton, S. O., 224

Houston, Sam, 216, 225

Hull, J. B., 123, 126, 162

Humboldt River, 2, 3, 31, 47, 49, 53, 56, 58, 65, 162, 215, 223

Illinois, 10, 11, 12, 13, 15

Indiana, 11

Iowa, 15

Ireland, 13

Jacob, R. T., 76

James, Noah, 15, 93, 131, 154

Jean Baptiste. *See* Trubode.

Job (quoted), 137

Johnson's Ranch, 74, 77, 82, 118-19, 120, 126, 127, 140, 141, 142, 145, 148, 155, 162, 166, 189, 190, 192, 193, 204, 217

Kearny, S. W., 219, 220

Kentucky, 11

Kern, E. M., 76, 120, 162, 225, 228, 235

Keseberg, Ada, 155, 156, 159, 160
Lewis, member of Donner Party, 16; in Reed-Snyder affair, 52; in Hardkoop af-